island people

Also by Coleman Dowell

One of the Children Is Crying (1968)
Mrs. October Was Here (1974)

One need not be a Chamber
to be Haunted
One need not be a House—
—EMILY DICKINSON

The only antidote to the irreversibility
of history is the faculty of forgiveness.
—HANNAH ARENDT

island people

COLEMAN DOWELL

A New Directions Book

Portions of this book first appeared in *Ambit, Edgeworks,* and *New Directions in Prose and Poetry* (nos. 26, 27, 29, and 30), to whose editors grateful
acknowledgment is made.

The epigraph by Hannah Arendt is quoted from *Eichmann in Jerusalem:
A Report on the Banality of Evil* (Copyright © 1963, 1964 by Hannah
Arendt), published by The Viking Press, Inc. Passages from D. H. Law-
rence's "Herman Melville's 'Moby Dick,' " in *Studies in Classic American
Literature* (Copyright 1923, 1951 by Frieda Lawrence; Copyright © 1961
by the Estate of the late Frieda Lawrence) are quoted in this book with
the permission of The Viking Press, Inc., Laurence Pollinger Ltd., and the
Estate of the late Mrs. Frieda Lawrence.

Manufactured in the United States of America
First published clothbound in 1976
Published simultaneously in Canada by McClelland & Stewart, Ltd.

Library of Congress Cataloging in Publication Data

Dowell, Coleman.
    Island people.

    (A New Directions Book)
    I. Title.
PZ4.D7396Is   [PS3554.O932]   813'.5'4   75–34150
ISBN 0–8112–0604–1

New Directions Books are published for James Laughlin
by New Directions Publishing Corporation,
333 Sixth Avenue, New York 10014

island people

THE GAME

THE KEEPSAKE

I told Beatrix "Yes!" gladdened to think that her friendliness, and Jeremiah's, apparently, had carried over the fall separation. It was at least plain that enough of our summer feeling remained for them to want to come to me at the farm for Christmas, and for me to want them. After we hung up, following mutual assurances that none of us could really wait (Jeremiah, too; Beatrix spoke for him), I checked the dates she had given me, inclusive only of mystery when she spoke, and found that they encompassed a week. I was accustomed to winter guests coming on The Eve of things and departing the day after The Day; the thought of someone willing to endure for a longer time touched me.

I have determinedly never set my cap for younger people, so the youngness of the Dresdens was an incidental in our success with each other, as I suppose my comparative oldness was. Granted that some of the most successful things we did together could be called "young" things: flying kites in my fields among the cropping sheep, sailing too far too late in the day, being bested for hours by the tide at the harbor mouth, the day sailer flapping to the dock at midnight like an exhausted bird. But I do these things on my own with just my dachshund bitch for company.

Incidental, too, I suppose was that the three of us roughly shared a profession: Jeremiah, poet; Beatrix, New Novelist; and I a more or less failed playwright: my very long-running (five years) play in Germany is to American recognition as sound waves from that falling unheard tree to ears.

When we met at the ferry slip, introduced by my dachshund,

Miss Gold, what we knew of each other was what we had surmised those several Fridays in succession, seeing each other waiting for the train-ferry. I had made no effort to find out who they were. I have been here long enough to say to myself "summer people" and let the description suffice. They were interesting looking, he classically handsome, she as ugly as an ape until you saw through to her simian but real beauty. I had seen through to it before we met; had seen through Jeremiah, too, or thought that I had; his niceness seemed both glass and shield. As we said, my house guests and I, passing judgment sometime in midsummer after several exposures to the Dresdens, Jeremiah was surely the kindliest poet, too nice to be really great perhaps. Among those passing judgment was a poet of enduring reputation, so maybe the consensus was partly satirical.

Concerning the Dresdens knowing "who" I was before we met, people generally can find out my identity by giving one of three clues to any passerby: the car, the only foreign one on the Island; Miss Gold, whose photograph adorned the cover of a collection (*Coursing*) of my plays; or any word at all of my own appearance, which is eccentric, especially among the plain-groomed Islanders, and summer people, who are not groomed at all.

But as I have said, Miss Gold introduced us, I don't think in complicity with Beatrix and Jeremiah, though if they had wanted to meet me, cultivating Miss Gold was the best way to go about it.

I mean through these incidentals to set up vibrations of suspicion, of the possibility of a kind of fortune hunting. I will go farther and say that my house is the only one on the Island where any kind of fortune hunting is possible, and let the matter rest there. We are all adventurers, and if vibrations are at this juncture misleading, then let us call the story a "mystery" and let us, preferably through a glass dark with Jameson's Irish, look for clues.

Beatrix's telephone call gave me two weeks' notice, and in those two weeks I accomplished more than I would ordinarily have done in a month. Before she called, my only guest was to be my best friend, the poet mentioned in the foregoing, who is this year's lion as he was last year's lion and my sole Christmas guest. Paul and I are too relaxed with each other for me to go to any real pains against his visits, but for the Dresdens the house was cleaned and rooms were opened.

In allusive tribute there would be a German Christmas dinner: goose and sauerkraut in Riesling and potatoes sautéed in goose fat and thick apple sauce domed with its own jelly. My yearly gift from the smokehouse of home, an aged Kentucky ham, could open the meal with Madeira-steeped figs; there would be custards and spiced beef and pork pie in a crust and plum pudding. To this extent is a host allowed, sorcererlike, to meddle with the future: the Dresdens would be flattered by the German motif, and Paul, a secret Pip, would be pleased by the Dickens touches.

But early on Christmas Eve morning Paul called; early, he said, to prove that he *had* got up in time to make the train . . . but. He is usually precise, admirably so to a discursive person like me, but I did not get much past the "but"; in any case he was not coming. He was not especially sorry; he knew that I would not be alone. I had not told him about the Dresdens; it seemed that they themselves had told him. It also seemed blatantly like a clue, but to what I could not imagine. Paul had liked Beatrix, with whom he had in common Brooklyn, an Eastern band I have found to be as strong as a wedding ring. He liked Jeremiah's poetry, liked his looks; as he put it, he even liked Jeremiah, when he remembered him.

Paul is not a cruel man, nor is he unusually just; he is mainly disinterested, and I had to admit that the précis was accurate of many an essay of Jeremiah. His lack of temperament, of eccentricity, of vice, apparently, bleached him out. Too frequently one gazed at the place where Jeremiah was without seeing him.

When one said, or wrote down, "the Dresdens," it was Beatrix's simianity that gave proper flesh to the noun; Jeremiah was an essence, flushing the tissue with blood, coursing, undoubtedly healthily, out of sight; but as we forget our blood until we are cut, so did we lose sight of Jeremiah. A quip about his combination of vivid looks and colorless personality — "Beside him, other men pale to significance" — was not successful because of his art, which *was* significant, rather Augustinian. If, as some maintained, he was a throwback, it was to the best traditions.

His lovely ape wife could never approach his art. Her own was imitative of Nathalie Sarraute, experimental of many things but never emotion. But in person she was dark emotional energy, faintly furred (in silhouette against artificial light she wore an aureole, the filaments of fuzz glowing uniformly). She gave the impression, in the electricity of life, of teetering on the edge of breakdown, or breakthrough, some volatile display or discovery a nod away, waiting only for her permissive recognition. One both longed for and feared the revelation of Beatrix.

Their visibility, or lack of it; their art or attempts manqués — these are further incidentals, as such extraneous matters always are in love and lust. They had won my allegiance and revived the intensity of long-dormant curiosity about others, and I don't know how they did it. Jeremiah could have been ectoplasm, Beatrix entirely without talent, and their effect upon me would have been the same. It is hindsight that tells me so, for I write from a knowledge of worse than pallor and pretentiousness, and still curiosity, if not allegiance, persists.

They called from the Island side of the ferry, and Miss Gold and I drove through immensely billowing curtains of snow to pick them up and welcome them with champagne in the car. They were swathed like papooses as though we were a Canadian outpost, great dark sunglassed eyes all that Miss Gold and I could see of them, both of us lightly clad in sweaters in the snow-warm air.

In a story by Beatrix the focus, endlessly circled, would be the hidden eyes, the muffled mouths; they would become the characters, the only physical properties referred to, and because they were hidden, thus missing, slowly we would realize that Beatrix's story was about two pairs of sunglasses, two scarves, incapable of emotion but possessing a curious molecular ability to deduce, finally to murder through subtraction. Simple behavior, catching at her imagination like a fishhook, could cause her to darken with visible passion and pain and her fingers to crook as though tearing in retaliation great laden chords from her typewriter.

I am more concerned with what can be barely intuited, with those actions and reasons explainable only by atavism, accessible only to instinct. I am not interested in the cult of game playing or the psychology behind the way people sit or hold their cigarettes, and this indifference to gesture, to the visual, actually, makes me rather an odd playwright. But concerning the Dresdens' appearance, whatever their wish may have been for concealment, they were thin-blooded city people with smog-weakened eyes; and it was soon apparent that Jeremiah had a very bad case of laryngitis; his voice was a ragged thread fraying further with the slightest use. What to make of this new effacement: Jeremiah become his Art entirely? . . . That is me still being Beatrix; it is not my style at all.

The Dresdens were grateful for the warmth of the car. The train had been bitterly cold. They remembered with pleasure the snugness of my house, the first fire, bright on the hearth (Beatrix, lyrical), that we had shared in late September. Did I seem to be protesting her memory when I said that the north wind changes things? Sometimes, I said, it pulls the heat out of the house and makes it hard to maintain a temperature much above 68°. But there are fireplaces —

Indifferently, I thought, Beatrix inquired how Paul was holding up under the cold. At my news the air in the car changed.

Miss Gold's reactions always engage me more than my own, and I watched her sensing the change, lifting her nose high and sniffing soundlessly. I have seen her smell my anger before it broke, and dishonesty in others when the dishonesty was, as it would turn out, ripe with consequences. But she does not draw conclusions and frequently I cannot; though I thought that the changed air was colder.

Jeremiah must go instantly to bed, there to be fed with honey and lemon and comforted with hot-water bottles and judicious visits. But Beatrix made a trip to their apartment and came down blue and trembling, asking if they could sleep by the fire. In alarm, thermometer in hand, I went up cursing the wind, felt somewhat cooler than the rooms when I discovered a uniform temperature of 74°, infernal in my house in winter. Beatrix, I thought, is being womanly; some women hate, so I have found, to be thought hardy, even when too stony to be chipped from. I recalled that she shivered a great deal in stillest summer nights, gathering to herself the garments of others, and I amended my thought to: Beatrix is being Beatrix.

I built the fire up to a roar (Beatrix, as I went to the kitchen: "Isn't he afraid of chimney fires?") and went to put the kettle on for tea, feeling in the third person like a domestic. I told myself (on paper; that day warranted three journal entries) that champagne, of which I had drunk a lot, being two thirds bubbles, is two thirds fancy. Winter adjustments to summer friends, I wrote, leads to suspicion, is trying of our resources, is frequently sad, frequently abandoned. Remember, I wrote, who these people are. *Were.*

Here is Beatrix:

Beatrix, asking what something cost; Beatrix, requesting the salt-cellar (it's onion soup, not salt soup). Her voice seemed to have got higher since summer and had acquired a habit of repeating what one was saying *under* what one was saying, not quite simultaneously but as close-tailing as an afterbeat in music. If spoken words were visible, then talking with Beatrix would be like speaking with face slightly askew above a mirror. But her charm grew apace, too, and by early nightfall she had woven a screen to block out nearly all her minor transgressions.

She and Jeremiah napped by the fire, she under a favorite winter-thing of Miss Gold's, a robe of South American rabbit in white and various browns, beautiful as vicuña. I took it out to her on impulse as she lay with her spread hair seeming to grow like ivy on the blue velvet cushions. In the firelight she and Jeremiah looked exotic, dark haired, both of them, Jeremiah burnished and Beatrix as swart as Heathcliff. Beatrix rubbed the fur vigorously as though frictionally to disclose its nature. The fur was like her own pelt; the rubbing made her seem to be looking for fleas or salt deposits. Unconsciously I had abetted the ape in her. Jeremiah, bent in his chair, stirred as though to question my propriety. But no, the shape he assumed in the chair was more commalike.

I turned on the Christmas lights. In the glowing room, fire fallen to embers, the Dresdens looked like young dreamers in a ballet. Each sleeping profile thrust upward carving out the wine-jelly Christmas sheen of the room. They were perfectly strange to me, characterless as people sleeping on a stage when the curtain goes up. Dimly felt tendrils ran from my breast to summer and turned back and groped for the Dresdens but did not touch them, restrained by my desire. If I had thought Beatrix vulgar today, it was *had* thought; this woman was a sleeping woman, no more. And if I had thought whatever I had thought about Jeremiah since arrival, I thought nothing of the sort about the sleeping man. As a result, perhaps, the evening was a lute tuned perfectly to our accordatura. The visit was saved, all was redeemed, reputations, judgments, friendliness, love – all saved. There is a relief like shock; the difference is that one must help the relief to voluntary numbness: third journal entry of the day with "clarify" in the margin. I never did.

Early morning scrambling, tissue paper, trailing ribbons leading like false clews radially outward from the tree through doorways. Was the tree then the beast?

The presents were fine: a kite sculpture in memoriam; Paul's wonderful new fantasy book in which, in disguise, Miss Gold and I figured; the silk scarves; the flowered set of mugs for the kitchen; new Mahler recordings, the unfinished Tenth Symphony underscoring the morning; sweaters, raincoats, carcoats for Miss Gold; Italian bottles of milk bath for everyone, and pomanders.

A box of fancy chocolates for Beatrix; her look of disbelief was fascinating. She put them on a table where they remained untouched throughout the visit, and where they were left when

Beatrix had gone. No mystery, now; no point in making one out of it. That night, late, in a tense discussion about Women's Liberation, Beatrix brought up the chocolates, tossed them figuratively at my head: Would I give a man a box of chocolates? Would I want to see a male placidly stuffing himself on heart attacks and hardened arteries, chocolate death dribbling down his chin onto his — I interjected "Slim volume of poetry?" looking to Jeremiah for lightness; none forthcame. I said I hoped my chocolate-eating protagonist would be neat enough not to dribble hardened arteries.

Vibrating like a uvula, Beatrix reminded me that a man could eat with both hands, could smear himself with food and belch and undo buttons and pick his teeth — other things, too, of course; Beatrix has a liberated tongue. I did not know if I was being allowed a glimpse of formative years. I was momentarily confused, thinking that we had, through the chocolates, reverted to our discussion of calories, the only topic at dinner: Beatrix had estimated that if each of us had one helping of everything on my encomium-intended menu we would have swallowed 25,000 calories apiece. Jeremiah, placidly eating, had been laconic: "Stuff a cold" . . . But we were not discussing calories at all: calories did not matter. According to Beatrix, all that mattered was that I and others like me readjust our thinking and attitudes, by surgery, if necessary, until the sight of Woman behaving exactly like Man under any and all circumstances would be no more objectionable than if it *were* a man.

For the first time between us, my age was mentioned: Beatrix thought it a factor, perhaps *the* factor, in my inflexibility. There was more, but I did not attend too closely.

I retain an impression of Beatrix stoutly defending Doris Lessing, though not of anyone attacking her. Had this been Beatrix, in the summer, requiring no offensive to launch a defensive? It seemed a clue to her, an important one — as my age has turned out to be to me. Perhaps she believed that all are guilty until cleared by her offices.

I have acquaintances who attend a sort of church — God figures vaguely — where they improve memories, learn, as they put it, to "relate," and where they study such as the elaborate system of inner antagonisms and reprisals against Self of which we everyone are composed. When a bad water skiing accident followed the failure of my play in New York, my friends were glad for me: the inner wound had had to be matched by an outer wound — the mind's insistence that the body share the pain — before balance was restored.

On my way to bed, having had my age inflicted upon me, I slid on a rug, and in flailing for balance I wrenched my vulnerable back. Beatrix, seeing me teetering, sprang up. As though she were in a nimbus, I saw her as the messenger come to remind me that I was purified again, inner and outer wounds nicely balanced.

Jeremiah spends the days in bed forcing liquids. At intervals Beatrix brings various cups and mugs down and sets them on the piano, from whence I hobble them to the kitchen and wash them. Women's Liberation has many radii. Some resemble crutches.

Beatrix, returning from a long walk (in her absence Jeremiah futilely summoned with dull poundings; Miss Gold replied with growls; a metaphysical dialogue), bright cheeked and giving, said to me, "You really are too good to your friends," and it was a summer voice speaking, shocking my eyes to water. With Francesca I believe that happiness recalled in misery is the greatest pain; just as dwelling upon it is the greatest folly.

I, walking Miss Gold, am reminded of a drawing of a man approaching a house whose shape has been assumed or consumed by a woman. Beatrix by dint of anger and frustration had consumed the house; all seemed now to be of her flesh, and the flesh was increasingly rank. Her pallor, the greenish cast of her shadowed complexion, aroused in me the aversion one feels for a corpse; odors were supplied by association: lilies, primarily. I would pass her in rooms of my mind with pomander pressed to my nostrils. The lily odor alternated with the after-odors of her milk baths, which were sour; she had sat too long bottled without being shaken or heated and was going bad under my nose. I thought that she, two years married, might be frustrated on ac-

count of Jeremiah's weakness, that it might be sexual frustration. I became obsessed with her frustration. I was pursued by
it.

I would sit by the fire, I am sitting by the fire trying to put
summer through myself again. I sit in the shambles of Christmas, among portents of a shattered winter. I do not recover
from aborted love sooner than I would regain strength following the loss of an organ. Fear of pain and the boredom of repetitive convalescence had driven me to seek a burrow at last in the
country and a companion in Miss Gold to make cozy the house
of roots.

Beatrix's importuning voice on the telephone winds about
summer recollections, changing their coloration through pressure at vital points:

Can it really be that she said about a play of mine in manu-
script that she would never theretofore have suspected my erudition? Or had she said intelligence, or was it education she had
not suspected? I see the setting — the table, the company showing off for each other: someone had seen Kokoschka in Switzerland, Bellow had said to someone, someone had "discovered"
William Gass; I heard her words in a lull, other words to lull
and then the ones about me, my play; others hear her words —
Yes, because Jeremiah (!) breaks in to say that he told his wife
the reason my erudition (education, intelligence) does not show
is because I am Southern. Beatrix professes not to understand.
She says, amusingly (coarsely!), that what you know, if you
are from Brooklyn, you let stick out all over you. I say — could
I have said? — that in my South the only things it is all right to
display are manners.

To my winter eyes, watching the summer scene, the little
shrug Beatrix replies with is as blatant as a belch.

Another table, another evening, dinner in the garden: Beatrix
and Jeremiah sitting lumpish and silent. Later, my reference to
my "silent dinner party." Beatrix, defensively: "We were comfortably turned inward" . . . Do I say (did I say) that a dinner
party is the last place to turn inward? No, nor had I made the
fittingly cold remark about manners. There were, are, never ex-

12

changes between us in that sense; there was, is, only Beatrix and heedless Jeremiah; and doting me. Was there not? Or had I hated them then, too — then, but in the future; hated them, knowing how they *would* be, but loving them helplessly then? Or is it now I love them, helplessly?

I ask my journal what I meant. Did I mean that summer excess as seen in winter is another thing? Did I mean that in summer the self, camouflaged in permissiveness — looseness of sports, cocktail parties, sexual misalliances — recognized laxness as part of earned leisure? It's true that in winter, lacking universal permission and nature's profligate example, the true self shows as surely as galls, leaf-hid in summer, do on trees. I try, but cannot tell whether it is truth or erroneous assessment or Charlus-streak unsuspected, that has ruined my Christmas and shocked my coming year. It becomes less and less accessible, retreats into being a parable of summer people and winter people, those races who visit each other's countries on off seasons. Paul is a winter person, pared down to his manners, the fat of summer extravagance always dieted away in time. I do not know what I am, but if I were a summer person I would kill myself by spring.

Miss Gold bit Beatrix in the following sequence of events.

1. Beatrix tries to coax Miss Gold to chase a ball, Miss Gold's expression of incredulity maddening to one untalented with drawing pen or camera.

2. Beatrix moves Miss Gold from the latter's favorite chair by the fire to one distant, taking the chair herself, though two others and a sofa stand empty.

3. Beatrix at dinner curtly refuses her hostess a morsel of food, saying, "You've had your dinner, now let me have mine." I think Miss Gold bit Beatrix as punishment for unoriginality rather than for stinginess or bad temper. I have followed the course of events and predicted the bite to myself. At my small nod and half-smile Beatrix locks herself in such a vise of self-concern that I can hear the clink of iron on iron, iron device on iron flesh.

Beatrix, out of some perversity that recalled manners to her when they were not wanted, was generous in her assurances that she was not hurt, but she was. I, in fact, could see no recovery for her.

I fear Beatrix's edges, her serration. I am drunk before the fire; her sharpness increases as though to pierce my protection to the heart. Will the blurring liquidly run and harden to edges again? Ask Beatrix.

Drunk, I am a victim; but drunk, I cannot be victimized. I talk back. I suggest that they have pursued me because of the people I know. I suggest that Paul's absence has turned her monster and isolated Jeremiah in an upper chamber from whence Assumption is but a thought away. I intimate that Miss Gold and I are helpless babes and she, Medea. Jeremiah's cough from above sounds a warning: *Don't actually speak; Beatrix is suggestible.*

She cast about her for satisfactory or outrageous victims, strayed into unexplored territory, lit on mutual acquaintances whom she had met through me in the summer and whom she and Jeremiah had seen several times in the fall in town.

She demolishes reputations and characters; finished, I think; but she proves still hungry and tears the limbs from the couple's two children and goes on and eats the younger, a boy of five. The illusion is astounding: Beatrix's mouth is gory and loops of saliva glisten in firelight. My skin blazes; the scarf she gave me for Christmas, ingratiatingly worn, touches me and burns. I tear it off.

Beatrix was aghast, unable to claim her words. It was, she said, as though she had been possessed. She begged for my belief, and I had no inclination after such excesses to doubt her. My willingness made Beatrix sullen; it was as though I had accused her.

With Miss Gold I nap secretly, tucked into a room I have shown to no one, a smoothly enclosed old inglenook unsuspected in the house's present symmetry, windowless as a womb. Do I hear her searching for me, calling, afraid of my escape? Do I hear him padding beside her, panting? Miss Gold's instincts lie still beneath sleep, her hackles consolingly quiescent. The smell from the useless fireplace is as fusty as Puritans. My house of roots, a long gallery of sensations more graphic than portraits. Their Puritan clothes, lye, ashes, leaching; leached of lies, from here one could emerge restored.

Jeremiah was in the yellow chair writing. As I came in he said, "I think my wife has deserted my bed for yours," and went back to his writing.

In my bedroom Beatrix was in my bed, propped upon my pillows, under the fur robe. One glance shows stacks of books about her, a box of Kleenex, a bottle of pills. Used Kleenexes strew the floor, a rough path by which the wastebasket may be reached. There is a negligee over the back of the desk chair. It is like the onset of mystery, or like the very end of mystery: soon Jeremiah will come in, and the three of us . . . Beatrix and Jeremiah and I . . . Miss Gold, too? Jeremiah comes in. He wants to lie down. It seems to me that I should move aside so that he may join his wife. Somehow I cannot.

When Jeremiah had gone upstairs to nap, Beatrix began. She mimicked voices, launching right in like a stand-up comic. Sometimes the voice was clear, at other times there was interference as though the sound were projected over water. The voice would be recognizable — Paul's, mine — and then not at all, though the words would seem to have been plucked from one's mind yesterday. Paul was excoriated, I berated; summer words reappeared in new contexts. A formidable writer she could have been, serving imagination and total recall, if she were not so pretentious as to be blind to her own gifts.

I heard my voice through the medium of Beatrix saying hateful things about Women's Liberationists, deploring women writers using dirty words; uncannily, my voice in Beatrix's throat said that a prurient attitude seemed to be growing among female writers, and it gave specimens; it had been a good year for proof; then Beatrix's voice corrected my pronunciation by example: I, she said, don't think women are at all pure-ient, her rebuttal as unfelicitous as her correction. I half expected Miss Gold, tucked uneasily under a corner of the fur robe, to bite

Beatrix for sloppiness. Pathetically, one charged and countered in the person of Beatrix; and one listened.

The telephone rang. My back twanged like a guitar string. Jeremiah's step was heard on the stair. All at once separate strings of a final knot place themselves at our finger tips.

As though the devoured child's father had by divine intervention been able to substitute himself for the child, he had died in the early morning. Our maligned acquaintance, even as Beatrix savaged him and his family, had lain dead . . . Had lain dying? It was a formidable weapon for Paul to hand me at such a time.

I listened to his voice that touched death with reason. The widow had asked him to help her make calls; the word was only that the dead man had (in his wife's recalled Viennese accent) died in sleep, for which we could all be grateful: "He had liked very much living." I wanted to shatter the quiet, to scream that Beatrix had killed him, that he had died in knowing horror . . . My acquaintance, or me?

Jeremiah, returning from the kitchen, gave me a look of surprise in passing. I wondered what my expression was like to give him such surprise. Carefully, perfectly aware of Beatrix listening, I inquired after "the little ones." Paul told me that the girl was fine, the boy, too, except that he expected to be allowed to keep his father's head.

"Don't" I said sharply. Paul understood. We said emotionally balanced good-bys. I retched dryly, keeping Beatrix waiting.

Beatrix leaned through a swarm or a gale that roiled her hair. *"What did you tell Jeremiah not to do?"* His mild presence behind me was like saneness. I stood aside to let him pass. What had she imagined had been going on between us? I was unable to duck the swarm of images, Beatrix's images surely, of what had taken place out of her sightlines. I let the swarm take me. I believed that I knew what the lining of a mad mind looked like.

In the therapeutic tub I planned how I best might use my acquaintance's death. The dead, I told myself, don't mind how we use them. I shall not mind when I am dead how many Beatrixes to further themselves manipulate my bones. The dead don't mind. But words came: In death there is other sleep, other closing/ Compared to which, death's dozing.

By the fireside they were still. Beatrix, unposed, stanceless, was disarmingly plain and young looking. Her reading glasses were askew, her mouth quirked. Her long arms reached the book out toward the hearth's light. A literate, uneasy ape. I could play on her vulnerability, catching her unawares with the news of death, the head; she would think that it was not the child she had devoured but the father, all but his head.

Jeremiah said that someone created his own light. Seeing Beatrix's look of sullenness at praise wasted on an absent someone, I thought, "Poor man, your wife creates her own darkness."

By my bed I found my journal where Beatrix had left it. She had told me not to leave letters lying about, for they were irresistible to her. We laughed together. So alike, the two of us. That was in the summer.

I went into the parlor and found Jeremiah's journal on the table by the yellow chair. From the number of pages written it was clear that he had been writing most of his waking hours during the visit — fifty close-written pages beginning with the plagiarism "Of the Farm."

With magnifying glass because of the smallness of the hand, I read me, us. I read that Paul and I were lovers. I read that Jeremiah had observed us together during the Christmas visit. Jeremiah did not like to be disappointed; like all poets, he created his own world as he wished it to be, or feared it to be, arranged and rearranged it for the effect wanted at the moment. Casual words, imaginary or not (some rang familiarly) were placed in contexts so alien to the characters of Paul and me that in comparison Beatrix's distortions were as the prattlings of children, who light briefly upon grotesquerie through buoyancy, like butterflies. A number of times Paul and I, halves of one narcissist, as it were, were pushed, peas in gelatin, into the framework of *Tamburlaine,* itself a good model of poetically reordered history. It was evident that Jeremiah was at work on a highly personal approach to dramatic/poetic explication, using friends as his medium.

There were diversions: graphs as classic-appearing as diagrams of chess moves—Jeremiah recording successful facial expressions as used at strategic times by himself during our holiday. In the summer he had looked at women newly met with subtle ruefulness which said, "If only (we were alone; were not married; were married to each other)"; it was a very effective look, more so when one knew that it had been rehearsed with Jamesian calculation. On graph paper; might a mirror have failed to reflect anything at all?

Finally it was what Jeremiah did on paper to Beatrix that I found most affecting. We all write about loved ones, friends, acquaintances, sometimes even with insight, sometimes even kindly. But there was no emotion, not even spleen, in Jeremiah's clinic; only the eye of a computer, among the chimeras of our modern world, could be so pitiless.

They were still awake, lying propped on cushions reading. Their bodies were close together, one stem under the covers, with their heads leaning away toward separate lights. They were a rich sight, dark and burnished blooms on a slender stalk. I was humbled by their beauty, by a trembling-kneed desire to be rid of it. My age bothered me unbeautifully at all joinings, humbling me further with faulty articulation.

I handed Jeremiah his journal and saw that the kindliest poet was waiting for a sign that I had read it. Of course I had been meant to. A man who plans his facial expressions does not forget his journal.

I told him about death. A plastic envelope of paranoia formed about Beatrix's head. I told them, "I know you'll want to be there." I mentioned the early train. I mentioned packing tonight. The room, I let them see me seeing, badly needed cleaning and airing; price tags littered the floor; they must have bought all new clothes for Christmas.

Beatrix softened for scarring made me sorry. I thought that

her abrasiveness and aggression could be meant to balance Jeremiah's secrecy: they were two wounds balancing each other. I imagined that she read his journal, each new installment soon as written. Reading herself would be like watching herself decay, seeing the pattern of her life and the end of her life as projected by God. Then I was less sorry for her: she had read herself in our journals, but where were we? What reality did we have, in some secret place of hers, that we did not know about? Her mimicry was awfully creative at times; what would the frozen static words do to us? Might she have made me a murderer, a pervert, lobotomized my memory, driven me insane? As though she were reading my mind, she scratched her head: Beatrix in the zoo.

I have decided that I do not fancy myself as Jeremiah wrote me, in the guise of half-Tamburlaine. I will be whole or nothing. We shepherds, when the world comes to us, can grow ambitious, and ambition can make us revert, forgetful of learned consequences. I was a stalker of quarry long before I wrote; in the South it is honorable to teach a child how to hunt; from the hunted he draws conclusions about survival.

I drove the Dresdens to the ferry, but Miss Gold and I did not share the wait with them. I told them, "At least you won't miss the boat." Beatrix's eyes were not too sure. Jeremiah briefly turned my meaning over and then withdrew into his famous decency.

Their bedroom was a shambles. Books had been pulled onto the floor — Beatrix might have written, "as though in a search for meaning." I don't know how she might have written about the old-fashioned device, obviously used, left slimily in plain sight; perhaps a discourse on the right of women to frustrations quite apart from men and their biological cofunctioning or failure. The floor was still strewn with price tags. I fancied that they were a Brooklyn version of manners: Beatrix's way of indicating that they had quietly shared the price of our Christmas together.

February 14

On the stroke of noon today I finished "The Keepsake"—
though "finished" would be more like it, for its reverberations
are yet to come — and sat back sharing the sense of a job well
done with executioners of all Ages. I noticed only then that it
is St. Valentine's Day, so my love tribute is appropriate. Stroke,
too, of noon lovingly fitting when one recalls Time's hand on
its prick. Skeet-shooters pull-banging since nine o'clock, the
sounds of orgy entering the nerves like parasites. I couldn't find
a place in the story for one vicious little vignette. It is perfectly
a mirror held to the vis of Clytie Steuber — did I ever really love
anybody so named? — but was quite wrong for tougher Beatrix
Dresden. I copy it here for the record, and because it makes me
laugh: "I fed Beatrix bread-and-butter pudding. She ate it
greedily; wearing a greasy moustache, she hugged herself and
walled up her eyes saying, 'It makes me feel like a little gur-ul.'
She looked like a gargoyle fallen to the pavement, trying to disarm passers-by until she could somehow clamber back up the
cathedral façade and crouch on the parapet and once again
frighten in earnest."
  This may be unfair to Clytie, but she, name and all, now,
brings to mind a haughty woman I used to see in the elevator in
town when the apartment was first bought. This lady was well
groomed — rather tacky phrase, like" tastefully appointed" — but
it was her demeanor that told one and all that she belonged to
the penthouse. She did, too, as I found out one day, sitting in
the window seat, looking up one floor, watching her sullen face
as she cleaned while her mistress stood behind her, apparently
chatting amiably.

I rather wish I could have kept my poet's name, Gabriel: I wonder if he blows.

Question: Are the Steubers exorcised? Answer: No. They are embedded in me like Trichinella spiralis. When I think of them I vomit, I shit, I bleed. But the Dresdens; I rather like them. Is that because of so much New York basic training? Certainly self-loathing was given a refresher course at that stony knee. Example: Clytie, reading the art page in the newspaper: "Jews praising Jews." Or the book review, or the magazine sections: "Jews praising Jews." Of course self-hate has a lot of complacency in it.

In a month or two, or a year, when I read what I've done will I still be stirred by Beatrix-Clytie's sexuality as I was, writing her? Superimposed over Beatrix is Clytie in a column of sea-green satin, bronzy hair in a Greek chignon, boy's body.

And superimposed over me, to my surprise, there is a name, *Chris;* it kept coming unbidden for the narrator of the story, which I would not weaken enough to set down. But he is there ... Entering Beatrix I came out the other side transformed: deep woman, labyrinthine woman, the clews of her guts misleading. Or: a river of a woman; entering her cunt I emerge full grown from her mouth, directed upstream by a — what may be a — superior will. Is Chris, then, Beatrix's idea? Her creature?

Midnight

Today, catching up on magazines, undeterred by the steady snow of flyers whereon each magazine advertises itself — having rejoined the world in all its trashiness, Steubers, thanks — today I was struck by the fact that EFRON (var., Ephron) has become as ubiquitous as Smith once was. Puzzled at first, why so prolific? until the thought: Efron (Ef., Eph.) WAS Smith, but as Eff-ing has risen, Smithing has declined ... All play and no work?

A new method of murder for my Handbook, using only the

self-advertising of popular magazines. I see myself sitting on the john beside someone in the tub, handing that person mag after mag: *Time, Newsweek, New York Magazine, Harper's, Atlantic,* and the advertising sifting quiet as lethal snow from between the leaves, sopping up the bath water until he-she-it is buried under a solid log of pulp. Then the victim can be flamed like a crepe or left there over the centuries to become the fossil in the lump of anthracite.

In an article on — what else? — drug abuse, someone's eyes meet someone's eyes and the famous reporter tells us that one pair of eyes was: vacant, unmistakably scared. For the first time since schoolboy days, I wrote in a margin: Fear is a formidable tenant.

February 15

My act of revenge, which I had thought would be like closing the door on a tomb, has, by an occultness in the structure, set up reverberations that have opened another door, perhaps other doors. Fancifully, in keeping with the story, I appended those words that were to haunt me all last night: *Is Chris, then, Beatrix's idea? Her creature?*

In the night I felt that she had come for me, that nothing could drive her out except at her own dictation. The substance that she could not have in life I had given her in the only form she could now assume: the form of words. But once words are set down a condition of permanence is established, and from the words other substance grows, the substance called ideas — ideas breeding ideas — and ideas can, must, take other shape. And so they have done: it looks as pure and irreversible as evolution.

All night in a weakened condition I thought of countermeasures: to burn the writing, the words; but for me she has emerged from the words and inhabits other space: after the brief sleep allowed me (by Beatrix?) I awoke expecting to find on the floor her spoor in spent Kleenex. Before I slept I had had the notion to give her her head, where "Chris" is concerned, to see what she would make of him. To deal with Clytie Steuber I invented an "I" who invented a "Beatrix." Which is to say that Beatrix may as easily have invented Chris, whose name appeared not in the story but afterward!

If I had "made" Beatrix a painter, as Clytie was, would this naming have occurred?

Hunting season opened today, this little autonomy out of step with the rest of the world. Dawn broke to the sounds of slaughter. Beefy men scuttle in and out of the woods. I could pick them off from my window.

February 16

Today, driving with Miss Gold, I pulled to the side of the road, drawn by a glimmer of white stone, to read the sad legend of somebody's brief span. Found: CABLEVISION. A grave marker under which lies sight and insight, a modest marker for the latest evolutionary casualty. Still, man is the only creature whose passing, bit by bit, is recorded in stone: the Sinai Tablets that were the beginning of his demise through Moses' *hubris*, which decreed that man's will must be as God's . . . the death of judgment. The death of the heart as recorded in monuments to war leaders; the death of Grace as commemorated in mountains re-made in man's image; and now, the death of vision. But we are grown modest through repetition, and the grasses will soon enough obscure the small white stone until the monument will seem Nature's, like a possible stalactite to the eyelessness of cave fishes.

Tonight on the box, a concert for us blind. Mr. Leinsdorf gestured; the unseen announcer told us that Mr. Leinsdorf had gestured. There was further delay; someone came on with an extra chair; the announcer told us what we might have seen if we had not been blinded: "Someone," he said, "is bringing on an extra chair." The conclusion of the program brought on a wildness of vision as the announcer, still — eternally — unseen, told us: "The first violinist is taking a bow; Mr. Leinsdorf is returning to the podium; Mr. Leinsdorf is gesturing to the orchestra to rise; the choirmaster is joining Mr. Leinsdorf on the podium; the choirmaster and Mr. Leinsdorf are shaking hands."

Why, one asks, proceed through life with these eyes, so frequently troublesome, needing the constantly updated furniture of spectacles, causing so often, by expedient of strain and cinder, the brain to ache in its cavity — why bother, when we have the true and clear and magnanimous vision of The Announcer, an entity so modest that he does not wish or require or expect to be seen . . . would, in fact, rather have us blind than to see him, a conclusion reached by extension, but EXTENSION is the very language of Cablevision, of T.V., of blindness, of, indeed, Evolution.

Deafness next? I would prefer it to being auditor to the hourly slaughter of our language. Tonight's folk hero on tonight's talk (!) show was so prodigal with his words that he used all of them up in a short speech, which ran the following gamut, only the tense inaccurate: Most people had bad hang-ups, but some, through staying loose and doing their own things, were getting it all together, which was where it was at. The other words he knew were offered as a coda: genocide; fascist; pig. The audience stood and applauded, a flock of penguins, until I sent them on a flight to oblivion, the vanishing silver ball like a bullet in slow motion.

3 a.m.

D.H. Lawrence on the meaning of *Moby Dick*: "Doom! Doom! Doom! Something seems to whisper it in the very dark trees of America. Doom!

"Doom of what?

"Doom of our white day. We are doomed, doomed. And the doom is in America. The doom of our white day. . . . The idealist, doomed. The spirit, doomed. . . . And in this maniacal conscious hunt of ourselves we get dark races and pale to help us, red, yellow, and black, east and west, Quaker and fire-worshiper, we get them all to help us in this ghastly maniacal hunt which is our doom and our suicide."

We, it seems, have finally found our Quaker, who, from the flanks of the White Whale in Washington, is administering the coup de grâce to our white day, our idealism, our spirit.

February 17

I had the illusion of having slept well, not once having mentioned in yesterday's journal entry what was becoming an obsession and which I thought to have exorcised by all omission of it, as simple-minded a thought as I may ever have had. This morning I came smugly to the desk to read what I vaguely remembered as "clever" observations, and found: Beatrix.

1. *Miss Gold* appears in the first sentence, rather than my lady's real name! Beatrix was writing, had taken possession of me during the concert. Further proof:

2. The style, the observations, are Beatrix's, down to making the unseen announcer the pivot of the piece. The program is what I would have written about — the so-so Beethoven, the superior Brahms. But Beatrix is, by her own admission, tone-deaf; acid rock is her ichor.

Why "ichor"? I ask this in stillness. We are now either into (as vulgar Clytie would say) pathology or godheads.

I would prefer to skip over the D.H. Lawrence, but can't. To my knowledge, I have never read those words, don't know where they appear, *if* they appear anywhere but in this journal. The political observation, or whatever it is, tagged onto the end, is like opening a letter and finding a turd. Among my other reasons for isolation is the need to escape that ubiquitous proof of the country's pathology, the shitslide that bore such a creature to enthronement on the nation's potty.

I am made to remember a line of my writing about Jeremiah — and is Beatrix going to defend him after what he did to her? — where I wrote in a preliminary sketch that he seemed perfectly amiable, but "what a good idea for ANOTHER character: one in which the ability and the intent are NOT amiable."

Helplessly, I see that my invective has gone her one better. Fuck you, apess. Go unfurl your tail and hang onto something.

February 18

Woke in the night, went outside as though drawn by fine wire. The stars were astounding. One understood "stellar," and its misapplication to show-biz types, seedy comedians, brassy girls, made one mourn for the death of the word. The populous western sky! Great masses of constellations, myths, fables — a great literary sky-city. And to the east, space and quiet. I did not know there was such a concentration of winter sights in the west and gaped and wondered. One mass of glitter puzzled me, and I wanted to run somewhere and look it up, and then I convinced myself that it was Orion's Belt — but surely too late for it? And now that I write this, was I not facing *east?* I see the skeleton of poplars through the memory, and there are none to the west.

I have just returned from trying to track myself down, to ascertain from my footprints in the snow the direction I faced, holding for support onto — *what?* — for nearly an hour. But something has erased my evidence. Perhaps this should worry me more than it does, but I rather take to the thought of astral bodies observing the stars. I would give a lot to get out of this body, if not permanently, then for the duration of the winter, and managed it, somewhat, after my stargazing last night, by drinking a large quantity of wine, Miss Gold sniffing in disdain. This morning a great gong woke me as though to danger or a Lucullan feast: *Who struck the sun with such force!* Miss Gold was sitting at the foot of the bed looking at me. It was she who caused the gong to sound. She wanted breakfast and a walk, the latter made dangerous by hunters. I ran to keep up with her, waving signals toward the woods where they skulk.

Later

An increasingly bitter day, like black ice, a slight thaw followed by a hard freeze, my lady's short legs breaking through the crusted snow so that she is held immovable, until I lift her, in the trap of winter. Returning to my desk, more bitterness when I see that Beatrix has been about her deeds, witness "Miss Gold" above. I too am caught in a trap with no one to lift me out. The car is immobile in the driveway where I foolishly left it, its wheels in a vise of frozen mud and snow. Exits locked and barred.

Late

The vertical door, the line of yellow light, slightly bellied, like a cat's eye. If memory lay beyond a black rubber wall, and the wall had a slit from top to bottom so that when you squeezed it the slit widened, especially in the middle, this would in the simplest way tell what it is like. Quick little squeezes like involuntary reflexes and quick little glimpses of what could be memories or could be another world — if memory is not already that — but quite close, not juxtaposed as much as superimposed, with all the figures lifelike and doing lifelike things. Comprehensible things, at least, which may not be the same. To strain at a simile — an old fault after early training: *Try to be precise. Yes, Mother* — but the simile has slipped away, maybe into that slit of yellow, and left only vague feelings of two T.V. stations on one channel at the same time, a figure I am sure is a cliché. To strain at precision and come up with cliché; that is defeat personified for me. It may be hours (a hateful imprecision) since the door opened, the yellow slit, but if I could be exact, then it would be a memory, which for some vague but strong reason I want to avoid. I don't want to risk anything beyond the immediate moment and its sensations and sights, mostly sensations because the primary sight is of these words on this paper, and the predominant sound is of the motor of the typewriter, and the main sensation is a mingling of relief and hope. Not too much of the latter, because that would be a projection into the future, and suppose a door began opening upon that!

February 19

If she is death, she must want me very much. An eternity of her style?

Later

February is the four o'clock in the morning of the year. The bars are closed, telephones are off their hooks, those who made no earlier arrangements for sex or companionship are fair game for their fancies until dawn.

Beatrix knows the darkness, its structures and protuberances, its lookouts and burrows. She would have me add: its barrows, too.

Question: Burial places of prehistory?
Answer: And castrated male swine.

Boum.
AU BOUM.

CAUGHT

ISLAND PEOPLE

Opening line for book: Journal entry:
I live in nightmare. My primary activity is concealing that fact. I am less and less successful.

Epigraph for the book, which may have turned out to be a novel:
Success is the degree to which we can conceal the fact that we live in nightmare.

From the particular to the general, or, better, from the personal to the collective, may be hopefully viewed at this time as a progression toward grace. The assumption is — will be? — that a sense of participation in the "human condition" is part of the composition of a state of grace. *The* state of grace, perhaps, or to go all the way, squeamishness cast aside, Grace.

To crib the imagery of an acquaintance, to paraphrase lengthily and restate the above, it would be like an island managing to throw out from itself with whatever enormous effort and depletion of certain hoarded materials enough matter to touch, however tenuously, a main body and thus become a peninsula. If one could find the causeway only at lowest tide — the walk to Mont. St. Michel — could this still with benevolence be called Grace? I suspect redundancy: benevolence surely is Grace, or its central atom. Back to the personal particular, if this atom lies within me (as leading character in this book) it is on some floor so many fathoms down, separated from light and air by so many nightmare creatures of the deep: plants that walk, stationary carnivores — that it is my apocrypha.

I (my character) sit (sits) by a window looking onto a snowy park where small figures ride, prance, jog; stand perhaps in awe. The connections between us are only those rays and vibrations of which sight is composed, which Will or an accident can sever in a moment.

In my opening melancholia, which I might call my Dresden-death if it made any sense, it seems to me more than ever, and in the unnatural brightness of winter sunlight, that my view, especially from the Red Study, is like a kind of Karnak seen by eyes asleep for a thousand years, through the horizontal slit-window of a tomb. All the sounds are memories today, I tell myself — and digress here to write down what I got up from a dream to write down in the nighttime:

I, Philippe Auguste, crowned at Etampe on May 29, 1180, the sixteenth anniversary of my birth.

. . . . all sounds are memories today; actually the view lies under a silence so prolonged as to have acquired the palpable and visual qualities of dust: so much time falling so quietly and steadily on the same view, undisturbed by sound or wind or night, becomes as visible as sand.

The dais on which I lie — on which my casket (the word here: precious; not coffin) lies and I atop it — is high, lofty. In death I am my own gisant, with perhaps some of my worldly worth in the casket itself. The interior of the tomb is light, lacking only the brilliancy of direct sunlight, but bright and clear and dry, and resonant with old pomp. And yet the interior, the room, is unfinished, the dais apparently resting on the peak of a cone of sandy stone, and though there is no rubble there are shards. I have never been inside a bunker, but the long horizontal window might be the same, or are a bunker's slits vertical? In my tomb the window is cut so precisely that a supine body a fraction of an inch lower or higher than my own could not have seen through it and beyond to the vast imaginary city which was not always a necropolis. This vague encroachment of city onto woodland began when the Dresdens brought it here for a Christmas surprise, but it is less vague with each experience, for its climate grows more real and influences my dreams, which are becoming city dreams: of conquests and restless burnings, burning restlessness that comes only from the knowledge of the proximity of particular possibility. One dream was simultaneous narration and experience, picked up on at some late point in the story, or life, so that for its duration I was writing itself; I was language. Do you know the terror of that? Here it is, the narration and experience, as precise as it then was, for I have endowed the "I" of this book with total recall — (though there will be a lot he will not want to recall, and will manage, sometimes, not to):

Even as he feared pain — at the very peak of his inward recoiling that the next thrust might be the one beyond endurance — part of his mind glimpsed a room wherein pain was the thing sought, longed for. At times, very rare, the experience became a textbook illustration of Platonism and the idea projected him into, or partly into, an actual room where pain, my own pain, is taking place, and I think: Yes, it *is* familiar; yes, this *is* reminiscence — straddling the threshold, part of me in the ecstasy of pain, part of me observing, fearing, reacting.

In my papers I find a paragraph whose significance only now I see: the first laborious attempt to form of particular pain one pebble for the causeway. (There are no "papers"; I compose now a tiny moment of compassion, one chord to disarm you before I attack the Dresdens, whose raging destroyer I intend to be.)

"She asked for two buns, as she always did. In the summertime it might be bagels she asked for, on a Sunday morning, or homemade cupcakes, but it was always two in quantity. The proprietor knew she could not afford two, and once he had learned her secret he fell into the habit of saying, 'Oh, Lord, there's only the one left!' except in circumstances when the goods were atop the counter instead of behind it, in sacks. And her response never failed to move him. It was not simple, was indeed complex for being made up of a kind of unacknowledged knowledge of his duplicity, and of gratitude, and of chagrin. It was the chagrin that got him, when she said, 'Well, the one will have to do for both of us.' For there was no 'us'; there was only herself and had, as far as anyone now knew, always been just herself, though she had fooled the entire Island for nearly a year by making them suppose that she had an invalid tucked away in her little house, to which she had come in the dead of night, on the last ferry, with the side curtains pulled on her ancient automobile and the back shade rolled down."

Even more shameless, I find in my papers (my "papers") this:

"Those who had just met him were told by those who knew him, or had known him: Try to get two things out of him: a dinner, and a letter. He was a person clearly at his best when not present in body. Even his telephone conversations were highly rated by some, and when tribute was paid him at his own dinner table it was paid to the person who, silent, absent in the kitchen throughout the evening, had constructed such magical dishes; in short, the chef with whom one does not often actually sit down to dine. It was this sense of his duality that let his own guests turn their backs on him without feeling in the least rude. As far as one could tell by appearances, no more did he find such exclusion rude. Usually he reacted not at all, sometimes with a slight smile which still did not seem to admit the boorishness but rather was a granting of permission (unsought) to the guest to turn away in the midst of some statement that he, the house, was trying to make. As for his letters, they marveled to each other that such grace, wit, perhaps for all they knew, such profundity, should have, however briefly, resided within the mottled and hairless walls of the skull of such a forgettable man."

The narrator of my book will, I think, like primitive people, set great store by the magic ritual of names and naming. If he has a particular succubus, female, he could call her Bea — to bea or not to bea; or Else — do this or that or Else; or a host of other reverberant names through which he might try to get beneath her guard to her heart. She could come to stand for all of his obsessions, but perhaps he is too shallow (she among others may have said so) to be continually obsessed. At times he could be free of her, hag-ridden only by her daily telephone calls, which he learns to confine with other matter in a cage upon whose specifications he has collaborated. When the cage is opened the possession is total, and it is these times when the rites of magic occur, such as naming. In the process he too assumes other names and identities into which he slips like a man into a river at night. Emerging, he is disorientated: at what place upstream had he slid out of his own skin? and in the darkness he makes his way, stumbling, sometimes panicked to think that his skin may have been assumed in his absence by another. The narrative of his life becomes erratic, its boundaries, watery due to his Island dwelling, drawn by Meander, but this erratic journeying is reserved for night.

A layering of his life occurs, which can be tentatively set down this way, subject to change:

1. Diurnal narrative (3rd person)
2. Journal entries (1st person)
3. Translation of experience (all persons)
4. Nocturnal narrative (?)

And "?" is a failure grown from ignorance: "who" the narrator of the nocturnal narrative is is not known, though "what" it is will be guessed at when he is groping on dark stairs or through the more remote corridors of the brain. Just as "not to name" is as well a form of magic, he does not name it, and if it is called *madness* he will not address it so. To hold at bay its identification, he settles upon personae for himself, for the succubus, or witch, and for his companion, the bitch. To these he will return when wanderings have taken them too far afield. For himself, Saint of Wanderers, Christopher, or plain Chris; for the witch, initially, Bea, or better, Beatrix; and for his bitch, *his* only by virtue of her goodness and willingness, still his only possession; sometimes he sees her as his salvation made manifest and he aspires to her — he chooses after much deliberation, Miss Gold: precious malleable strut of the earth.

Revised epigraph, with themes and a faint allusion to old religious affiliation:

Where is charity? Where compassion? Did you expect to find them here? This is a house of threats.

Too, of threads, leading nowhere. This labyrinth is sealed with lead. This is the house some children dreamt of, some silently baying with throat too open to scream; for those silent screamers, all sphincters opened in the horror of that sleep; mother was furious.

This is a house of doors and behind each, darkness, and behind the darkness, this house.

This is a house beyond philosphy, which is the lees in the cup when the wine of Art has been drained. Groups of artists walk through the rooms of this house cleaving unto each other not by choice but for the cold nurture of mutual venom. They are beyond philosophy; they are this house.

Beyond this house? Only a bell, sometimes heard in the evenings, stirring in some minds a chiming word — complin — and the faint sadness of old bereavement, a feeling, as distant as charity and compassion, that the bell is the sole survivor of a family of seven.

CHRIS

That first winter on the Island was haunted from its onset, which arrived with one of those rare snows that clings to all surfaces no matter their convolutions, so that each twig of each branch of each tree is furred with ermine. The snow stuck to walls of buildings as though glued there, and then it all froze hard as stone, and the bay with a great crackling in the night threw onto the beach for a distance of fifty yards immense blocks of ice which the natives called ice cubes.

Once, inspecting the phenomenon by torchlight while his convalescent bitch strove to relieve herself, grunting as the effort caused her stitches to strain and hurt her, Chris heard over her gallantry a peculiar whirring. It was a dry sound like old breath. He turned the torch about the beach and saw the long grasses bent low by a wind and saw how they turned like compasses, drawing on the sand perfect circles. The results were like impressions left by the landing gear of flying saucers.

He would sit in the glassed-in garden room, back to the roar of the new fireplace, holding his dachshund on his lap, and watch the trees riot as dusk came on, always to the waterflow of Chopin, and would see, as though they were cut out of the same piece of paper, the frieze of squirrels mounting from the feeding stations to their various caches in the trees. They looked Blakean to him, unimaginably tortured or afflicted with joy, though at their extreme, he thought, the emotional effect was the same. All was greatly heightened by the music, which could cause the most banal scene in a film to seem to be permeated with meaning.

The trees up which the squirrels clambered in endless transport were the kind loved by mistletoe, the growth for him most likely to force a tendril through the closed door beyond which superstition had been gathering dust. Ash trees, holly trees, rowan trees, ivy, and mistletoe: one or all of those words or realities could cause him to set burning mental fires on hillsides. One gray siege of a day he bought entrails from the butcher in the village and twined a tree with them.

Once, feeling something nameless in the car with him, in which he returned through the stormy night without his bitch, whom he had left in the Animal Hospital, on the Mainland, distended with peritonitis — feeling the space in the car grow less, he stopped the motor and fell out onto the road and rolled about, protecting his head with hands and arms, and in the ditches bordering the road, brackish with glints of ice, he heard sounds he would not try to describe for fear of success.

Though the winter was haunted, unavoidably because of his bitch's lingering illness, which mysteriously caused her to lose patches of fur, there were long stretches of days and nights whose coloration, psychically speaking, never varied. He read Cicero's letters: sed heus tu, manum de tabula! magister adest citius quam putaramus — and tried to update witticisms and simultaneously, through translation into Greek, to rediscover his small knowledge lost like a penny in the long grasses of a life gone random. Veroer ne in Catonium Catoninos was a natural when Kennedy was substituted for Cato, and he was amused to let Κατω, which means "the world below," stand for Kennedy Airport, but he became despondent at where κατ led: to curse, and bribe, and abomination; to despise, stone, attack; and eventually to shoot down. That was before the second assassination.

That winter he fought a rosebush. It had torn at his bitch's coat so fiercely that she could not free herself. He had been standing gazing at the distorted sea under a glaring moon, open to the rush of atavism of which her pained grunts had become a prolonged part before he turned and saw her predicament. He freed her and took her back to the fireside, then dressed in leather: long coat, gauntlets. The rosebush flailed thorny arms in the wind at his approach. He grasped one end of the tough trailer with one hand and with the other, grotesque in its heavy mail of leather, he began to flog the rosevine. At first the vine was resilient and took his blows meekly, but as he continued it seemed to stiffen, as though the loss of a number of its thorns actually got its back up. *Best be polite to those whose temperaments are unknown to us, especially on nights of storm and wind. Nature covers so many unpleasant sounds that mortals make — screams; sounds of expiration — with her own cacophony. Yes, indeed, even little boys should know that it's best to save our bad tempers for those times of guaranteed continuing calm. Now kiss Mother good night.* Tensile as a snake the vine curled and coiled, rising from the pressure of each whack higher and higher until it was swiping at his trousers below the knee, then above, then at his shirt, then clawing at his neck as though to tear the heart vein. In the house the bitch howled; on the beach the ice groaned; long whips of smoke from the chimney lashed the treetops which clawed at the sky. He stood, when sanity returned, over the rosebush with the ax from the woodpile, visions of blood slowly sifting into a mirage of summer blossoming. Retracing his steps to return the ax, he found the place where he had fallen in his murderous haste, the huge imprint of his hands in the snow.

Though it did not seem to him a noteworthy addition to his opus privatus cognitio, that night he wrote in his journals:

"Is it the talk of violence, the constant talk, that makes one think so much of buying a gun? It may be therapeutic for the dark races to be able to talk aloud about killing whites; to be able to exhort each other to buy guns; but a climate does not merely affect those who created it by seeding clouds. Once the clouds are seeded and the hard rains fall, all are affected who stand within the radius of storm, Therefore, everyone who hears the dinning words about guns and death, regardless of color, will be affected in at least one of several ways: he will feel fear; he will want to hide; he will want to buy a gun and use it; he will feel fear and want to buy a gun and hide and use it; a sniper is born."

It is true that you have feared violence all your life and just as true that you have abhorred it, and because of it, at least partly, you have put cities behind you. In violence you see the violation of all privacy because, being of arbitrary nature, violence is entirely directionless once unleashed, so that a stranger can, in the reign of anarchy, walk up to another stranger — you — and violate the privacy of your person, a much more secret entity than that of the mind. You inhabit your mind without cease; even in sleep you are a mind-dweller, therefore you know your mind — its quirks, method of logic, strongest and weakest points — quite well; your conscious mind, at least, and it is for your conscious body that you feel fear. You inhabit your body and know its appetites — the why of them — but its functions are mysterious, and toward them you feel tender, and for them you feel fearful. The minutiae of its decay is pure anomaly, as was, in its brief day, your beauty. Therefore, when anyone touches you or speaks of touching you, they violate you in a way you are not able to understand, condone, tolerate. It is the total mindlessness, the lack of a tinge of the conscious or of the familiar, in the threats that have become public — threats which leave only the terribly private bodies to clash — that unpens the mindless wild boar that has guarded your body for so long. It is the feeling of that upthrusting tusk needing to be touched with blood that translates itself into such violent action as tonight's.

All that day the hunters had ranged the drifted woods slaughtering the furred and feathered, among which he placed, out of loyalty to Emily Dickinson, hope. His own days of blood sport were so tangled in underbrush that their memory was as rare as glimpses of his atavistic nature. As once he had been roused on snowy days, from reading or listening to his mother play the piano, by the sound of hunters, and been driven to take his rifle from the rack and join the blood feast, so did he now feel the balance of the piece (killing and études become one) and the weight of ammunition in the pockets of his mac, and he tracked the hunters in imagination, and topping the rise, zeroed in on their scarlet, against which blood would reluctantly show, and shot them down one by one; until, ravenous and impatient, he imagined the light rifle into a submachine gun and whirled on his hilltop, slicing them off where flower joined stem like a field of red poppies; and at the same time he was killing music, Scarlatti, unavoidably, though his mother had played nothing but Bach.

"Look," she had said, commending the day to him, "how beautifully new." Sulky, he replied, "I've seen it before." She told him — peculiar that he could recall each word, perhaps because the words were peculiar in such quantity from her, but he imagined later that she had known she was to die in a matter of days ("Be precise if you can"—"Yes, Mother"), in four days' time. She told him, "You have never seen this place before," and when he looked at her, frightened, for it was their own woodland they walked in, she said: "Never, never, never have the leaves bent precisely so in the wind; never has the sedge faced us from just that angle of the bog; never has decay been at this particular point visible on the wood of fence, tree; never has this peculiar collection of detritus edged the road; never have so many, so precisely many, leaves hung dead at the same time, nor has the illusion of blue between been so precisely *this* blue, never." But it was not hindsight that told him of her impending death. It was language, her use of language, the mystery of language itself. She had, in an odd way, herself become a Bach structure, knowing that she would not, with woefully inadequate ghost hands, be able to find particular oblivion. He, surely her instrument on that day, as later, responded to her sureness by learning all that he was meant to know in his persona as sonata verging upon nocturne.

By spring he realized that he had no idea of the look, much less of the personality, of one single Islander. At the post office people nodded and he nodded back; driving on the narrow roads hands were flung up in greeting, or, a more Island habit, one finger was lifted from the steering wheel, which slightly comic, slightly insulting gesture he returned. But the nodders and wavers and finger-signalers had no more solidity for him then he imagined he had for them. They had existed side by side through the winter like ghosts of different centuries in a house: sensing the other presence, perhaps, in passage, but never really seeing.

Nowhere in his new life was there a thought or wish for another person. Sex was a closed fist, conversation was in books or in his head, invented or recalled; in either case, an improvement over the real thing. If he had only substituted one kind of emptiness for another, there was no one in his present life to know. A shallow man, alone, may gain a distant reputation for depth. He may be talked about, with surprise, for his suddenly revealed inner resources. The inability, so pronounced by prolonged human contacts, either to experience or translate into art the expected passions, becomes suspect, is seen — perhaps — as a cover-up, and his attempts at art may be re-reviewed and the cool, even, precise, and passionless surface may tantalize with the suspicion that its opacity is not dullness but deliberate obscuration!

The visitation occurred when Chris was asleep in the old master bedroom, a room he had never used nor slept in, whose door he usually kept closed because of a vague instinct that it was the right thing to do. On its own the door swung nearly shut, a soundless slow swing as though pushed by a breath, or by someone's long-armed, sleepy reach. When he first arrived at the house he had concluded that the room's capacious lightless closet was just the place for things he never expected to use again: ski and squash clothes, squash and tennis rackets, skates, riding breeches and boots, the closet a repository of youth and community, which he had come to believe was an alliance irrevocably broken off from the mainland of a life — floating in the past like a secure and unreachable island — by the certainty, a sudden, riving force, of one's growing old.

It was a sleety sleepy day that drew him to take Miss Gold and go to the room, to the bed by the window where one might watch the rain striking the roof of the porch and, beyond, the moor and what wild things that might venture out into the freakish winter revival to crop and root.

Miss Gold's rising hackles under his soothing hand brought him, or so he imagined, wide awake and into another's life. He thought that he was a young girl. In any case, he was a weeping female. The two people behind him were plain to him in all details of features and dress though he did not turn around. It was as though he had watched them dress, watched them leave, and had imagined until that moment that they were still out of the house — at church, he thought at first, until some intensified carnality made the thought profane. Seeing the man on a street in another country, a stranger would have recognized the sea in him. He was salt cured, permanently darkened. He would have looked foreign on any land.

The woman rustled like a listener in a closet. It was as though she were forgetful, in her need to hear, of the garments hung about her.

Chris was mesmerized by his duality. He felt himself chambered, hermaphroditic, the two sexes and sex itself clamorous within him. The force of sexual desire in the other half, which had commandeered his body so newly, was shocking to his mental celibacy. More than the ghostly possession, the assault of desire threatened his mind. The tenderness of self-regard that he had felt for a moment, when the weeping began, the softness, vulnerability of a young wounded thing, maiden in all respects, was clamped about with a fist of knotty need, perverse and breath-stopping. It was associated with a killing instinct, primal as a cave. Side by side, he felt the swelling of his cock and the opening of another organ as though he moistened and gaped to receive himself. With great effort, over the distinct beating of two hearts, he called out. At his voice his bitch's tail beat the bed hard, a frantic recognition of familiarity, and something — perhaps a need to reassure her — brought him back to himself.

He lay stupified, feeling himself sorely hurt by the occurrence as though he bled internally. His effort to cry out whipped at his mind like a flail to induce a remembrance that was not there.

Escaping to the garden room with the bitch, it was as though he carried with them the dark salty man and the voyeuse.

His journal entry for that night was: "What form?"

The shiny new kitchen is like nacre in the twilight, a series of glimmers from shined surfaces as you pass and then out like

brief candles. Then to your — is it dismay — one light will not
be doused, and you see that it is an old kerosene lamp hanging
from the ceiling, no ceiling you have ever seen but bare rafters,
and when you turn for reassurance to the glass door and the
pear trees beyond you find a wooden door as solid as finality,
heavy oak to keep out a frost that struck summer a killing blow
that hard early winter in 1884.

ONE TWO THREE MUDDIED RIMED STEPS on the wide splintery
clean boards of the kitchen floor; three steps from the door
into the kitchen and then it's as if the walker had been lifted from the earthly plane leaving as evidence of his Assumption only a trail of dark drops from the last footprint
toward, and disappearing behind, the stove. Under the
stovepipe whose red-rashed elbow is being damper-sooth-
ed; around the woodbox containing no new litter, no charming mewling creature nor kindly settled one (ants in the
hastily stacked wood seep sluggish in the heat, unloved,
trap-doomed, admired for industry), and here the shoes:
deep-creviced, ankle-bulged, organic appearing as the recently severed pads of a very old beast; the right shoe has
a loosened sole; through the interstice the exposed stitching hangs like ruptured tendons.

"I admire you, I certainly do that, being so wrapped up
in your business that you couldn't smell the frost."

The shoes stand drying, curling with inaudible sounds of
striction, as masculine as barns in their odorous gathering
pools.

"About a third, I guess, salvaged; the rest turning black
before my eyes. Oh, I called. All I got for my troubles was
the old rooster. Thought I was calling him to feed. Thinks
about nothing but his appetite now. Too old for ought else."

The shoes' owner — or their possession; he would sleep

44

in them if allowed — sits at the oilcloth-covered table bending over boiling soup, his heel-propped feet in steaming wool stretched out and pointed like a dropped doll's. Between bending and sucking at the soup and grunting he watches his wife, who is able to scold through tight lips, as she hurriedly preserves the frost-rushed harvest, and wonders if out of her innate and admired frugality she is making the ultimate gesture of waste by stirring into the jars her own death in botulins. (You know where your death is but do not yet know its guise.) Under the swinging lamp the grizzled cheeks seem encrusted with the hoarfrost that lights the night beyond windows down which drops of inscriptive condensation slide.

"Stew him, I guess, next time ary brave soul ventures to come see us. They better hurry, though, before winter closes down the ferryboat. If they want to see all here as it is. Spring will break on a different homestead, is my guess. A winter of change, I'm sure of that as I stand here on killing feet. The first fall in a lifetime that has got more of the garden than I have. If that's not omen there's no such a thing. It's plainly saying, 'Look out for the coming winter.' The *coming* winter, mind, for I'd wager on changes before the first snow flies. Oh, when I called and you didn't come help me gather in my garden, that was change enough. But it won't be the last, mark my words. For once change sets in, it piles on up. No, it won't hardly be the last by a big margin."

In the long portentous pause following her prediction, he makes a prediction of his own, waits for it to come true with the soup dribbling from the suspended spoon like the last drops of a life too scalding hot for pleasurable consumption; when it is taken it is taken in pain and doggedness. His prediction is that she will remind him of this quality of his life, for such reminders have never been slow from her lips, or absent from the eyes and manners of others. This thought has stitched his day together, held it taut like lacing on a football. Now he wishes to deflate the day, withdraw the stitching, burst the swollen thing too much like an idiot's head for his liking.

His wife draws in her breath as though it were a bitter brew and attests to his talent for prophecy.

"It's like your forgetting whether or not you helped that girl to murder —"

He slams the plate of soup at her back, wishing that the red tomato stains imparted to her dress were from the seepage of her blood, which would make her screams entirely bearable to him.

He stumbles from the kitchen through the enclosed breezeway dark as a mole's house. The parlor is lit by a feeble lamp, a child's lamp of tinware with its trimmed wick turned low. It was a gift from his stepmother, the murdered woman whose face he has encountered at every turning through the long day. Beyond its dimly glowing chimney she may be nodding and beckoning, knowing something about his day's voyage that he himself does not yet fully comprehend, though he is filled with suspicion as sweet as a lover's to whom the prospect of reconciliation makes the quarrel desirable. In case she really is there, he, all hackles, makes obeisance, hurried and in spite of disquiet, half forgetful, for in passing the lamp he seems to be leaving her too, seems to be making his way toward a time that did not contain her nor a seed of her. In the process of passing the lamp and her he thinks briefly that in a way he is restoring her to life, raising her from the grave to which she went a murdered soul (for in condemning her as a witch posthumously they had taken from her her immortality) and placing her in the future with all the horror still to come, and then he reaches a threshold over which she has not yet stepped and walks across it into his parents' bedroom.

A man in his last days may be simultaneously in many places. All of life is compressed like a checkerboard so that he may step from light to dark square, from past to present (the future is now the past) with no effort to speak of.

All the day he has been accompanied by his death without being able to determine its ultimate guise; all day he has stepped from square to square, has stood at times with one foot in shadow and another in light, wearing simultaneously the joy and sorrow of his life like a harlequin suit.

Now he stands within a bedroom in which he has sired children by the screaming shrew (her voice faint as some memory), and it is as it looked to him fifty years ago when it contained his mother's joy and his father's mystery: clutter. His mother was an untidy saint. A capacious room but the furniture was larger. High dark headboard and footboard like a king's bed, billows of feather mattresses, bolsters aslant and askew, goose-down comforters held together by large stitches. A heavy chair — mahogany? — and a stool, his father's pride, covered in cordwinder's leather. But when he gazed into the room as it had been the stool was not there, or rather it was insubstantial, wavering in uneven lines of light as though to find, piecemeal, its place. Had his father wanted such a stool, and had he, returned from Spain, brought the cordwain — cordovan — as some kind of offering? Two immense wardrobes, the Dutch "kas," painted, carved as sarcophagi, with massive mirrors on the insides of the doors, probably a New World addition. Tables, one scallop-edged and inlaid *at which she, doomed, sat, forestalling the sword of Schahriah* Lamps, candlesticks, framed needlework. A small, tiled, lady's fireplace hiding timidly behind enormous poker and shovel and tongs. Curtains of rusty plush with ballfringe edging and ties. Silent clock of bronze, part of his mother's bride effects, hushed by his father who did not like its voice; he said it spoke a foreign tongue, by which he meant, not Dutch. That was the room in winter, which was how he nearly always thought of it in connection with parents. In summer it was stripped to the bare boards. Then, the bed wore a flat pad of flock, and thin pillows. The fireplace was lightly filled with greenery. The windows were barely veiled in panels of white linen, woven from their own flax by his mother, which seemed always to be blowing into the room and catching on things.

He sees both rooms at once, the winter room with its long heavy nights, the sprightly summer room as slim as a young girl. He starts toward his mother, who stands, as though she waits in an entranceway, between the two rooms in an oblong of light. He walks cautiously, for all his longing to touch and be touched by her, watching with foxy eyes for the least hint of change. When it comes he is nearly prepared, and he wheels away a fraction after the first flicker, but in the split second it takes his brain to direct his body to turn, his mother's face has been overlaid with that of the other woman, only his mother's eyes peering through those of the other woman a bit wistfully and then out like a light.

February 28

I turned for reassurance to the child's lamp of tinware and finding my bedroom lamp, rheostat turned low, I ran, ignoring my lady's whimper of alarm, toward the kitchen to stay his flight, but midway a sense of foolishness caught up with me.

Time compresses and becomes itself indivisible; I believe this; but I do not know the reverse equation. I do know whose face it was peering through "my mother's" and replacing it. I address her, you: Beatrix, it is your game but I am willing to play, for this reason: two heads *are* better than one and I do not care, especially, which skull forms the outer covering at what time (if we are like a set of Chinese boxes). If we interpret events turn by turn, can illumination fail us? for you are, like me, in darkness until another intelligence acknowledges you. I acknowledge you: "I," not Chris; and "you," not Beatrix, though the meaning had gone from that clause before I could set it down. Perhaps "you" were the voyeuse, the ghost-lady. All I know is that in giving you your head, I found mine, briefly, though I am not certain why this conviction is so strong: an old man, perhaps a murderer, dying, perhaps, when my grandfather was crying his first greeting to the world: my liberation? And yet I admit to the sense of it. If you were a prism and I could turn you in the sunlight, I would ask you (as Beatrix had Chris ask himself): "What form?" meaning, what of the voyeuse can you show me? The old boy was (is) experienced, unshockable, I think. But how would she, in her rusty pose of sanctity, respond to some post-mid-twentieth-century spells (if she is the hidden witch?) Would she revel, smoke pot, fuck? There was, in her silence, a knowledge to match his of the ways of the world — would you say? She knows its structures and protuberances, its lookouts and burrows, perhaps. Its barrows, too? Winding red twine onto a cocklebur, did she ever catch a glimpse of this, of us, in those rifts between worlds?

MIDSUMMER—SEXTET / *for E. and S.*

They look well together. She is small, zaftik, thick-cream skin, slowmoving — a Sabra who chooses to be called Sabra. He is reedy, sinewy, with a carven face, and quite black; after a day in the sun, fishing off Buoy #16, there is a rosy undertone to the black, something I would have thought impossible to discern. Both have pronounced accents, hers Israeli, his Brazilian — no, for he advised me of the difference: the Brazilian English is generally American, whereas his inflections are British (upper-class, though he did not say this). They met while he was at Eton. What she was doing in London at the time, neither of them say, but her stay there was long enough for his schoolboy crush to grow to match her mature, if that's the word, passion; she is twenty years his senior, or thereabouts. I will say that he is twenty-three and let her carry the ball.

She is American by adoption, as he now is; she was American when they met. When asked about her defection from Israel she says only that she found the country confining. What greater liberties she finds in New York are not too clear beyond the cultural; she is critical of the city without the endless conditionals supplied by most New Yorkers when denigrating the city of their choice.

They live together just off Riverside Drive on 101st Street. One is prodigal with the few details one has. How they came to the Island is not too interesting: the casual introduction at a party, the fervid invitation offered after too many drinks, the promise to keep in touch. The only surprise was the letter, months later, remindful of the offer to put them up.

It has been raining for weeks. The prospect of being housebound with total strangers is not captivating. One wonders especially about her: will there be a problem about food? The lobsters are just beginning to be plentiful, beef and lamb, except for the goatlike New Zealand, are in short, outrageously priced supply, the clam bake season is upon us. All the old irritation at the persistence of dietary laws long outmoded by refrigeration is revived. One is never able to reconcile the surface sophistication with the mumbo jumbo of culinary taboos; one bristles in advance against the reappearance of superstition in the Space Age. Not, as it turns out, unfounded this time around. Sabra bypasses the clam dip, the mussels, favors the quiche only after inquiring about the presence in it of the traditional pork, which has been left out.

I believe in bad beginnings, for there is no place left to go but up.

They are good at conversation, charmingly challenging. They do not allow small talk, for upon the most trivial subject they turn their lively curiosity and dissecting abilities. After brief exposure to them, this time, one no longer wonders what they see in each other. They are each other's audience, constantly renewed, always stimulating. Even silent, they speak to each other with glances and small gestures, with half-smiles and nearly imperceptible nods and shakes of the head; sighs, inaudibly, eloquently, affect silk jersey and batik halter. One becomes aware of the underlying conversation, their world of code. By the end of dinner, celebrating with cognac, I have broken the code, they all unwitting.

I described someone who, though in her fifties, looks thirty-five. Sabra is incensed, and I for her; it was tactless — or would have been if I had not calculated word and response. She says, "Your youth cult is one of the most depraved things about this country. What, please tell me, is wrong with a fifty-year-old face looking fifty?"

We, it evolves, are in earnest agreement. She then confides that she avoids, like the very plague, looking at herself. I see that on this subject she can be reckless, or perhaps must be, for it evokes — the response has a rote tone — his reassurances. Discreetly I inquire about the art, which must be precise, of make-up (I do not say "especially in your case"). It seems that she knows her face so well that she can do even a subtle job without watching herself do it. "Still," I say, sympathetically candid, "you cannot go through life avoiding mirrors." He is pleased. It could be a line from a Tennessee Williams play. Together he and I recall Giraudoux's "Madwoman" and the polished brass gong on the closet door. Sabra does not know the play; he and I share secret knowledge of the harridan who dwells in mirrors, necessitating the gong; his eyes ask me not to quote the speech. It is not a pleading look, nor peremptory; it is a reminder of noblesse oblige. I am a sucker for noblesse oblige. Sabra has not missed the byplay. He and I now have a code, and she has the task of deciphering it.

I do not remember how she and I established a code of our own. I would not have tried, being certain of rebuff, so it must have been at her behest. Let us pretend it went this way: He misses some reference; he is lighting a cigarette, which he does with absorption, like a child first enamored of a match; returning to earth, Prometheus with the gift of fire, he has to ask to be enlightened. My mouth open to comply, I see her signals flaming across the darkness to which we are to consign him; my craft, if floundering, is to be saved, but his must crash into the meteor. If he is hurt, he does not cry out nor does he repeat his request for rescue.

By bedtime we are all allies, all antagonists, three groups of two — a larger week end than I had — no, not *imagined;* than I had counted on.

Freedom. "It does not extend to include giving pain." One is emphatic. They have brought the sun with them. The Sound is blue and clear, barely ruffled, though our faces are cooled by constant lightly moving air. I am at the wheel, they are trolling astern, Sabra sturdy in shorts, rakishly shaded by an old sombrero found in the barn. Efraim's white ducks are wet to the knees and his cuffs give off the faint stench of marsh mud picked up when incautiously boarding the boat. He wears a dark blue skivvy. The only other craft at Buoy #16 is crowded with Negroes from the Mainland casting for blues. They are interested in Efraim, who appears to be unaware of them or their interest. As far as one can tell, his obliviousness is not feigned.

"What if the pain is wanted?" As though I might have heard *wonted*, Efraim amends the sentence: "What if the pain is sought?"

I see him bent under the cane at Eton, submissive before Sabra in her native androgynous army uniform. I ask:

"Are there Penitentes in Brazil?" I refrain from quickly turning to catch their silent communication, but when I finally do turn, Sabra's profile retains the squinch of distaste, held patiently, I am sure, for my notice. Noted, it fades, and she gives me a quick darting smile which he cannot see — the sombrero tilted against him — but must divine, because she wishes him to. Ah. We dislike him for his Catholic link with flagellantism.

Efraim apologizes for his slow response to my question. His mind is oddly blank on the subject, even after intense effort. It seems that he should know about the Penitentes, or Brazilian equivalent, but he muses that perhaps the Portuguese Catholics are too reserved. He is sorry, but he does not know. Can we look it up in some reference book at my house?

He is rueful. "The freedom to know is surely one we all abuse through specializing? We are educated —" His smile is amused at the assumption. He gestures with the lightly held fishing rod which tautens the line and snags something. Only his hands show his excitement. As they reel in the line his voice keeps its polite academic tone. "Some research among us should have unearthed that fact. Actually, basically —" the latter word his identification, like a birdcall — "it might be made to fit biology as well as psychology —" neatly combining his and Sabra's fields, "but it is religious and extremist, and bigotry is what basically stands between us and such knowledge."

As a thesis it has possibilities, but as comment in toto it is unsatisfactory. A bluefish a foot long flashes at the end of his line before it makes a dash for freedom, the reel humming with its flight. Efraim plays it calmly, his British inflection growing pronounced, so that the mechanics of its use, a most particular form of coolness, is revealed. "Willfully not knowing is a form of bigotry, don't you think so?" The fishback clears the water. "For instance, Sabra, what do you know of Catholics?" There is a thorn in his voice.

"Hardly anything at all." I wait for her to be baited further. Instead, he asks me, "And you, of Jews?"

"Some of the 'don'ts.' Something of the self-absorption, justified, no doubt, and the paranoia."

"The pluses?"

"Everyone knows those. They are widely publicized." I do not resist adding, "By Jews."

"Trumpets blow down walls," Sabra says easily. They smile at each other without code.

"Physiognomy?" he asks me, and as his hands tense on the rod to land the fish, I detect the planned drama: curtain line and coup exactly to coincide.

"Jewish?" I ask, all at once certain of my footing. "No, you and Sabra, for example, have no similarities." The fish is lowered into the boat gently, a last minute change, so that the anticlimax is minimal. I say, unnecessarily, "But it's a religion, after all, isn't it, and not a race," knowing that the often controversial words will elicit, this time, no response.

I am sorry to let go the image of him rapt before the altar, or as acolyte genuflecting, taper in hand. He is a poetical man, and Catholicism has the visual aspects of poetry in a limited edition: the placement on the vellum page, the illuminated capitals; with the horrors of the ages confined, or nearly, to the spaces between the lines.

We have transformed the garden with dozens of candles in colored glasses set among the flowers. In the afternoon while Sabra naps and I spy on him, Efraim has cleared the fountain of last autumn's detritus, frugally carting the rich mass of leaves and twigs, compacted as hashish, to the leaf-mold pit, and set the rusty little pump going. The faint drone of the pump under the gush and fall of the water (from a salmon's mouth; the bronze salmon stands on its tail and arches over the basin) sets us voyaging on the night. We dine under a vast umbrella. The most distant candles, among the calendulas, mark for us the shoreline.

I have not been fair about the spacing of the three of us on the perimeter of the round slate table. I have set them close together and myself opposite, but they are either grateful or indifferent; they do not comment. If I have denied them the ease of steadily observing each other, intending to make their silent communications more difficult, I have given them the surely more satisfying alternative of frequent touches. But after all I have put myself at a disadvantage, for I cannot see over the candleflames whether it is only illusion or fantasy that she keeps one hand on him under the table, throughout the meal. It is no fantasy that tension builds in him. His leg, stretched out, presses against mine, and I feel the knotted calf muscle.

With interesting undertones Sabra begins to speak of their yearly winter vacation in Puerto Rico. As though there were some connection, Efraim jerks his leg away from mine. As she speaks warmly, he grows morose; I imagine that he is feeling on his tropical skin the cold that must precede their exodus, for they — Sabra is saying — always leave on January the 28th ("JAN-u-dee twenty et-t-th"). I say — one is tempted to write "idly," but it is no longer so; I am certain none of us any longer affords that luxury, and I wonder as I speak what her reason is for telling the story in just such a tone — I say, not idly, "I have never been there." No one springs to immediate action. There is a silence in which they somehow communicate, perhaps argue; his defeat is barely marked, a shrug too small to be imagination, irony passing across his eyes like a cloud shadow, but I know his position when Sabra, victorious, says, "Then you must, by all means, *come*. We keep a flat there —"

My surprise is not intended to be polite; they have talked so much, without saying the words, about being poor. As though she hears my question: "On what do you keep this flat?" — she says, "A modest flat, but there's a spare room."

I am satisfied. I have heard that Puerto Rico can be a bargain.

I intend to decline with thanks and explain that if I go anywhere in winter it is to deeper cold, characterizing myself as
engaged in an eternal search for the Splendide-Hôtel, the polar
wastes. But . . . and without that conjunction there would be no
fiction. But . . . her insistence weighs a ton, offending her lover
whose spareness proclaims at every point his loathing of the
self-indulgence which leads to any obesity. He takes the narrative from her, and his recital is an exercise in subdued savagery.
An attempt to duplicate his words or manner would result in
failure, but when he offers me the spare room I would have
agreed to occupy it, if for no other reason, out of a kind of fear:
perhaps by intrigue, I have been drawn up to the boundaries of
indiscretion which, stepped over, will have me pleading that we
leave for Old San Juan at once, at my expense. Such is the pull
of that spare room.

Dining on bluefish we talk about food. Efraim is nostalgic
for the potted shrimp of England. Sabra gives him a playful
swat which admonishes: *Shrimp?* Politeness to the winds, I ask
a pointed question. She can be pedantic, and is, on the subject of
the Jewish dietary laws. Her observance is a reminder of who
"we" are, where "we" came from, where "we" could wind up
without such reminders. Pressed, she adds, "It's about the only
gesture of solidarity of which I'm now capable, and others feel
this way, too." Weary, condemnatory, she says: "*Assimilation.*"
Suddenly resentful of my lack of sympathy, she asks me if I
really feel Christian about anything — when I celebrate, for example, Christmas or Easter? I tell her, no; what I mainly feel is
oppressed. She persists: What makes you feel Christian, then?
I ponder, at a real loss, and have to tell her, "Nothing." She
smiles. It has been a game of one-upmanship. We turn to Efraim, who spreads his hands: Don't ask me; then he says to Sabra, lazily sexual, "You." She apparently is his only link with his
Jewishness, a handsome, stalwart link. She snorts in amusement,
then assumes an expression of parodied sensuality. "I'm kvelling,
darling."

Efraim receives a telephone call. It is late, after midnight. We are still at the table. The garden phone is at my elbow. I hand him the receiver across the table. He will take the call inside, if I don't mind. When he has picked up, at the desk just inside the window, I tantalizingly hold onto the receiver until Sabra takes it from me in a masterful performance of absent-mindedness — as though her hand has become my hand — and replaces it. As much as a half minute has passed, but all that has issued from the telephone into the garden has been someone's "Hullo."

She explains: They had simply forgot to tell me that his sister had written to say that she would call from Brazil at such and such a time, and the answering service obviously had passed the call along to the Island. There has been none of the clangor and alarms of long distance, none of the gabble and static. I know the vagarious nature of telephoning to and from South America, of which the North American experience nowadays is a not too faint echo; add to that the peculiarities of the independent Island system — I do not tell her — and chaos could result. But perhaps she is Christian in her belief in miracles. It would surely be a miracle if I believed a word she is saying. She knows this and challenges me to pursuit. Behind me, at the desk telephone, Efraim listens, asks "When?"; a pen scratches on paper, he says, "Yes, certainly," and hangs up.

I can barely wait for his return. His slow steps sound palsied to me, but when he is in the garden the gravel crunches briskly under his energetic stride and the candleflames rise to the swirl of air he brings with him, a clean stirring as though he flings salt in his wake.

"How is your sister?" Is anyone vindictive enough for the question? If so he answers, "Puffectly fine, thank you." Curiously demonstrative, as though riding the rush of an injection of amphetamines, he slaps Sabra's arm with his open palm, a quite hard slap. What has this told her? for there must have been pain. She smiles, sad and fatalistic, Mona Lisa. The sad fatalism throttles beginning speculations about stock market coups: their celebrating broker detained by martinis and envy; and yet I think that only money and love (and drugs) can release inhibitions to such a degree.

The brandy, Efraim pouring, clouds my vision and covers

my intuition in vaporous fumes like the ground fog created with dry ice. They look — eyes veiled with wine and candlelight — to me like blind people reading each other by touch, using both hands and feet. Under the table her sandals and his canvas loafers, searching each other out, find my bare feet. The sandal leather is chilly, authoritarian; the corrugated rubber of his loafer warmer, submissive. In the market place I choose, shift so that his two soles rest on my insteps. His eyebrows lift, but he questions the night, head thrown abruptly back, and does not move his feet. Her sandal ascertains the indiscretion.

In a clipped tone that I can only characterize as professional she says, "You'll like him," and before I can say, drunken and very earnest, "I *do*," she has risen and gone with no disturbance to mark her passage. Efraim gives me a long direct look, composed of waiting. An underlying candor makes me fearful of an abrupt stripping of defenses, and I retreat behind closed eyelids. When I open my eyes he is standing beside me, asking or offering still. Relief inhabits his "Good night."

From their window above the garden, in a while I hear her: "You're a dirty boy, but boys are supposed to be dirty."

I cannot decipher the runes they have cast before me. I move to a long chair and sleep among the candles, my hand in the dewy calendulas. I wake up to a series of sounds, only momentarily puzzling, as dew and burned-out candles break the colored glass bubbles that held the fire, the bubbles imprisoned in plastic fishnet. The dull pops of breakage continue for a long while, a sequence with an odd order of its own: several pops, a reviving rest, another series, rest, renewed vigor; there are two dozen in all and in my suspense I find myself counting, fearing that sleep had deprived me of some speck of release. The morning birds are singing overhead when the last pop occurs, soft and enervated, like the bubble-bursting sound sleeping lips make. I would like to add that a cry or a sigh came from their windows above me, but only the birds sang there on the long limb of the mimosa tree, stoned on the smell of nutmeg from the heart of the pink blooms.

They are charming at my party. I watch them with pleasure.

The summer colony has turned out in costumes hardly this side of parody, a queer spectacle in the blaze of afternoon until liquor and grass and pills equalize sight and expectation. The long party will last from brunch until breakfast, and most have dressed for those hours of fullest release that stretch onward from the late dusk.

My admiration for my houseguests expands like a drug vision when, breasting an oncoming wave of celebrants escaping from the garden, some with cheeks comically ballooned like fish, I find them rapt before one of the legends of the Island summer. The woman, a power on Wall Street, is an ennuyante of stature. In a crowd of silent listeners she resembles an outcropping in the sea (birth trauma long forgot) composed of those negative virtues of speech which hold in themselves a kind of enthrallment. But she also occupies herself, sprawling across her own broad base like a degenerate siren. When one by one thralls are broken and we cast off our bonds and escape, looking back we could hope for a Parthenopean response, but she is both enchanter and rock, and perhaps the feat of diving from herself is complex beyond her imagination. Whatever the answer to her longevity, her tactic is a practical one, which is to draw within her range yet another unwary Odysseus and begin again the long excruciating song. One imagines that the unvarying chanson must hurt even her own deeply buried sensibilities, now and then, but if so she gives no sign. All summer long we have heard the chant of her husband's newly discovered perfidy. She has perfected the tale until no syllable, no emphasis, shifts. The garden is murmurous with other voices — the hardy, the stoned — in unison with the litany. After some time of these theatrics only Sabra and Efraim and I are left. I am eager to witness their resolution of the problem, certain that it will be original.

Efraim sits on the brick steps beside the Lorelei, Sabra perches a step lower, facing them. The late afternoon casts the shadow of the house upon them. Sabra sympathetically takes the hand of the droning woman and holds it, then gently carries it to Efraim's lap. As though the hand were modeling clay she kneads and shapes it around some structure there, erected perhaps for that purpose. There is sudden silence in the garden.

From beyond the shadow of the house a paean arises to the sunset.

It is a party of hands which can never seem to tan enough to hide in the darkness as unsmiling faces can. Or it is a party of hands because their natural placement is so near the primary objectives at such parties. I see four hands in Sabra's lap, none of them her own (costume my sole means now of identification). Roaming in certain quest, I see through a window the hands of the Wall Street boss-lady smoothing her skirt as she descends the stairs. Before her face emerges into the light of the lower hall, just as familiar canvas loafers and the cuffs of white ducks tentatively appear on a line with her breasts, one of her hands reaches for the light pull and the hallway goes dark.

In the circumscribed light of the piano lamp I see famous hands, campily exaggerated — distinctive links flashing — as they accompany a star of the City Opera whose pure voice rolls across my dewy fields: "Come on and fly me"; "I Went Looking for a Noodle." She prefaces an encore by reading from the current *Time* magazine the reviewer's praise for a recently dead troubador's "curious American genius for capturing in lyrics the America of the 'little man,'" then sings:

> Lord, it's hard,
> It's hard, Lord;
> Lord lord lordy
> It's hard!

Hands write busily, tear leaves from address books, search in wallets and outlandish reticules for cards, laundry lists, deposit slips. One frantic hand writes on the back of a child's photograph and pushes the photograph into Efraim's white-duck pocket, lingering there. Is the photograph of the first-born? The face I clearly saw was that of an anxious baby.

Sabra's hands. Above them I see her face absorbed. There is nothing apparently to connect face and hands, so that another's brain could be directing the hands to write. My literary party, everyone busily scribbling. I walk up behind her without stealth and bend to her straightforward script: not her own name but Efraim's, first and last, and "Calle Magdelena, telefono —"

She gives the paper to the waiting woman, someone I see at other such parties. If either of them looks at me with challenge or defiance I am too full of imagined revelation to respond. And a kind of sorrow for the woman, counting the months until Jan-u-dee. Why she must wait until then is her own cross.

I go to bed alone, neither amused nor sorry. The party murmurs around the house and grounds through my sleep. At one point, as though belatedly to gratify me, there is a sound from above, from the guest room: a prolonged whimpering moan. Miss Gold, hunting in her sleep, grinds her teeth as though she has tracked down her quarry and is devouring it. I come fully awake when the local woman arrives to cook eggs and pancakes for the remaining debauchees.

There are many loose threads, I know, which only time can knit up, but I am honor bound to one fact: I will not seek out that woman, receiver of the slip of paper from Sabra, to ask her to corroborate what I believe I know. Some knowledge does not require corroboration, some is destroyed by it. In my sleep I have set a price for Efraim based on what I believe is a sense of his worth — speculation being my strong point, indeed my stock in trade — and the price is high. To have this woman's word as proof of why they go to Puerto Rico, how they maintain the flat there, is unessential, but to have her adjust by a fraction the price I have set for him would be a destruction of my knowledge, which has become a strut for my imagination and its frequent consequences. In nocturnal imagery I see Sabra in that spare room, sleeping or listening nightly in their holiday time. Sometimes I see — no, I *feel* — myself in that room, where she would in fact have placed me, but this is fictive and complicated and, for the purposes of this narrative, discursive.

For some of us, convictions are fluid, rising and falling with the tides, bits and pieces left behind on the shore until in the daily scramble we come not to recognize the scraps of original premise among the lately acquired. For others, conviction is an edifice to which we add, without going in for actual research, any small scrap that will appear to fill a crevice. One small scrap — for I am an edifice builder — that fits and clings of its own rightness is that the former great bore of Wall Street has become a contemplative woman, who sits and smiles and plucks at her garments for a long time before she will venture an opinion on any subject. If I were Beatrix, I would imply here something about the healing power of instinctual behavior.

But back to Efraim and Sabra. I would be shocked, I think, to discover that she had set a low price for him. I cannot define it further than that.

Our farewell that summer morning at the ferry is nothing to write about.

March 14

"Where is Charity," indeed. I am plunged into summer like a sore thumb into a rotting pie to discover — what? An assuredly putrid plum. My style is cleverly mocked — brava, Beatrix, you hairy ape, you — but the promised *insight*, meant to show my vacuity in a clear light, is as fashionably empty as anything I could have written myself. I return to March, against which there is no rebuttal, to find a dizzying world of mirrors: "I" have created a Beatrix who has created a Chris who emulates, through Beatrix, "my" style, replete with hints of queerness and a nagging anti-Semitism. My original judgment — o.k., "judgment" — passed on Beatrix's technique was hardly refuted but has been borne out. (I love that touch at the end: *If I were Beatrix I would imply here* etc. You are farcical, Beatrix.) All is hints, innuendo, endless circling, *Coursing*. No gun is fired, no conclusion is reached, they fade away, like Beatrix and Jeremiah, into the mists of the Bay. "I" would write to them, at least to Efraim if he had engaged my libido to that extent. As I am writing to you, Beatrix. Within limits you set for him, he was certainly an attractive man, though you would reduce him to an easily accessible cock — like the dark glasses and scarves in "The Keepsake" — with no intimations beyond the power of his cock of how one might otherwise have responded to him. Is that because he is a "nigger," or because "Chris" is a queer? Sabra, the Jewess, is given a philosophy, a stance, while the other two minorities are left one-dimensional. That was hardly what I meant by collaboration, baby. "I" would have made Efraim listen to my philosophy, or to circumlocutions that might have intrigued him enough to reveal some of his own. I would have written to him:

"Dear Boy,

Have you read *The Counterfeiters*, I wonder? I have just bought a copy at the Library sale here. Of course I read it when it was fashionable — just after the Nobel Prize in 1947 — but I realize that I did not really understand it. In fact, I remember practically nothing about it. I see now how audacious — though I dislike the word for art or person — it is: the total exposure of self and technique and evolution of idea — while, of course, at the same time concealing all those things . . . But reading it has made me wonder (I am now at a conversation between "friends" when Edouard tries to talk about his writing) just what you had expected of me, conversationally, as a writer. All week end I wanted to say to you: I am not a conversationalist! I passionately believe this: that I would, could, not expend one idea in conversation. If one occurs, I carefully husband it until I can reach a typewriter. For me, conversation must never, under some awful penalty, be "serious"; it always should be artificial, whether the artifice is bitchery, subtlety, or — again those quotes — "serious." I would not dream of exposing myself to anyone in talk, idle or otherwise, and for me all talk becomes idle by nature of its impermanence. And this could not be changed — this idea, ideal — even if someone were recording it. The point of verbal communication, as I see it, may be to explore the possibilities of insincerity in oneself and others. This has a deadly serious — no quotes this time — purpose for me: the game of divining *how* one uses insincerity to cover *what*. I flee from confession, or what I am made to believe is real confession, as I would from an avalanche, and my own talk is composed nearly entirely of confessions. These I, perhaps recklessly, trust my audience to recognize as artificial, no matter what "real" details I throw in to season the game.

When you asked me if the story I let you read, at your insistence — "The Keepsake" — was a record of my actual experience on this Island, I felt dismay. I would not have let you read the story if it had been, and the question made me fearful that I had been badly misunderstood. In other words, which we always seem to need, I would no more put my own experience

64

into a story than I would into a conversation. The difference is that in writing I draw on the emotional side of experience and distort facts; whereas in conversation I include obvious facts and distort everything else, especially emotions. If I tell you, for example, that I adore you and give you reasons why: manners, mind, sweetness, honesty, sometimes confusion and even boredom — believe the reasons but distrust with all your mind the adoration. You can invert that directive without my help, but I imagine you won't: if I give you recognizable reasons why I could not adore you: intellectuality, skepticism, snobbism, the perverse games you play — acknowledge the facts, as you must, but completely distrust the conclusion: that I do not adore you.

As you were given neither of those choices, both can be seen as academic. And as this, being in the nature of "a letter to a friend," can also be seen as a conversation, you can conclude its insincerity and if it amuses you, try to figure out *how* it is used to cover *what*."

By which, Beatrix, I endeavor to tell you that overtness has its points. If I'm to be a queer, then make me queer. Are you a deus ex machina, or just an ex? One true thing about your tale: we all do listen in on blacks making love. Though of course you had to make Everyman-woman Jewish, did the black have to be? Obscure, circuitous, monomaniacal. But melting into you, the very type growing faint on the page (printer, take note), I know that you will doom me to the circuitous until I am weakened beyond my ability to resist (survive?) the fatal knife. Ah, there are other downtrodden misunderstood. How about a Wasp for my next summer adventure?

"Christopher"

P.S. Are we to dedicate our stories now? Then I dedicate all of "mine": For Beatrix.

In his youth, Chris would boast, he would have slept with a leper if one had been available. He always admitted that what he sought was not the brief spasm of the body but the prolonged one of the soul — as desirable, he would say with chilling effect, as epilepsy. A perfect body, he would say, was an end in itself and needed no soul within it for ballast, comfort, and so forth, and the words varied, and usually sounded witty enough for his friends, most of whom were indifferent to language.

But Chris, believing himself soulless — perfect body, decent brain, supreme uninterest in all but the shallows of life — actually was superstitious about the soul. He did not think one could grow one; he did not believe in achieved Grace by any means; he believed that Grace (soul) befell one at birth, and that it was inextricably connected with calamity. Nor did he believe that the soul, or Grace, was a "good" thing, but rather could as easily be a malignancy. Thus a fall from Grace could be a healing process: if God was Bestower, and God was malign — evidence abounded — the conclusion was, or could be, foregone.

Actually, good and evil did not engage him at all. Reaction engaged him, and vulnerability, and prolonged vulnerable reaction was what he secretly meant when he spoke of the prolonged spasm of the soul. He battened on misfortune, and when surfeited, momentarily, he would seek out his giddiest companions and go on a binge. That, and moderate drinking, and less moderate use of pot and cocaine, comprised what he termed his "human virtues."

In Low he sensed a small lode (his phrase, Lowd or Load, funny to him) and then a mine, and before he knew it he was panning the nuggets in a frenzy that became an adequate substitute for eroticism. Low was a dreadful lover, virginal and foolish. Even the way he ate, if he had to use his bare hands, reflected his terror of sensualism. He picked up a chicken leg as though he had worms on his fingers.

But he worshipped Chris — Chris's body, Chris's mind, his poems and plays, and had evolved a litany of worshipful words that he murmured whenever possible, which both soothed and repelled Chris. Lying on Chris's breast, pied as a little pony — or, pale pink and lavender, a garden of anemones — he would praise Chris in a kind of cadence, and if Chris pretended to sleep, Low would mouth the words silently while Chris watched through veiled eyes, wondering how he could get rid of the succubus.

One ending to the affair had Chris flaying him, literally taking the birthmark off, but when experimentally he gave it a dry run he was aghast at the blood, the bloody knives, and saw Miss Gold lapping at the spilled gore and then ravening it, swelling like a leech. That was the decisive image: Chris would not have her get fat for any reason.

Well, he said, Low's triturable, isn't he, like the rest of us? and mentally put Low through the apple press, dried the remains in the barn, and pounded them to powder in the Mexican mortar with the lava pestle. But scattering ashes demanded some ritual, and Chris would have no part of anything smacking of religion, pagan or otherwise, in his daily life.

Once, feeling something that out of laziness he called gallantry, he wrote his own end, at Low's hands:

"Chris began horribly to quake and shake and fell to his knees, sliding from the sofa like ectoplasm. Directly ahead of him the space under the table was as urgently inviting as a cave when wild things were about. He made for it, all homing instinct, pointing, glad of having four limbs to propel him. A voice — 'Here, you can't do that in my house —' The eyes he turned upward were certain of no mercy. The first blow was numbing, the second astounding, the third — just behind the ear — was crippling. He lay in some throes, unnamable, composed of twitches, and saw objects being strewn around him, drawers opened, a radio wrapped in its own cord put to his hand. He seemed to recall that he was in a place not his own, a place belonging to Low or a relative of Low's, and some old gift of analysis let him anticipate the arrival of the law. With a kind of satisfaction he heard that he was an interloper, and those informed of this took him away to cage him. 'Caught in the act' he heard quite often, and there was condonement for his crippling because 'they' were 'going too far.' Sometimes he wondered what happened to her, the warm companion who had curled into his arms, against his chest, who needed protection, and in the wondering times he would try to make a place for her in case she should come back to him, but he could not move, and finally he only imagined that he could think and imagine, and then he could not." Beatrix you bitch leave my lady out of this I warn you At last before he gave up worrying the subject of endings he wrote:

"Chris heard the car revving up behind him. He turned and sensed Low's triumph. 'No,' Chris said in the darkness, 'I will not be a high-bouncing lover.' Instead he stepped into the path of the car so that the headlights' abrupt beams impaled him precisely. He felt Low's black panic as he spun the wheel. The narrow road could not contain the attempted ellipse. For a moment it seemed as though Low, luck intact, would clear the slit between the trees and wind up harmlessly and unharmed in the bamboo grove, but the absurd automobile bulged in the middle as Low was beginning to do, and with full impact Low struck the virginal slit and died there.

"Chris always said that Low had been trying to avoid him, helpless at the wheel with the stuck accelerator."

THE BIRTHMARK

Low came out of the Post Office and found the car waiting at the curb. The previous night it was parked in front of the movie, the day before that it had come to an erratic stop in the middle of a green light, seeing him stranded on the traffic island. Today he found it difficult to turn his back and walk away. A superstitious child in him reminded him that the third time was the charm, but what the thirty-four-year-old man felt was longing and dread in equal measure. What he knew, the other two times as now, walking away, was that the eyes of the driver were tracing through his clothes the outlines of his birthmark, down the right side of his back and hip, like a schoolboy belatedly preparing his lesson by using tissue paper to copy a map. Low waited for his back to try to tuck in like a dog's tail. In childhood he had imagined a flowing motion, the red tide rushing up from his leg and hip and across his back and under the bridge of his backbone to be hidden there.

It was early in a springlike day, and the sun and the bay winking back at it down at the end of Water Street were drawing people out of their houses and shops, out of themselves. But the top-down foreign car was trying to drive him into himself, into the darkness that had been there since Gym Class, Fourth Grade — which he thought of in Caps, like Christmas — when the instructor had made him take off his sweat shirt like the rest of the boys and he had been exposed in his difference. Until that day his birthmark had been a family legend with something of romance about it: his mother, pregnant with him, standing at a window watching a fire that had marked him in the womb.

Before the revelation in Gym Class it was as though God's hand had touched him, alone among his brothers, with a kind of privilege. Within the family there was subtle acknowledgment of the bond he shared with his mother, and he had sensed an affinity with fire.

When even as a small boy he was dressed in long pants, it had seemed to be a tacit conferring on him by his mother of the manhood he had possessed from birth. Long pants were something aspired to by others his age, and he wore their solemnity well; he was a grave child. His brothers, one of them older than he, had continually pointed out the inequity. That the birthmark wrapped around his leg and ended pointedly just at the right instep was never seen as the reason, not by himself nor by his brothers, and his older brother had been his enemy because Low had always been accepted as the elder and treated accordingly.

None of his brothers had been witness to his disillusionment, an inadequate word, in the gym class, but talk had gone around, and Low had suffered, especially from his older brother's sudden, frightening, irreversible superiority. His smugness and cruelty — he called Low "Blaze" in private — kept the revelation constantly new and renewable. Low was not allowed to sink into despair but had to retaliate daily. With each retaliation the surface became more impermeable, for it was as though his defenses were forming into a crust, and the crust was growing beneath his birthmark where his real skin was, setting the birthmark, which was mainly smooth, into bas-relief. What had been supernaturally his, shared only with his mother and with fire, became through his own efforts, which he could not cease, like a badge forged at the world's insistence and pinned to him. He could feel the dowel pin in his back, and the space of air, and then the badge.

He wore it as Jews wore the Star of David in Germany, because they were forced to. Thinking of himself as a Jew, he believed he knew how they must have longed to tear the star from their bodies and disappear in the mass, and he believed he could share their defiance and their self-loathing, which was one of the faces of pride.

Another face of his pride made it necessary for him to hate and blame his mother in secret, for carrying the taint which was the ability to set him apart from his fellows before he was born. But he was open in his refusal to share her religion with its fiery censers and candles for all occasions. At his final confession he told the priest that fires in a church, in a world where Jews had been burned alive, were obscene reminders, and that he turned his back (laughing at the contradiction) on God's Passion. Low was certain that he heard the priest yawn.

His first job was among Jews. He sought them out, trusting them to sense his difference that was like theirs. It was a retirement hotel that employed him and gave him on-the-job training in hotel management, and he worked for the title and position with great concentration. Once he was wrapped in its protection he was tireless and good-humored; it was discovered that he had a remarkable affinity for the old and aging and an equally remarkable intuition. He responded to wishes and whims sometimes before they were voiced, and could be stern when he sensed it was required. The tips were good, his pampering was returned, there was sometimes talk of codicils. Accolade of accolades, public declarations were made that he must be Jewish, and yarmolke- and phylactery-clad he shared the morning services. He became liaison between aging lovers. He held dying hands and loved and was loved in return.

He would have stayed on forever except for the nephew of a hotel guest. The man, a problem and a failure by his aunt's admission, was given a job as desk clerk and simultaneously, or so he said, fell in love with Low.

The nephew's besiegement of that fortified citadel with the emblazoned shield which was Low's body was constant, unrelenting, and at last desperate. He was emotional and wept for Low; he was like Salome lusting for Jokhanan's head. He grew thin and more erratic, and his aunt ferreted out the reason and took his part.

She tried cajolery. She told Low, "Now we are sophisticates, I hope. On the Riviera, on the Costa Brava . . . Capri! The Parco Agosto! You wouldn't believe!" She tried bribery. "Here's a hundred. Buy something nice." Very softly and pleasantly, with her nephew pale and wet eyed in imploring attendance, she threatened.

Low did not know, or believe, that he was beautiful. Any reference to his physical appearance turned his mind's eye upon his birthmark, and that eye grew stony. He never went beyond, in his imaginings, to an actual scene where his naked body was exposed to another's gaze. The exposure to himself was sufficient to allow him to inhabit the other's sensibilities. That last session with aunt and nephew the stoniness of his manner, though they could not know it, was the nephew's after gazing on Medusa's head. Low was denounced for his arrogance. He left the hotel before he could be fired.

Heavily carapaced and aimless, like a turtle in the road, he drove, and at some point remembered the oblivion he had been able to find in mathematics at school. He sought out and enrolled in night classes where he learned the three systems — NCR, IBM and Univac — of electronic auditing then beginning to be used in banking. When he had finished the course he thought that he was armored in systems and numbers and would be employed among people who were rationally without passion, who had chosen to block out with machinery and abstractions the fires of the body.

A state auditor, impressed with Low's ability, lured him away from his job in a bank. Phil Rose was the first close friend Low had ever had. They worked side by side, as Phil said, "putting the morons on the spot." Traveling to banks throughout the state, increasingly they rode, as Low began to notice, thigh to thigh. When Low drove, the man's hand rode on his knee, then embraced the sartorius muscle, making prolonged point, pressing without knowing into Low's birthmark. At that vulnerable part of Low's body, high up near the genitals where the birthmark quixotically scattered into a firmament, a constellation of bright blisters which Low had never allowed himself to rub, the man's fingers rested and smoothed the cloth alternately as he spoke of mysterious debits. Once in the middle of a speculative sentence he had stopped talking, and his fingers had worked on as though using an abacus, and his head had turned toward Low, startled.

In Low's sixth month as manager of a Montauk hotel (no Jews allowed), a guest settled in for the winter repeated the nephew's pattern of behavior, a pattern to which the auditor had been forming himself when Low disappeared. It was a progression from veiled hint to plot to open injunction. Through the duplicity of a hotel bellhop, a homosexual who had become disgusted with Low's remoteness, Low found himself in the guest's room with the key to the locked door in the man's dressing gown pocket.

Such open beseechments as those of the nephew and the hotel guest were not strange to Low. He had grown up in a resort village that in the summertime overflowed with their kind. Several of his contemporaries, unlike Low, had from the age of sixteen or thereabouts cashed in their opportunities, acquiring techniques and an attendant vocabulary that they spouted among themselves, such words as John and Mark making them sound to the innocent like Bible students. The recitals were complex for not being composed entirely of easy fortune and occasional violence. The boys sometimes repeated with a particular mark and obscure hints of pleasure crept in. And touches of bizarreness. These latter Low recalled in the guest's room.

A confluence of the events of Low's young life occurred in that room. As he stood locked in, perfectly still, waiting, slowly a wholeness formed of which his birthmark was seen, for the first time since early childhood, as the nucleus. The birthmark pressed into his back and lapped his leg like flesh returning to flesh after a long separation. As the prodigal is accorded the ordering of the house, so did Low's body efface itself, and in so doing he imagined that he became the birthmark. It was what he was; of all he had, it was the sought-after thing, the sense of it being what made him the target of thrill-seekers.

Taking off his clothes, it was as though he were simultaneously present in the guest's room and in the Gym Class; his present belief re-formed the earlier day to a different mold. For the guest and his classmates and the gym instructor and his older brother he was a butterfly emerging in all his colors from the chrysalis. He was not proud, but his lack of confusion was complete. And all the while the man spoke soothingly of perfection.

Low went to a psychiatrist for a while with some of the money the guest had given him, a large sum at Low's insistence, payment for putting on his clothes and leaving. The man had babbled queasily, fumbling with his checkbook, begging Low to somehow understand that the perfectionist's eternal quest was knowingly for perfection forever unattainable, but that the failure was not in the imperfect object (the guest could not bear to think of the "Venus de Milo" or the "Winged Victory") but was in the seeker. He told Low about the Platonic ideal; Low told him the discussion, interesting as it was, should have occurred earlier. The man, checkbook unopened, spoke of Platonism, of things being copies of ideas with the copies always falling short. Low said, not necessarily. Perfectionists, the guest said, lived in their minds, which was as close, surrounded by pure Ideas, as they could get to God. He spoke of *reminiscense* as Low reminisced and then told the guest his idea. The guest gave up and wrote to Low's dictation. Low admitted that he wrote very well, indeed. Low told him that *his* copy of Low's idea was just about perfect.

Most of this he related to his psychiatrist, trying to remember as precisely as possible, though he prudently skipped the part about the money and his own words, and the guest's attempt to have him arrested when the stop-payment on the check had proved too late. Low had, after all, been paid for his birthmark, and his birthmark was paying for the psychiatrist's services, and to have told him so would have been rude.

Finally, there was a draw: by seeking help to eliminate the traumas resulting from his birthmark, Low was asking to be relieved, as he saw in the midst of the last session, of his vocation and livelihood.

After that the troubles he ran into were by design, the results of careful planning. His interior vocabulary had coarsened to the level of the boys' back home, so that he thought of himself as going where the meat was, and then discovered, or remembered, that the meat was wherever he was.

His face and clothed body awoke in others, as they had in the nephew and the auditor and the hotel guest, dreams of perfection and perfect fulfillment. He learned, though again it was

74

more like remembering something momentarily forgotten, how to play upon those visible dreams. He learned the stresses and tensions of dreams which, like the strings on an instrument, had their breaking point. What he practiced was a tediously slow profession, necessarily so, for he must first stretch the dream at all points to the outermost rim of the instrument, which was the dreamer, and fasten it there, and then go away. The judging of tensibility became an art, as did his sense of the duration before snap or sag would occur. He categorized his victims as the Snappers and Saggers.

Sag was worse than Snap because a sagged dream was nothing but disillusionment, which does not pay off in any currency except wisdom, of little use to him in another person, though occasionally he could feel like a philanthropist when that was a side-effect of a plan gone awry.

But a Snapper, if caught just at the snap, might and usually did in the hysteria of the pain, pay off, believing salvage possible if the payment were sincere enough. Subliminally, Low instructed them that sincere meant large. He concentrated on the middle-aged and postmiddle-aged, for their brittleness and accumulation of worldly effects, and their despair. Because he knew about the latter, he was, so he told himself, both victim and victimizer. Their pain became his, and became ultimately erotic. To have attempted the game with women, the middle-aged and the old, would have been, as he saw in one brief but bright corner of the eye glimpse, more than dangerous, probably ending in his murdering his mother by proxy.

The ploy he found most effective was to stretch and nail the dream, arrange an hour for fulfillment, disappear, gauge the tensions, and then telephone or reappear, distraught and helpless and cleanly bewildered, his faith stretched like the dream unendurably. He had co-signed . . . and now was stuck with paying off the loan, the automobile, the mortgage. His job, nameless but he said he went there every day, paid him just enough to get by; the only thing he could do now was to take off and hope the law wouldn't catch up with him. He was, in fact — the clincher — actually impotent with worry.

He worked alone, without confidant or confederate. He

turned aside any effort at acquaintanceship that came from another obviously his kind, and unless the moment was hot for
harvest, he would leave, recognition being enough to drive him
away. His work was too concentrated to give him much time
to speculate upon the motivations of others, but if it could be
called security, he was fairly secure in the knowledge that he
was unique. In the motley crew of hustlers his intuition and
their different kind of assurance informed him that he was alone
in wearing the motley on his skin.

Low lived well enough; he traveled; his clothes were what
clothes should be at the given moment in fashion, though modified hippie and only longish hair was as far as he would go in
that direction, and he avoided drugs and smelled of soap. Sometimes his fare was paid from coast to coast — working two tautly stretched victims at once — so that fulfillment could occur,
It never did. As a dealer in dreams, he knew that the dream deferred was the permanent dream, without which one became a
Sagger. He dreamed permanently of clear skin and so was able
to work, and move on, his dream kept aloft by others' belief that
he was perfect.

How he came to the Island was a mystery to him. The ferry
was no mystery nor was the Island's existence; but *why* he
crossed over to the windswept place — five dollars round trip
meant to discourage the aimless — was mysterious. He had no desire to see the Island, which was visible from the pear tree in his
mother's garden. No curiosity had ever taken him to the ferry
slip in his years of growing up. What he knew about the Island
was what he had heard: that the people were surly and poor,
that anyone not an Islander was questioned at will by any local
as to the stranger's reason for being there. The place had been
religious — Quakers or Shakers or something of that ilk — and
somewhat communistic; what was left, when the religious
moved on, was the dregs. The girls — all that interested his contemporaries — were reported to be dim and ugly as the result of
inbreeding.

Low had gone home classically, seeking answers. After ten

years of playing victim-victimizer he knew less about himself than he had before he began. What he knew was that mental pain had been his stimulus and fulfillment and that it had ceased to work for him. His birthmark had become an idea; at times he could imagine that it was there only in his mind. He hungered for the sense of its physical presence, which looking at it in a mirror could not give him. It was as though he had used it up and had no magic left.

That the magic had failed had one proof: there had been a death. The mark waiting for him had died; a female voice on the other end of the wire had informed Low of the death but not of the cause. In the silence he had considered telling her, "It's because my birthmark is gone."

The word *victim* gained new meaning, or an old one brought up to date. Low had never asked if the fire that marked him had claimed a life or lives. He saw his failure to ask as possibly more psychotic than the result: his life. On his way East he could hear his mothers' reply to his future question: a baby had died in the fire. It was the only answer, a return to the legend that had bred him. But when questioned she said, no; vaguely, for she was old and burned out; no, they got the baby out. Low was sorry for her, still unable to give him a rationale for his life.

On the Island a deer in a field made him stop his car. As he watched, a bounding herd of them came from the surrounding woods and ranged themselves in three circles: the fawns frisking circularly in a circle of does, the bucks ranged on the periphery, facing outward, looking for enemies.

He got out of his car and leaned against it, breathing the air with the beasts. He wished that he could take in innocence through his nostrils. The fawns were marked with youngness, some of them as pied as himself. He saw how safe they were within the two circles, the mothers nudging at them, letting them know how privileged, marks and all, they were in their natures, and the fathers teaching them courage by osmosis. His own life had lacked the outer circle.

That the markings on the fawns would fade did not bother him as he expected, edging up to the idea. He palpated the thought, wondering why there was no resentment. He thought that it was because when the birthmarks faded the beasts would become victims by the law of the state. There was a penalty for shooting a fawn, but when it became a doe or a buck it was fair game, in season.

When he was spoken to he turned at once, all directness and deep dimple and cleft chin pronounced by his nice smile. He had learned that a slow response marked you as a caser of joints, a calculator. Clean directness, learned as a stock in trade, was not easily abandoned.

The man puzzled him. He was middle-aged, dressed in denim pants and jacket, with a face like Low's own, strong and open. Low was puzzled because the tug between them was so strong; it was as though the man had snared him before he could turn and now was pulling him forward, but not beyond safety; just to the edge of the circle, to point out something to him.

The illusion made Low wary, remote inside. What the man, whose name was Chris, said, Low could not have repeated an hour later, but in their talk it was Low who did the questioning, almost surly at first, and he thought that if the man was an Islander, then they had changed places, for Chris was polite and open. When he turned to leave it was Low who asked if he could buy the man a drink.

Chris shook his head and to his distress, Low felt his spirits drop. "It's Sunday," Chris said, and invited him to have a drink at his house. On the way Low tried to think that this was more like it, but as part of an old formula it did not work; his going with the man was an isolated fact, the move had been Low's own, as it never had been in the past, and Chris's manner was as cool as a tree's. He seemed to belong to impersonal nature as much as the grass and woods and sky.

Sometime later Low went back for his car and crossed the ferry to his mother's house to pick up his clothes. On the way he thought of nothing at all, not of the fulfillment, his first — the painful stab both punishment and reward — nor of what he was doing, going to get his clothes and move in with a stranger. He had thought of some of these things at the moment they were suggested or at the moment they were occurring, but once in his car he seemed to be encased in the circle of a dream both present and deferred. He was free of plots.

Chris really lost his temper with Low only once. The birthmark had never been mentioned between them, though Low wore it more and more openly around the house and garden and on the private beach as the weather warmed. After a childhood and youth spent variously carrying the burden, and a large chunk of his adulthood concretely based upon it like a house on its cellar, Low could not accept the absence. The manner in which it was absent, with Chris, was worse than when it had become a powerless mental thing that could let a man die for lack of its physical magic.

Low's feelings on the subject of the silence were twofold. He, as he had told Chris early on, was a brooder, and in brooding upon the silence he came to see it as a denial — a denial perhaps built on shock — of himself, which meant that Chris had to imagine him as something he was *not*, which made Chris as bad as any mark Low fed such illusions to. Or, worse for Low, it bespoke a blindness in Chris, a flaw like the birthmark, a glaring imperfection. In this case, inability to see was worse than seeing. He subjected himself before Chris out of a strong need to have his subjector a perfect thing; not for Low, either, the headless statue.

He had unearthed for Chris a sense of ethics buried when he was twenty-five and was prepared one day to come clean about himself, a painful gift for Chris, which was what he had to give. But honesty must begin with basic materials, and without Chris's acknowledgement of the birthmark no further honesty would be possible. He believed that there was a dam in Chris which must be broken to let the pent-up waters through or they would both drown.

Chris disliked weakness; Low became weak. "Thanks for loving me in spite of my birthmark," he said, having calculated the timing perfectly. He watched the rage grow and break out. At the top of his rage Chris shouted, "We're all birthmarked, you little bastard," and as though the crack in the mold would save the world from birthmarks, Chris took a large rare shell, one of the few perfect ones in the world, and raised it up to smash it on the floor when Low stopped him.

Frustration and a deep sense of something lacking began to wake Low up in the middle of the night. At first he would wonder in terror whose weight was pressing down the other side of the bed. In the old days he had dreaded the idea of that weight, following the exposure of his birthmark, as much as he dreaded death, for in his emotions the weight would have to belong *to* death. He, marked with the fire that had killed a baby (he denied his mother's denial), believed in the present moments of waking up that he was marked as death's lover.

But he would go back to sleep, lulled by the palpable life in Chris.

And another night he awoke and consulted his watch and thought that this used to be a particularly good hour for him, when the bars were about to close and the dread of dreams deferred rose and clouded the air, enhancing his beauty, which he thought of as sticky and malodorous like the insides of a Venus's-flytrap. Fire-backed, flower-faced, he had gloried, like any great magician, in the illusion he created. Out of these lowly elements I make this: a rose from a filthy (thank you madam) handkerchief, snot into money just like that, gents, and hear that crackle! Red back into greenbacks!

And Chris moved, enveloped him, carried him into sleep.

And then another night he lay and thought of Chris's friends, the great and the excellent, their books inscribed to him with love and thanks; photographs of stars, opera albums signed by the living composers — all because Chris was rich. Chris's money kept Low, transported him, bought him. He was being paid for his body, the one thing not for sale.

And Chris woke up, and they talked and got up and had a cup of tea and a cigarette and went back to sleep twined together.

At the end of eleven months with Chris, Low knew very little about him. He knew that Chris wrote, and that what he wrote was published in little quarterlies: a poem, a story or two without endings, one static play called *Coursing* that Chris said had been produced in Berlin. When Chris worked at his writing, in a carefully closed room, for portions of every day including week ends, Low incredibly suffered from the separation and the secrecy, the closed door like a hand in his face.

He had met some of Chris's friends, who came out mainly in the summertime, exhausted and green looking, and lay without moving on the beach until sunset, and counted the calories in what they ate and drank — they called Chris's house The Spa — and were as noncommittal as Chris.

But Low did not know what state Chris came from, nor where the money came from, nor how much there was of it, nor much of anything else about him. With Chris his intuition was as dead as a dried leaf.

In the evenings, listening to music, Low sat close to Chris, pressing his leg against Chris's long leg, wanting to be taken in through the muscles and tissues and gristle and blood until the legs became one. He imagined himself in Chris's body, Chris's smooth back covering his own, and then cynically he would see that the birthmark would still be there, maybe worse for not being able to be seen, and talked about. He said to Chris, meaning to tell him the whole thought, "I think sometimes that I'm inside you," and Chris said, startled, "You are. You live in me every day." A flash, like a sign he could not read, made Low ask him, "For how long?" but Chris did not answer. The Grateful Dead or The Temptations or Scarlatti would take precedence over Low's need.

He wondered, if it was true as Chris said that all are birthmarked, what Chris's birthmark was. The need to know obsessed him and he became physically ill.

Chris nursed him through chills and fever; Low would see him clearly and then he would be gone, and then it was Low who would go, traveling his delirium back to where he had come from. In that place he would think of Chris with longing and would somehow return, but eventually his strength ebbed until he could not manage the return trip, and he lay defeated with half his known world between him and Chris. Fever was like a web whose filaments he counted as though they were an equation in the center of which strength would be found. The need to find was transformed by an old process into the need to extract. The telephone was his instrument for extractions. He dialed Chris.

"This is Low." The old thrill traveled the wire between Coasts.

"Come home." Chris's voice was like breaking wood. "Come home, boy."

"I'm on my way," Low told him, jubilant, revving up hope, paused and said, "— as soon as you can wire me home-coming bread." He waited for the conflict, the necessary conflict in Chris, and the idea of the good pain caused by separation of man from money. It was like taking a turtle's shell. Overcoming conflict, reconciling pain and desire, was his art.

Chris, torn, said, "Listen, be sure you know what you're doing this time. I can't take much more of this. I can't change for you. I've tried, but I have this other life. You'll have to accept it or —" But he had said too much. Anxiously, he asked, "Will you?"

Low waited a long time, too long for Chris, who had begun to speak when Low said, "O.K., then." "You're coming?" The long pause had worked. There was nothing but relieved gladness in Chris's voice.

Shaking his head as though he could be seen, Low said, "No. I guess I'd hoped for too much. Have a good life, Chris." "Wait!" Chris was calling as Low hung up.

Low started back anyway, mindlessly driving through the still fog that suspended him at Fresno, then when the fog lifted, on into Arizona — the southern route because it was a bitter winter — pushing on to Albuquerque and Oklahoma City and Knoxville and Philadelphia, where he turned back. He altered the road stops as though to lose himself that way; in streaks of neon he glimpsed Nashville and Elk City and Gallup, and the barren wastes in between drew his eyelids down as though permanently to fasten them with metal, and the fog and Fresno caught him again, halting the ferry, and in some place there he lay and saw Chris pacing the floor at The Spa, going upstairs and down, opening drawers as though looking for himself, a compact bundle to hand over to Low. What was finally found was like a package that had been badly misused in the mails, parts of it missing, but it lay in Chris's hands and gazed up at his worried face. Seeing the concern, reading into it willingness to accept Low's rules, Low thought he told Chris, "I want my birthmark back." He thought he said, "I'm lost without it, so much that love and desire and health and even you have no meaning for me, because there's no one at all in my body for those things to mean anything to." He thought of the coarseness of life, good strong fibers holding you together no matter what color they were, that kept you from falling apart in the face of death and silence. He thought he said, in Chris's terms so that he would not fail to understand, "Without my birthmark I'm as blank as a piece of paper not written on."

Convalescing reluctantly, Low would get up and go through Chris's things, looking for clues to him, to his secrecy, and it was as if every gesture found in Low's imagination a mirror turned upon his own past. So might someone have gone through *his* jacket left hanging on a chair, riffling through his papers with hope and fear for the impending disclosure. His tears were the nephew's; his need to believe Chris perfect was the hotel guest's; his leg pressing Chris's was the auditor's. And his frustration belonged to that host of men which he had left poorer for knowing him. They were all in him, maimed, helpless. He was an island of ruined men.

Low woke up one morning feeling clean as a line drawing. There were no details, just the outline of himself drawn with one confident continuous stroke. He traced himself with his hands and liked the bareness well enough for a while, but not quite enough to settle for it. He began to fill in details. The final copy of the idea was the same old imperfect, impermanent one with a major difference: by some process, occurring somehow in his long illness, he had learned how to draw with perspective. He knew what he meant by that and knew that he really meant it. It would be a new man who walked in on Chris today, yet paradoxically unchanged. He believed that Chris would grasp the complexity.

Teetering on new legs, he sought out Chris and found him in his room, the usually closed door standing open, Chris at his desk. Chris turned, smiling, taking up a sheaf of yellow paper and tapping it on the desk into a compact rectangle. Saying welcoming words, chiding a little, he put the papers face down on the desk, and then with a curious look at Low he turned them face up. Low, hand on Chris's shoulder, glanced at the handwritten pages. There was a title, printed large: THE BIRTHMARK. Gazing back at Chris, he felt nothing but the newness and lightness. Chris lit a cigarette, said, "Tea, toast," and got up and left Low alone with the papers.

When Low heard him come back in he looked up; to the question in Chris's eyes he shook his head. "Not a bit," he said thickly, and cleared the mucus with a hack and cough into a piece of tissue. "Not a bit like that." He said it in wonderment: this was *Chris* he was correcting. He imagined that his chest felt burdened because of lingering sickness in it. Watching Chris set the teapot and cups down, and the rack of toast, he said, "I'm afraid your imagination is just plain lousy." He couldn't help raising his voice when he said, "You didn't want the real thing to get in the way of your story. That's why you wouldn't let me talk about it." Chris sat down and said, "It's finished anyway." Low asked him, "You mean the story?" Chris did not speak for a while and then gulped his tea and mentioned the process of Art. He sounded as fouled-up as the perfectionist in the hotel room, and a little bit smug, which stung. Low said, "ART? THAT?"

In the story the man was passive, full of quiet despair and poetic thoughts. He was as malleable as clay, hoping for a sort of Master to come along and shape him differently. There was a repetitive dawn image that the birthmarked man compared to the colors on his skin as well as the new day when he would

84

rise up, the story did not say where to. His tentative thoughts about his birthmark were as soft as feathers about to settle down on a strange egg in a nest, but only to hatch it, never to break it in fury. Low told Chris, "Like a neon sign going on, BIRTHMARK. Big as hell; even a hand on the shoulder, or the leg – BIRTHMARK, in neon. Red, hard, poison. Never easy, never soft. Not goddamned feathers." Puzzled, he asked, "Don't you ever hate anything and want to change it?"

In Chris's face that opened and shut like a gate on a lumpy beast, his returned intuition read a different answer: he saw that Chris was revealing his own birthmark. It was a deeper tale than the story Chris had written; it might even be Art. Thinking of that, and the singularity of motivation, and of the fever that had gone on and on, once up to 107°, he had been told, melting him down and re-forming him, he grimaced and said, "I know who died in that fire."

Chris's face sprang into life, eager and young, as Low had expected it to.

"What fire? Who died?" He tried to hold Low back. He stood around while Low packed. "Come on, what did you mean?" Finally, with tired petulance, he asked, "Why are you going *now?*" Low heard the extended sentence: Now that I really need you.

Crossing the ferry Low thought that it was the symbols that had got through to Chris, the symbols of the fire and the dead. He thought Chris's story could have used some of life and death.

On the springlike Saturday street, turning his back on Chris's car and on Chris for the third time in three days, his back after all would not try to tuck itself in like a dog's tail. It rode under his jacket like an arrogant creature, a mean old parrot. If anything, it rattled its feathers trying them out. Behind him he could feel the questions as strong as the sun on his back: What fire? Whose death?

He turned and looked at Chris in the car, looking *at* him for the first time since he had left the house. He shook his head at

Chris, trying to let Chris know that he knew: I wasn't supposed to survive this. Then, to even things between them, uncertainty on all sides, he shook his head again, a different mime: Was I?

He walked on, not minding too much that he could be seen crying by old acquaintances, some of them classmates who, it was now plain, had been marked in their DNA for early-middle-aged unpleasantnesses such as fatness, or baldness, or alcoholism, or a tendency to talk to themselves on public streets.

Here came an old acquaintance, one who had been a hustler at sixteen, nodding now and smiling and laughing and waving toward friends, many of them long gone to other towns, some of them to the grave. As they passed each other, Low told him, "Schultzie, I'm crying for somebody else."

Schultzie smiled on him like the sun, in circular impartial beneficence. The two of them stood raining and shining together for a minute. Low didn't mind if people thought that he was high like Schultzie, because, as a matter of fact, it was true. He took a cue from Schultzie, who just *was*. Under the drug he was pure, unexplained and unexplaining. Low had been going to push on and take advantage of Schultzie's good trip and tell him in full: "I'm crying for somebody else for the first time in my marked-up, crossed-out life," but to the sun in Schultzie's face he could not, prone and waiting to be burned, present himself as a masochist. And so he walked on home.

Chris rewrote the story. He sent it to his agent, who had known Low in the year he lived with Chris, before he was enticed back to California and jailed for extortion. The note to the agent was a little pompous and sentimental, the way she always hoped his stories would turn out to be. He wrote: "I wonder if the boy will ever see this, and in a curious way, like it? If so, I hope he can forgive me for curing him on paper. But I doubt it."

March 10

Beatrix. Damn it.

Two suspicions.

1. That knowing how a maligned woman feels is meant to arise from understanding a birthmarked homosexual hustler.

2. That the real birthmark in the story is Chris's, whom neither you nor I are supposed to like or even feel sympathy for, because (?) he is rich, has a measure of "success," is physically unmarked (i.e., not excessively hairy; that "smooth" body gives you away time and again), and whose mind is attracted by, to, flaws, disabilities, baseness, disease. Your sensibilities astound me. Shall I attempt to defend myself — sorry — "Chris" — by laying on the altar the Mass of literature and visual art? Clytie would understand; she painted people in trusses, back braces; you know that painting of a waiting room filled with prosthetic devices abandoned in haste, which she calls "Exodus": the disability is all there is. Or the immense pair of dark glasses reflecting, barely, some throes, which she named "Epilepsy." From "the Mass of literature and visual art" to Clytie's morbidity is, I admit, like pushing oneself off a World Trade tower into a stopped-up gutter, but as she is your prototype I know the analogy is not lost. What is lost on me is your humor, where queers and their audience are concerned. Queer revenge, like Puerto Rican and female revenge, can, if we are able to accept it, amuse as well as instruct.

But there is some "insight" here, and do I congratulate you, or Chris, or me? As you demonstrated, people tend to turn to the ends of stories about queers *first*, to where the fellow gets him comeuppance, which allows them to go back and read the piece through, knowing that the status quo is not being disturbed. In your preface of "endings" you were nearer, for all the violence and blood, flayings and maimings, to the queer status quo than at anytime in your rather soft (if sometimes moving) organ recital — an infelicity, for they had no organs; it was the relentless tremolo that led me astray. But where is the homosexual desire, consuming as sickness, that threatens John and Jane Doe, and, regularly as menstrual flow, tables "humane" legislation — the two perhaps inextricably connected? Where the real duplicity, the truth, the "reality" (who said we should always put reality in quotes?) of that sixth man? Hit hard, Beatrix, or don't hit at all. The dark tower is there even in the daylight, like the moon; and on rainy afternoons in country stores:

There were some men in the narrow aisle; at Childe's approach they squeezed back against the shelves on either side to make a passage for him, then closed up behind him when he had gone through. He thanked them with a nod and smile, his eyes gazing at each face; he did not know any of them. Waiting for Tommy to appear from behind his curtained-off resting place, where it was said he lolled and morosely sucked on a bottle of heavily fortified elderberry wine, clinging to an age-old belief that it would restore his power of speech, Childe self-consciously took inventory of the meat case, too aware of his short shorts and bare feet. He tapped on the glass with his fingers, hoping to attract Tommy's attention. All the men, five of them, turned in his direction. Was Tommy filling some large secret order of theirs, rummaging in the cellar among scuttling things? An electric hum filled the small store, all the refrigerated cases going about their business. One car swept by, tires swishing in the rain. A throat was cleared.

"Where'd you get that sun tan?"

Childe turned, relieved at the normal question, although his movement was in its abruptness a betrayal.

"In my garden, mostly."

"In the fog?" The tone was impertinent with a snicker at the core. Childe gave the man a cold look.

"My tans last." His abrupt turning away was no mistake this time. Or was it?

"Well, where'd you get it?" Another voice. Childe's teeth set.

"Garden."

" 'Garden' where?" The mimicry was accurate, a perfect little bite. Something informed Childe to play the game.

"My house."

" 'My house' where?"

"Island."

" 'Island' where?"

"Old Road." Childe was staring at the shelf of Gourmet Foods, kept well out of reach of thieving epicures; only Tommy had access to the high-priced cans whose names he began reading off in his mind. His knuckles against the glass of the meat case were pressing his hand to sleep.

"Which house?" Childe did not answer. "Which house?" Without any sound at all they were moving toward him, floating at the corner of his eyes. "Which house?" He waited to give each a turn to ask, if they liked, in the silence reading WHOLE GOOSE LIVER.

"Old — old house."

" 'Old old house'? How 'old old'?" Childe thought, "About as old as all of your ages put together." He hit the showcase with his fist, to wake his hand up. In extremity any impulse seems to be permissible; he wheeled on them and asked, "Are you the house?" Let them laugh at him now. But they did not. He could think without trying of any number of reasons the house might take on flesh and crowd him into a cul-de-sac, pressing him against a display of meat.

TO THE DARK TOWER

Childe slept under furs in the winter and wore velvet a lot, but when he went among the frugal Islanders he presented a denim front and a convincing simplicity. In his third winter there, itself a test of character, they began to mention him among themselves with the irony usually reserved for each other. When Jim Gratz, after installing bookcases that he had made for Childe, told an anecdote about him in The Schooner with only regulars present, they all tacitly concurred in taking it as a sign of probationary acceptance. That Christmas, Childe got a number of identical cards with the printed greeting "To a Good Neighbor" and inside a poem of felicitation.

He had, by metaphorically standing still for three years, worked hard for their approval. His standing still had been in making no advances of any sort to any Islander. Metaphor to one side, he himself had worked hard, mowing his own acres on a tractor, planting a garden, and reviving the orchard – doing in fact those things for which no one was to be hired but scrupulously making use of carpenter (Gratz) and painter (Micawber) and other artisans, and spreading his business equally among the three stores and two garages.

When the bartender, an off-Islander, meeting him in the fish market, related the story as told by Gratz, and Childe realized what the story meant, he loosened up a bit and soon was flinging his hand up in greeting, automobile to automobile, without waiting for the other's signal. This sufficed for the remainder of the hard winter, and in spring he consulted a few neighbors about gardening methods and let that suffice for the spring.

Summer, as usual, was hectic for everyone, for it was then the bulk of the Islanders earned what money they did earn by catering to the tourists, and Childe reverted somewhat to summer person with guests out from the city, but that year there was a slight telling difference: the conspiratorial nods and looks given him by Islanders as though he too were engaged in hustling the foreigners. In the market a husky voice (an Island peculiarity among the men like the crossed eyes of a Greek island) at his ear — "How you makin it, fella?" — could bring almost painfully alive the longing that had settled him in that place and kept him there for over three years.

In the tapering-off fall with its small harvests, he shared with his neighbors, leaving baskets of tomatoes and pears and eggplants on doorsteps, always without a card, knowing that the grapevine would reveal the benefactor. It was an Island rule, indeed a necessity, that there be one witness to any event, and how it was arranged nobody knew, but no dead-of-night occurrence of any significance, however remote its locale, was without its observer; at least there were no unsolved crimes on the Island.

In the late fall when the thudding of walnuts and hickory nuts resounded in the woods like drumbeats, and the hedge known as bodark was bare except for the great convoluted balls of its brainlike, poisonous, green fruit, Childe paid his first visit to the church. He had seen the Islanders dressed only for work and play, and part of his longing was to see them in the austerity of Sunday beauty, dark suited and white collared, shoes polished and hair slicked down. He had an almost ecclesiastical attraction to the face of repentance though its suasion was sensual to him; the thought of thighs in warm dark loose clothing was so mystical as to resemble religion: the marble bone in the dark mummy; the holiness within the damned act; hysterical abbesses clawing at the dark habiliments of the forbidden abbot.

The Island itself was a dusky firred sleeve of land three miles by five and within it the Islanders, dark blond and sturdy, were kerneled.

Childe wore his sunglasses to the church and kept them on

during the service, not minding that he attracted attention; that he could observe without being caught out was the greater consideration. Afterward at the church door he offered the explanation of badly strained eyes.

One night Childe lay awake, head thudding with hangover from daylong drinking. His body was torn with fires like grief. Sleep had rejected him for hours, as lover or violent suitor, and still it was only one o'clock.

He turned in bed until it seemed to him that he revolved over heated sheets as though on a roasting spit. His mind went out in search of cleanness, of innocence, an earnest search until he remembered what it meant. He got out of bed and wrote, bending in his myopia, "In love with death." It was a magic phrase intended to be a restraining reminder. Back in bed he sought the diseased sleep he had earned, from which he might emerge like Lazarus from the winding sheet bearing only the marks of restraints.

It was not until the very rim of sleep was reached that he would allow himself the luxury of imagining himself to be an epileptic. Seldom did he fall into such a tranced sleep, into the arms of divine disease, for it was allowed him only as a reward for having tried and managed for long stretches of time to deny himself access to his own nature. And then, like a homecoming to a dreamed childhood, with pomp and distant music and carnival in store, he would tumble over the rim into the smells and the decay.

But his denial had been far too lengthy. He had forgotten the progression of necessary steps that was like a blasphemous version of the Stations of the Cross. He worked at his memory like a thief at a safe, honor at stake and cops in the alley, but no tumblers dropped. Too assiduously he had filed away at the whorls of his identity, with inhibiting callouses the result.

In the shower he concentrated on strategy. He would not make this particular debut in The Schooner, hangout of hunters and fishermen, loud and hyperbolic. The Cove Inn was quiet, dimly lit with a small flickering fire, the atmosphere a gratuity of the owner's Scotchness, where the conversation was generally about motors, for these tended to be the mechanics, the ferry crews, the boys hopelessly in love with propulsion, however circumscribed. The idea of sublimated recklessness appealed to Childe, as well as the precision of the talk, for he was in many respects a purist.

It took him an hour of conversation — his Ferrari was the catalyst — and subtle probing and, as it evolved, misunderstanding on both sides to present himself without disguise and to be rejected. Not unkindly; the young man was recently "back from Nam" and knew the score. Leaving, he laid his hand on Childe's arm and said, "But listen, not everybody's like me," and it was as though he were pointing. Watching him limp out, Childe was glad that he had not been accepted by a cripple.

A handful of patrons were left, only two of them possibilities. Deciding between them, Childe went to the bar. MacGraw, the owner-bartender, watched him approach, and when Childe set his glass down for a refill, MacGraw very slightly shook his head. Childe picked up the glass and set it down again, testing. When the head shake was repeated Childe saw that it was no illusion and saw also, in the man's eyes, that somehow the important fact had been guessed.

To the detriment of his planned life, Childe became a nightly habitué of The Schooner. Some adjustments were necessary, for in his old life, though he was seldom quarrelsome, he could be assertive, and he disliked, in the extreme, inaccuracy. In The Schooner his finest hurdle was to incorporate into his scheme the dogmatic and frequently idiotic pronouncements of the other patrons — he learned to murmur assent, when it did not mean taking sides — and to use their famous independence through the discovery that it was not collectively operative. Specifically, if he offered to buy an individual a drink he was refused, often surlily, but he found that he could set up the house as often as he chose. On this discovery he based the progression of his generosity, moving easily and slowly to allow its meaning to sink in. The new sense of affluence at large need not be consciously attributed to him, in fact he did not desire it; he wanted only that the assimilation include him as a vital but hidden particle. By this method he managed also to conceal from them that he had become a kind of center to the gatherings, for to have named it would have been to lose it. It was enough that he was considered agreeable under all circumstances, one of those being that he adroitly managed to help the emergence, nightly or weekly, of a new Island personality. The way he bent to the favorite's remarks, answers, dogma, stupidity, the way he deferred to his aggression, if need be, had the others doing it without knowing why, for Childe knew the psychology of drunks. All they knew was that the next day they found themselves discussing one of their number, sometimes in puzzlement as to why; but they seldom any longer discussed Childe.

In March a supreme test came when, in response to a nearly subliminal suggestion patiently repeated that they should have a drink on him even when he was not present, he stayed away from the bar for several days. He admitted to himself that the test was crucial, and also that he feared defeat. But when he returned and was at his request given his bar bill and saw that it was composed of many tabs run up by others, he knew that he had won his round.

Slowly — in exasperated amusement he would say to himself, "Slowly! Slowly!" no matter what he was doing — he began to invite men who did not frequent The Schooner but were loyal to The Cove to meet him for a drink. On the ferry or during a discussion of tachometers or torque at a garage he would say, jovial in the Island manner, that he "dared" them to come "see how the other half lives!"

Thus, slowly, he began to siphon off the lifeblood of The Cove, because free liquor, however euphemistically taken, is an enemy to loyalty. His sense of timing was satisfied with the position achieved, and he would have rested there, allowing time itself to absorb and harden into other usable forms the debris, but his friend, The Schooner's bartender, caused him to alter and accelerate his plans. On his off-nights the bartender would occasionally stay on the Island and visit around, including The Cove in his itinerary. After one such visit, he reported to Childe in a gleeful whisper that MacGraw had said about him — unmistakably, though naming no names; the remark came after another's reference to Childe: "Fella was a black-headed fella when he first came to this Island, but now his hair's as gold as my late first wife's." Smiling without making a demurral, Childe murmured, "Was hers from grief, too, I wonder." He had not expected the bartender to understand the reference and was bemused when the man said, "Poor old Wilde." He reflected that it was the kind of opening he might have used under other circumstances, idly playing a line through it to gauge its depth, but he saw with real excitement that other game, another game, had come into view.

As though sewing a hem on the proceedings, he instituted and footed the bill for a Saturday Nite Buffet at The Schooner. His excuse, when he needed one, was that his house could not accommodate all his friends for a weekly blast, but The Schooner was — wasn't it? — his home away from home. And his circle of friends was widening weekly.

One night he saw for the first time in The Schooner the young man toward whom he had been heading after his rejection by the cripple, and found out that he was the son of Mac-Graw. Childe saw him as a spy, and saw his presence as harbinger of worked-for, waited-for developments.

He was not really surprised to see the owner of The Cove standing on his back-door step. The man had pulled around the house where his car could be hidden by the lilac bushes from sight of the road. Childe had not seen him since Twelfth Night and now the lilacs were in full bloom.

They sat in the kitchen, Childe drinking coffee. He emphasized MacGraw's dilemma by adding cognac to the coffee without offering the man any.

"Maybe I was wrong."

"Wrong about what, Mr. MacGraw?"

"What I thought I knew."

"There's no way for me to know what you thought you knew."

"Wrong about what I thought I overheard, then."

95

"No."

"Sir?" MacGraw, badly thrown, wanted a replay.

"No, you weren't wrong."

Childe watched the man's hands, saw by them when the silence would be broken, as though they were hands on a clock face approaching the hour.

"I can't make it with everybody goin' to The Schooner. Sat'dy was always my big night."

Childe was sympathetic. "Mine too."

Fighting himself, the man took the meaning as given. Childe saw that he was causing another person to try to understand and incorporate within his life a fact or series of facts as alien as moonrocks would be in his fields. He could not plow the rocks under for fear of what they might do to his soil, though he would look at them in passing, speculate upon them, and finally accept them there. But he would never, under pain of death, touch one.

"It happens," MacGraw said. "I know it happens. I'm no school kid." Seeing Childe's face he said quietly, oddly abashed, "Well, school kids —" The hands excused the very young, including himself in some past barn loft or stabled automobile on a rainy afternoon. MacGraw said, "But people grow up, and I never wanted none of that in my place. Hard in the summer to keep it out, but I managed. My fam'ly in the back, there; my son, now, in the bar —" His hands asked Childe to understand his efforts on behalf of purity. Seeing this noted, the businessman returned. "But I can't make it, with everybody down at The Schooner. Free eats, free drinks —"

Amazed, Childe saw the man's face dehiscent, feared the releasing of his teeth to take root in the grime on the floor, a new Thebes! Of necessity, though, a synthetic army would spring up for his taking: the large even teeth were too dazzling and, released by the huge smile, clicked artificially among themselves as though at a party. As Childe gazed at the glare in the middle of the suddenly terribly good-humored and ruddy face, a horny hand pounded the table between them and a big voice boomed out, "Hey, why'on't chew bring yer gang on down to my joint? See how th'other half lives, huh?"

After a silence the smile diminished a bit, but MacGraw, still jovial said, "Hell, anything goes down there. Just like at The Schooner." Before self-hatred could set in he made it to the door. Childe was aware, on MacGraw's own terms, of the size of the gesture, but on the back stoop, seeing MacGraw's dread that he might be offered a hand to touch, Childe told him flatly, "Nothing goes at The Schooner."

The dread stayed on MacGraw's face though it changed sources.

"Huh?"

"I said, nothing goes. It's just like The Cove, I'm afraid." He waited, spread his hands in eloquence, stated the obvious: "So there's no point in changing bars, is there?"

One of The Cove's defectors had said that MacGraw was a preacher: "Runs his place like a goddamned church. Not even no tabs there — honor system and all that shit. Hell, you can't even say 'goddamn' in there, afraid his wife might hear." In The Schooner there was dart-playing for money, but MacGraw would not allow betting over his pool table.

Watching the incorruptible man, Childe saw him struggle with the fact just handed him.

Finally MacGraw mumbled, "You come on down there, hear? You're welcome." He did not look at Childe, but his mouth, tasting decay, was as eloquent as eyes. Childe walked with him to the car, said (it was a Monday), "We'll be down on Saturday," stressing the plural so not to be misunderstood. He felt the man waiting and told him, "I'll be down Wednesday." MacGraw nodded and got into the car. This time his eyes, direct, asked Childe to let him go without further words, but Childe could not do that. Humiliation must reap itself, one of the oldest laws to be learned. Even as he formed words, he visualized the time when it would again be his turn, with MacGraw, or someone else, in the position he now occupied. Changing the metaphor, it was as though, in turn, one man stood above the other and watched the throes of epilepsy, safety pin in hand to pierce the tongue and attach it to the collar, for accidental death was the one thing not allowed.

"I don't know your crowd, MacGraw. Maybe you'll be good

enough to introduce me." MacGraw, silent, started the car. Childe put a restraining hand on the doorframe. He was surfeited as though from food too rich, but the almost imperceptible recoil at the sight of his hand on the door let him finish.

"By Wednesday you may have turned up somebody who wouldn't mind meeting me." In half-mourning for old subtlety, he refined the sentence, smiling charmingly though unseen, for MacGraw sat as though unable to turn his head lest he reveal his swollen tongue. "Of course I meant somebody who would *like* me." Childe behaved as though there had been some amiable, verbal commitment and told the figure, after a pause for the unsaid response, "If you change your mind, of course, just call me."

He was fairly certain that there would be no telephone call. With the arrival of thirsty summer people Childe would be on even surer ground, though MacGraw might surprise him by choosing the alternative and closing down his business.

Childe gave the dummy in the car another gracious smile and a wave and watched the lurching departure, clucking his tongue in rehearsal for Wednesday when he would say to MacGraw, controversial on the right subject, "Looks like that first gear on your automobile's like mine — not worth a damn. I usually skip it and start in second." (He could see the engine-loving boys in the bar turning at his voice.) "When she's really warm — like from July through October — I can practically kick off in third. Plays hell with the works, I imagine, but gets to the point a lot faster."

It was a rough draft, only a mock-up, and the fun was in the refinement. By Wednesday the nuances would be considerable. Taking cognac in a perfect glass — the crude coffee cup in the sink with the other litter — he wondered if MacGraw's son would be interested by such an opening.

You drive, walk, eat, look at television, read, and all the while, beyond you and the cozy circle created by your lady around herself and you, like the natural emanations of stars, other lives circle yours, seeds still winged and wind-borne, looking for sympathetic soil. You feel the juices and solids of your body in attempted rearrangement, or, more disturbing, making an effort to create a stillness that approximates death, beyond which the body does become soil, receptive to all wind-borne seeds. In a not especially prolonged stillness, as though no chances could be taken that you might decide to become perpetual motion, words fall out of the air, a random fall from which you might be tempted to make selection, and as you do not move, cannot, a string of words falls onto you, and from you, onto the paper: winter rye greening up, smoothing the old brown earth with a fine new plane: Carpenter Rye, neighbor.

WHEN ISLAND WEATHER SETS IN it will become like a sea, billows and waves of rye in winds of fifty knots, whole gales for days on end. A young man's dream was to be isolated behind such a wind with a true love, "three whole days together." An old man thinks somehow to survive it, to come out the other side, one day in spring, and crawl out of his flannels and wool and have the only reminder of winter be the smell in his clothes — of liniment, mainly; an old body tough and lean as jerky hasn't much smell of its own. It's juice that makes odor, juice that carnifies even plants. My

99

god, the stink of youngness; high-tided sperm smell, sea-like. The smell of a split-sapling could turn a maiden stomach. Females digging deep for handkerchiefs to stop up their noses to the smell of scythed grass! Intuitive recognition, instinctive rejection: seed — carpenter — sea — Christ?

"Soul to the wind, eye to the sun"—a prayer for dispersement and blindness, true prayer for the dead. A prayer for the living would be "Eye to the wind, soul to the sun," an island boy's prayer, for it was through the wind's eye that first was seen the sameness of field and sea; the immeasurable differences . . . thus the making of a sailor. It was through the wind's eye that first was seen the battle between the intractile and the fluid and it was then that imagination saw the battle reflected in a man's fight with himself, the daily war, continuing to death, between juice and substance. Death's final victory is in the draining of juice, the extraction of salt from clay.

The wind's eye was a round attic window, small as a porthole. Looking from it to the left you could see the west field which favored grain crops. Looking right, you saw the bottle-shaped harbor so thin-necked that from some angles it looked like a pond. But the wind's eye saw the neck opening to the long passage from harbor to sea and in bad weather watched the inpouring of trade boats and ferries, and observed how those most storm-tossed seemed to reassemble themselves piece by piece in the bottle of the harbor. Through spyglasses, any of the captains returning the gaze could have seen, beneath the eaves of the house, above the wind's eye, in ill-matched letters assembled from every kind of sign, the motto:

come *hi*ther—here *no en*emy but win*ter and* rough wea*ther*

Through circumstances of hasty sizing, collaborative worms, a millimeter's superior thickness here and there, and perhaps some irony in nature's reaction to the incantation, the dark green paint had flaked from the wooden reassurance so that what was discernible to all but minutest scrutiny were the words: come . . . *winter and rough weather*

And come they did.

Sometimes you woke in the winter mornings to find that snow had retraced the patterns of the dress-goods in the patchwork quilts and sat about the attic in peaked little piles like salt pyramids. And still, brittle-toed and frosty-shanked, you crawled to the porthole and checked on the two seas — first the real one, then its reflection. Remarkable how the grainfield could give the effect of throwing spume at the sky. It was like gallantry, or, later thought, art, and almost won you by its surpassing cleverness. Or by its desire, for land is itself a former sailor, reliving in countless ways — waves in deserts, heat mirages of surf and becalm, grassy wakes — its watery beginnings.

That part of you tending toward the field, the earth part of you, felt the call strong as religion during revival season to the warm reeky kitchen whose walls were so steeped in pork and coffee and yeast smells that they could let a hungry night prowler think he had found the spence. The earth side of you favored too the clangorous proof of earthiness of pails being scoured for the milking by the tellurian bond-maid who shared with you (though her share was niggardly, ladder-reached, set apart from yours by a wall) the eaves' cantic domain. Her rising was precursor to the sun's, her retiring was the official binding of the day's log, and more than robin, swallow, or wild goose did the journey of her petticoats to and from her clothespress serve as harbingers to the turning seasons. Herald of turning manhood as well was she; proof the dilated chink, like a pupil permanently astonished by belladonna, in the lath and plaster between your room and her cell. An ageless activity, that reaming of chinkholes in walls between genders, but seriousness of purpose separating man from prankish boy was shown by the care with which every grain of plaster and splinter of lathing was coaxed to fall, not a mean feat, your side of the peephole. Even the twelve-year-old mouth of in-cipient Tom was employed as leech to suck out evidence of pathology. The resulting hole was so clean of a morbid past that one spring night when the moon's high tide washed her whiter than she had ever been in your imaginings, your dis-appointment in the rest of her seemed unconnected with original desire and was tempered with pity (her breast rat-ite, hollowed as an old stump) and acknowledgment of a certain justice. But still, unseen, her mysteriously woman-ly breathing in the night all of her that you could make use of, her call was as potent as ever — the call of earth, of field and barn and proper nature itself; her banging of milk pails in the kitchen continued to seem like Euterpean over-tures to a mating dance.

Other sounds of morning pulled like small kin at the tail of your nightshirt: your father's muffled hack and sputum like the cry of a winter bird; your father's water-making aimed at the center of the chamber pot loud enough to seem a bullying defense of his condition as Sire Billy One Kid, a nickname you had heard him called, not to his face, and you shook to think of the day when he might be called it openly. The name-caller had gone on to say: "Sire Billy One Kid will not ever be able to squeeze nor pump another out of his present Nanny *(your stepmother, whose murmuring rose and bumped along the ceiling just under you as though looking for a crack to climb through)* or if he does fertilize her, by his hook or her crook, the thing is bound to be black and cry meeow."

The dread of trouble ambuscading and fear of witchcraft within the walls of your gentle dead mother's sewing room made you turn your face to the watery sea, the case settled in its favor *the frozen grainfield creaking at the back of your head as if made suddenly old by rejection. Was it youth and softheartedness that gave tenacity to the illu-sion, and the power to become visible at will? Above a vo-lant ship cristate with storm, it would appear and hang stationary like a waxen carving, a model of a gisant for the land's tomb, or rise up from the ocean's stilled pulse, the fatal bubble, when the vessel lay suspended within the glassy globe of the fused eternities of land and sea. When you lay dying aboard a plague ship off the coast of Spain, à trois with buboes the size of lovers' heads in groin and axilla, it hovered your bed's obscenity, pale bride, dutiful virgin; it was her distillate whiteness, strength of light's untapped source, that unmired you from pus and blood, gave you courage, and the muscle to escape.*

But choice is an action, and action, as soon as accomplished, is past action; its characterization — of stupidity, greatness, ignobility — is the future's task; therefore an action exists only in past and future, and the boy in the attic in that present time — still there, looking; you see him now and again . . . there! that flash, like a mirror aimed at the sun; that was the boy, his innocence — the boy in the attic is and was guiltless of all but turning his head, and such an action, unless doubled or tripled, a willful turning from side to side, cannot be seen as denial. Therefore he does not have to remain there, haunting the spot. He is guiltless. The boy can leave.

Leave boy! Uproot your feet from the bitter floor. Take them down the backstairs and give them into her hands; tell her *my feet are cold* in the whine of babyhood, and trust her not to have seen the growth of chinkhole and boy, so that in her mind smallness and harmlessness abide, and because she is sole observer of you, you are once more innocent of becoming a man, expander of scuppers, betrayer; give your small boy's feet to the warm rough clothing of her palms, and turn your head once again, away from the future. Hear the then present fire sing in the stove. Watch the flicker until it is now present. Save your soul, boy.

March 15

Gone, my Beatrice? Five days without you is like a no-return trip to Elba. It is as though, awake and dreaming, I search for you in the past, through corridors of language, through the spectrum of the stages of Man (sorry: stages of Persons). You are like Low's birthmark: without you etc. etc. Last night I dreamed you burnished by a Southern sun, uncircumcised (is it true about Jewish girls?), forgiving of my dalliance (enforced by you!) with the street boys; dreamed you Catholic and catholic, pearls twined in your hair. I struggled with your tongue, my Anglo consonants aspiring to your liquid flow. Mel et lac sub lingua tua. My unliberated darling, you wrote to me, your words, in answer to mine, delivered through teeming streets by torchlight:

Mio Caro,

Per quando ho notato dal tuo grazioso biglietto, scritto nel senso piu-charatteristico e poetico, che la tua piu maggiore, pre-occupazione, e quella di tradurre la lingua, in Italiano. Ebbene, mio caro, non puoi sapere la mia contentezza, nel vedere, e sentire, come palpiti nel cuore, tutte le tue piu belle parole, che veramente mi fanno commovere, e nello stesso tempo la piu nostalgica comunicazione amorosa scritta della tue mani, in lingua Italiana. Come potrei ignorare quel grande gesto cosi docile e sentimentale. Perciò faro tutto il mio possibile di in-coraggiarti sempre di piu, sperando que nel prossima lettera tuo Italiano amoroso sera molto piu facile e naturale. Chiudo, sperando que tu continuerai a scriverme con la stessa amore con la quale ho scritto questa lettera.

Tuo per sempre
Beatrice

I bear witness to the liberty of the past, to simpler values, to the cleanness of developing normality. The theme of an old murder which hangs in that ancient air strikes me as "literary," a trap to catch attention which, once caught, must needs (the language is infectious) pay heed, willy-nilly, to the moral that, undetected, was the original intent, the hidden bait. The past is: restorative of trust. However that time travel is being achieved, it places us, you and me, safely — by a century — in a time pre-calumny, so that when I "invent" you, it is as a trusting composer of love letters. If you "invent" me, it must be — surely? — as a man (or woman) abiding by the older precepts of duty, loyalty, fidelity. Thus, arriving once again *here* — in this place and time — our bones will have knit differently, our imaginations will be grounded in salvation rather than destruction. It is a matter of perspective through imagined experience, perhaps: "the only antidote to the irreversibility of history is the faculty of forgiveness," and the ultimate act of imagination *is* forgiveness, and this includes creation: by the act of creation, we "forgive" the objects of our imagination for not having existed before, and for the necessity of our efforts to create them (even, and I put a fence around it, if the purpose was for revenge).

Ah, Beatrix, I trust you, but — forgive me! — only for the moment with my past, "his" past — that curiously bereft child, that Island boy — and, if you still insist, with "Chris's" past. Remember, I gave you pearls for your hair, and the language of love, however spoiled by pretentiousness and bad scholarship. What will you give us?

At nine o'clock the sky was a fixed mass of gray, like concrete. The wind flowed over the apex of the barn roof among the gulls set there like a line of stones caught at the lip of a dam. As though at the barn eaves the wind straightened out into an even river-flow fifteen feet above the ground level, it snagged the tops of lilac trees outside the kitchen windows before it threw its force shatteringly against the upper panes.

In the fifteen minutes she had been watching it the wind had broken a pane and was working at another, had placed in the top right-hand corner of it, like a brand, a small mark with built-in obliquity; she would watch, unmoving beside the washtubs, until the diagonal was effected.

The kitchen reeked of February, of the pent-up smells of smoked and salted foods and odorous tubers and naphtha. The influence of the scummy steep in the tubs, which were never empty, extended through the dining room and into the parlor. The stench of bacon and parsnips reached further, up the stairs and into the bedrooms, in the smallest of which the boy was still bound by sleep, or, she expected, bound by a dread of seeing her. Most four-year-olds were up and about at dawn, waking the household, clamoring for this, that, or the other thing, begging to be let outside to play, no matter how dark or cold or messy the weather. But not this one. When he finally came downstairs, at her command — and not at her first, either; she would have to call and call — it would be at a snail's pace, a kind of sidling creep that could get under her skin on bad days. Most four-year-olds were hungry, begging another biscuit, a piece of specially fried bacon, or trying to wheedle a big pale sugared teacake for breakfast. But not this one. She would have to threat-en him, or worse, to make him eat his oatmeal, on which morning after morning he gagged, turning her already queasy stomach.

When she was fat with him she had known whole moments of joy in which she had not minded that the baby might not be the girl she wanted, and when he was handed to her and she saw the grub at the base of the belly, that irreversible fact was overshadowed by her relief to have him out of her body. She had fed him dutifully, dragging herself out of sleep at his need. She had cradled and tended him with fidelity, and tried to sing to him, tone-deaf as she was and puzzled by what purpose such noises could serve, glad at least for his silence, for he seldom cried, and woke her without a sound, as his father had done, with his hands.

But his silence was like the crack growing on the windowpane as she watched: it sprang from some built-in flaw, and what that flaw was, and whose responsibility, and where it could lead, was what was driving her down the crazy road.

Because he was not a mute. As shuddery as that would have been, springing such a thing from her loins, it could not have been as maddening as his willful hush, as though he walked among the dead and knew it. She had heard him scream and knew the power of his lungs, but what it took to get a sound out of him was dangerous and had become an obsession.

Last night, standing beside his bed in the dark, she had told him, trying to sound calm, "From now on you will ask for anything that you get. If you have to pee in the night you will come into my room and ask for the pot. Else you will burst open. One drop on the bed will get you you-know-what, but worse this time. Tomorrow you will ask for breakfast, dinner, supper. You will say, 'Christine, I want—' and you will tell me exactly what you want to eat, and I will fix it. But only. YOU WILL NOT TOUCH THE DIPPER IN THE BUCKET—" (he drank water as though inwardly bathing). "When you want a drink you will say, 'Christine—' and you will say, 'Please.' You will not touch the Bible nor any other picture book without asking permission. I will close all the doors in the house, and you will not go from one room to another without calling to me to let you through — 'Christine,' you will say, and state your piece. That is just a beginning."

Turning to go she had heard a sound. If he had only known it, a sniffle would have won him a measure of probation, but when the sound continued she recognized it as a disturbance in his stomach and had remembered to take the chamber pot from under the bed, rapping the china with her fist so that he would know where he stood. She had closed his door and the door of the storeroom that lay between his bedroom and hers. The other door into his room was from the steep and narrow backstairs which slanted, enclosed and pitch black at high noon, from the attic to the dining room, with a pause outside his door to collect his fears (if he was human). It was up this narrow stairway she had to yell, like someone at the bottom of a cistern, when his quiet during the days oppressed her beyond endurance, and when she needed finally to get him up in the mornings.

He was over two years old when her isolation with him reached inside her like a hand and twisted something there, some organ or a mass of nerves. Through the kitchen window she had watched him as he sat unmoving where she had placed him under the pear trees. It was a summer day; the uncut grass, always heavier under the trees, fed by the richness of rot, had hidden his scrawny legs and grown up his thighs like green feathers. He had sat leaning back, hands and wrists cut off by the grass, and gazed up into the trees until she had wanted to scream. She had wanted to throw a rock at him, or a kitchen pot, or the hot flat-iron gripped in her fist; anything to draw a sound out of him, or to make him move. It was then his silence first reached her consciousness in the form it permanently assumed and which since then had worried her mind and her vitals without cease: it was the dead-weight disapproval of all she was and did, of her very mind and its thoughts, which she could not help and which had lost her the grudging presence of the boy's foreign father. As though in the boy he had given her a substitute for himself, the man (no legal husband, a guinea hired hand with no apology in him and hardly a word in the language that she could understand) had left when the boy was under a year in age. She had never been much on the Island, having no legacy of family and only the house and ten acres in property, but the man's going had left her less than she had been. That day, watching the boy under the pear trees and feeling the tension grow, she had seen him as his father's absence made flesh so that she could not forget it.

She saw herself running out the kitchen door, snatching the boy up, his flat eyes unsurprised as though he had been expecting her. She hurried with him to the bodark hedge with the twisted trunks like a black wall and pushed him into the thorns. His face and neck and shielding hands were torn by the toxic spines. His screams were real, then, no longer in her mind. In satisfaction she had put him down, his bare feet writhing among the old thorns in the weeds, and left him to find his way to safety.

His screams had reminded her of the way her father would test a dog's voice by grasping its ears and lifting it from the ground.

Not long after that day, watchful for any opportunity, she had found a rabbit in the fenced-in garden. As she went to fetch the boy she heard the rabbit begin its panicked beating among the fruited bushes and the lettuces, beating around the fence, stupidly passing the hole it got in by, cutting across its own trail as though it knew. She took the boy and stood him at the fence, his hands holding the chicken wire where she placed them, his nose and mouth and eyes pressed to it as he watched the rabbit. She gave them both time for anticipation before she began to stone the rodent. Time after time she deliberately missed the mark, letting her own need say when the moment was ripe. As though he could tell by reading her mind, the boy's first moan preceded the killing rock by a matter of seconds. The rock was so precisely aimed that the rabbit died in midair, in attempted flight over the fence, and it seemed its coat turned dull with death before it fell to earth without a twitch.

The boy had sprung a fever; the rabbit's death had affected him, it appeared, much more than his own pain among the thorns.

For nearly two years afterward she had taxed her ingenuity, when need became demand, to devise ways to break his silence, but he had learned foxiness, learned to hold in most of the sounds so that she had trouble getting more than grunts and groans out of him.

She could forget for weeks, for a month or over, that the only sounds produced in her isolated house by a human being were made by her: her voice, her footsteps, her bodily functions, even. It went beyond any understanding that the dried beans, staple of their winter diet, should distend her body with torrents of gas that had to be let out as noisily as childbirth, and from his nearly emaciated body produced not a "poot," as she had called it as a child; not when he sat on the pot, in her presence at her insistence, or when he was alone in his room with her outside the door listening to the quiet in the throes of something like superstition. She imagined then that when the door was closed he took wing and flew away to Italy.

But as though endurance were a measurable substance that could be weighed on a scale, her body would become overburdened; she would have trouble walking, and in the night could feel the lump shift in her as she turned from side to side in her bed. She would lie awake imagining the absences she suffered: his feet like snowflakes, in shoes or bare, on the bare floors; his body that never rustled a cornhusk in his mattress ticking when he turned — if he turned — in his sleep; his pee aimed at the side of the chamber pot to trickle soundlessly down. In the dark she would imagine that she had given birth to a corpse, and for a few times she had managed to frighten him by creeping into his room and laying a hand on him or making an eerie noise, causing him to cry out. But afterward it was worse, for she could imagine him lying awake all night staring at the door, waiting for her, and she would be the fearful one, seeing his large unmoving eyes hanging in the darkness two rooms away.

She had given him a cat, hoping as much to hear him croon gently to it as to have her way, but his fondness, if he felt any, for the animal was as silent as his hatred and suspicion of her, and when she thought of hurting the cat, seeing her hands breaking its leg under the boy's flat gaze, she felt certain that the only cry would come from the animal.

The boy read her intentions concerning the cat in her eyes, for he refused to play with it and then would not let it in the house when it mewed and scratched at the door, and finally he had taken it time and again to the barn and closed it in with the rats and mice until the cat had given up and accepted its own well-fed isolation.

In the past year, up until cold weather made it impossible for her to do so, she had turned the boy's treatment of her against him. She would sit by the water in the evenings for many hours, afraid in the dark of the moon, hearing the rushes parting and the slither of bodies entering and leaving the marsh grass and rattling the scallop and mussel shells. The boy would be alone in the house, forbidden to light a lamp or a candle. The night sounds of the house, the ticking death watches in the walls that made her flesh creep, were for him alone. But when she returned, worn-out and dead for sleep, he had no tales to tell her, no word at all that was not forcibly wrung out of him. If it was possible, he became more silent out of spite.

When the first cold snap drove her back into the house with him, she came to believe, in reviewing the summer and fall nights by the water with her terrible thoughts, she had been nearly happy, almost content. She saw then that she desired his absence more than she wanted or needed proof of his presence.

Muffled by doors, as though from another continent, the clock in the parlor sounded, but it was not the quarter hour of her expectations; bonging on and on, now close, now far, as the wind dictated, it became like the tolling of a buoy. Discombobulated by the failure of her sense of time, a daily rack upon which she was stretched and made to count, some days, even the seconds, timing them to strokes on the washboard or the cadences of other chores, she tried to imagine that it was in fact the buoy at the channel mouth, but at the count of ten the noise stopped.

She had been fooled by the growth of the crack in the pane, thinking it lengthened at a steady pace, into standing immobile for one hour. Now she saw that it had stopped short of the center of the pane, on its diagonal tack, because the wind had shifted east, she had been standing for she didn't know how long with its blast on her back; it battered the window behind the tubs, the worst window in the house, with a great racket that she had never heard, and slipping her fingers into the water that had been too hot for even her calloused hands, she found that it was stone cold.

As though a malevolence as big as a boulder had slipped into her eye she laboriously turned her gaze upon the heavy iron kettle she would have to swing off the stove to fill with water for heating. The kettle was pitted and scarred like a huge cinder, and the stove lid beneath it was gray and cold as ashes, telling her that the fire had nearly gone out. The woodbox was almost empty. It was the boy's chore to keep it filled, toting two sticks of stovewood at a time, one in each hand, trailing the ends on the ground. His path from the woodpile had a groove on each side of it as though a narrow cart's wheels had worn them there. There were no marks of deviation from the path, from the grooves.

The unnatural enormity of the precision had not struck her until now. A child wandered, a normal child wandered, his curiosity taking him far afield no matter the task engaged in. In the unwavering grooves she read the boy's single-mindedness. His sole preoccupation was her; straight from her and to her ran the tracks of his distrust. The path between, the black, compacted earth like an unbroken strip of slate, was the record of his plotting. It was there he perfected the discipline of his silence. It was as cold as ice. Only the boiling, blazing climate of hell could melt it and cause it to run. In her mind she saw, as it would be, the red-hot stove, the steaming cauldron, the air of the kitchen roiling with its effluence.

She heard his feet just beyond the kitchen door. It was as though he had crept there and listened to her and was stamping a challenge to her thoughts. The boulder in her eye twitched, and she had to stifle an outcry of pain. BEATRIX I CANNOT AND WILL NOT AND WILL NOT ALLOW YOU. THIS IS NOT THE PAST IN WHICH UNACCOUNT-

ABLY I TOOK REFUGE AND OFFERED REFUGE TO
YOU, IN WHICH I HAD FOOLISHLY ENVISAGED
OUR COMFORTABLE COLLABORATION. YOU DIS-
ARMED ME WITH THE SETTING, THE PROPS SO
FAR REMOVED FROM THOSE OF A SOUTHERN
GARDEN THAT I COULD NOT TRANSLATE WHAT
YOU WERE ABOUT. IF PHYSICAL TORTURE IS
WHAT LED THE BOY TO MURDER I CONDONE IT,
BUT WILL NOT RELIVE, I WILL NOT BEAR HIS
SCARS. I WILL NOT GROW WITH HIM. GIVE ME
HIS OLD AGE, HIS DEATH. I WOULD TAKE MY
OWN DEATH NOW RATHER THAN LEAVE THIS
SHEET OF PAPER, THIS MACHINE, OPEN TO YOUR
SLY ATTEMPT AT PARALLELS. I KNOW IT IS YOU
FOR I KNOW MY MIND, I LIVE THERE, THIS IS
NOT POSSIBLE FOR ME TO REMEMBER OR WRITE.
AT WHAT MOMENT DID YOU BECOME ACTUAL?
WHEN I ALLOWED YOU FOR A MOMENT TO AS-
SUME THE IDENTITY OF BEATRICE PORTINARI
WITH PEARLS IN YOUR HAIR (AND *BAD* MODERN
ITALIAN IN YOUR PEN! IGNORANCE HAS LED ME
HERE!) BUT YOU ARE A BORGIA AND I WILL
BURN BEFORE I WILL SIP THIS POTION. I WILL
GIVE YOU AN ENDING FOR *YOUR* STORY, HERE
WE COLLABORATE, IF NEED BE, OVER YOUR DEAD
BODY. TELL ME, ARE YOU SO SECURE, SECURE
ENOUGH IN YOUR CHILDHOOD TO CONTEMPLATE
WHAT YOU WERE MEANING TO DO? MINE WAS
SO BAD THAT I HAVE BEEN RUNNING FROM IT
EVER SINCE, INTO PREMATURE OLD AGE, INTO
SENILITY WITH DREAMS OF A MURDER TO PRO-
PEL ME. BUT I AM STRONG, AS YOU SEE, AND AS I
SEE TO MY NEARLY HUMBLE SURPRISE. EACH
MAN *IS* AN ISLAND, BUT I HAVE BEEN TOUCHED
BY WAVES OF GRANITE AND LAVA, BY A MAIN-
LAND THAT I SHALL IF I MUST BLOW TO KING-
DOM COME. AND BOTH OF US, ALL OF US, WITH
IT.

Here is the child grown up and old. Sterile. Is there a deeper silence than that? Old, lustful, sterile, alone. Praying. Praying to be rid of his cock. Can we offer you more than that for your liberation?

Take Thou the root of life's replenishment again from me and with it all motive divine and base, for the vessel of its containment is brittle and withered, too porous in sereness to hold the honey of enticement and fulfillment. Take Thou this and all Thy servant's thoughts and actions from this day forward.

ON ERRANDS IN THE VILLAGE he would watch the young cocks strutting and would experience the complexity of seeing himself young watching himself old, watching the young watching themselves old in him, and he would wonder what punishment, behind their arrogant façades, their old selves were plotting to inflict upon them.

With senses long turned inward he measures the day and is appalled at its length, as though he were the father of a child who, through practices of witchcraft stumbled onto in an attic-concealed book, has in a trice grown beyond easy recognition. It looms above him, more shadow than substance for a moment, and he sees the terrible growth, in the outlines of the shadow of his own growth, read diminishment.

He looked toward what motion there was in his world, what he took to be the waving of grasses, and he moved toward it and found that it was a squirrel, plumed tail swollen in indignation, whose motion had caught his eye.

On the wagon trail by which grain and harvest were transported to and from the fields there lay a squirrel newly dead. It had been crushed. Eyeballs hung from sockets dripping new blood, entrails protruded from rectum like an attempt at borning. He felt his eyes' deceit; despite the scolding of the dead squirrel's mate he lifted the tiny corpse and felt its warmth and flexibility. A gobbet of blood, as though expectorated, issued from the agape mouth and fell onto his shirt sleeve. The mate chattered, directing him to put the maimed body where he had found it, and when he did so, she (he believed automatically that it was the male who had been killed) set about tugging with her paws, trying to draw the body to some imagined safety, chittering like a shrew.

It had been crushed; impossible; it had been crushed. It had been crushed by a vehicle, for the mark of a narrow wheel lay like a sash across its middle. Who, what? No vehicles here, no carts, wagons, barrows. Harvesters had long since gone, and he had been here, a matter of a dozen feet away, for the length of a revery, longer than the squirrel's immortality, mortality, death.

Who, what? What conveyance is crossing the land, narrow wheeled and noiseless, killing wild things? The only moving presence through this day besides his has been the sun's. Time moving across the heavens, mortal below like the gnomon of a sundial, and at his feet the mystery of death's conveyance, unseen and unheard in passage; unimaginable in shape — plumed, dark, carven, white, pristine as chaos — only known factor is the wheel's involvement, the narrow wheel — a radiance of spokes or solid, tired or metal rimmed, unknown. Only the wheel's complicity with what is carried in whatever vehicle cannot be imagined by a man of the earth.

Bereavement in a small creature seems to him unbelievably weighty; he had not known it inhabited such tiny quarters. He is in the state of suspension of all disbelief that accompanies revelation, and fears the grieving squirrel will press its paws to its eyes and weep in human language; he rather wishes it would, for the chattering has grown from its noisy center a blade of panic that, if it grows higher, he feels could sever the chambers of his heart. Small noisy beast!

He stops himself, freezes as though in a children's game of "statues," and standing apart beyond horror's range observes himself: caught one-footed, the other brogaaned foot suspended above the bereft squirrel. Frozen in the act of crushing mourning out of the squirrel along with eyeballs and entrails and the throat's blood. Imagination pushes the foot downward — difficult, through the frozen air holding it in suspension — and inhabits it and feels the first brush with the furred lively victim, all the small signals of life that proclaim the difference between stone and heart beneath the foot, the most upsetting being the slower breathing of a creature which believes that it is being caressed; but once over that hurdle — oddly, now — the rest, the completion, goes smoothly, without arousing ugly emotions; the giving bones, the fine elasticity of well-tuned flesh, the lessening of returned pressure as blood, finding several outlets, goes forth; murderous foot and victim having become one, there is even exhilaration in the departure of the blood, as though with it, it carries the morbid humors of the foot's affliction — an old, untended wound. Interesting to find that the impulse to murder, the closing of the physical gap between instrument of murder and victim, the initial violating touch, is the effortful part; the actual maiming, killing, act of final deprivation, is as simple as an afterthought — which of course it is, if thing or act is merely a copy of an idea. Thus the worst part of murder or mayhem or assault, or, to begin at the beginning, the depriving of a right, is in the idea, wish, desire — the more so for there being no punishment to assuage guilt — so that his wish to crush the squirrel is seen by him as truly human and truly himself, and in his horror at the death of its mate he suspects a cover for *kicking the chair away, then grabbing at the rope with both hands, beginning to laugh inside, feeling the reprieve of the thick safe rope in your hands above your head, and then feeling something begin to yield and thinking, or beginning to think "I will not, after all, I will not —" but the thought and a kind of blackness seem to melt and become one . . . thing . . . so that to finish the thought is no more necessary than to positively identify the blackness, because the thought and your affliction and the thing and you and time . . . all of it, all, all of it, are at last, seen as one* "I had forgot that." Humbly, he tells the squirrel, "I had forgot that," wondering at the sensation of stain on his cheeks.

With a switch of the tail as though it could sever memory, the widowed animal scurries away, parting the pinkgold grasses bordering the hedgerow. He attends her progress as told stealthily by the sudden half nods of weeds, like neighbors surprised by news of the murder, then he sees her reappear, full-plumed at the foot of the nut tree. Without emotion he observes her as she scales the trunk and dives — as if the bright tree were a river of forgetfulness — into the shivering leaves.

He sets a courtroom in his mind, populates it, enthrones Justice, and lights the scene with the sunlight of high summer. Invisibly, in the hush preceding the first solemn words, he roams, admiring the scrubbed wood and shined windows, the starched bonnets and freshly blacked shoes, the pervasive proclamation of impeccable intent. He nods, ticking off presences as though conducting silent roll call by occupation: Tanner, Taylor, Fuller; Glazier; Cutler; Wheelwright, Joiner, Cooper, Weaver, Cordwinder. Here, man and wife; here, the wife only; here, widower newly formed in the crucible of summer.

That morning he had felt Reisefieber like winesap and had kegged it within seasoned staves of chores until he was alone with it in the sunlight, so spanking new a result of the season's concentrated alchemy, that it was molten in the center while the edges still creaked with the chill of spring. Standing in the dooryard with head thrown back he had felt the nucleus of the crystal in his skull and the brittle edges in the fingertips of his outflung hands. Behind his closed eyelids touched with heat as steady as passion recalled or imagined, he had seen the shadows of birds as they warily circled him, motionless scarecrow, before they settled on his outstretched arms, and flung himself skyward flapping and screeching, flaking the silence like rapped pottery. The abrupt exercise strung his blood to a singing race as astringent within his veins as new wine on a frosty night. Recalled, he thought: Thus do we reward trust.

In the courtroom, unseen, he stands before himself, trying to assess loss. A stormy man, riddled with temper: his scars abase him with public testimony to his lack of self-control like the remnants of innumerable gunfights. But where is grief? Does it sit, a darker star, somewhere among the visible constellations of his self-distrust?

He suspects, dreads, then clear and clean sees: it is not the trial of the witch that he attends but his own, old and recurrent, conducting of his own trial for the murder of a love — nameless, undefined; whether of person or pride, his own or other's or others', or of talent or judgment, he cannot tell. He is plunged back to the resounding hollow of bereavement, a whirlpool whose sides honed him into the shape he was to wear through life, through time travel and down the corridors of his brain.

He believes, standing before himself in the courtroom, that he is in the final days of his mortal existence. Not believing in the immortal with any part of himself that can count in the Beyond, he finds only the potential peace of blackness and yearns for it as does a tired man who would willingly pull the curtains against delayed night if chores did not demand another hour of his time.

TRIALS

June 22

Today is the first day of summer. In the past there was a cre-
scendo that began in mid-spring and chugged, how slowly, up
the hill toward summer like an old funicular; one's impulse was
to get out and run up the hill, shedding clothes on the way.
There is a confusion now about seasons so that their advent is
neither marked nor their going mourned.

How can I convey for some future brain the impressions of
this room, now, and make that brain sense the complexity of this
particular confusion? The white-fringed curtains blow, the mimosa trees dance beyond the screens; the effect, within and
without, is of rippling: the shimmering fringed curtains, the red
silk tassels on a velvet cushion shivering, the moving surface in
Miss Gold's bowl of water, the yellow roses stirring in the vase,
the window shade pulls swaying; and in the sunlight on the
floor, the shadows of these things. More. The shadows on the
grass; the glinting gliding water in the gap in the liquid hedge,
waves of the bodark hedge framing waves of—no, tufts of—bay
water. The papier-mâché hawk has weathered the winter and
spins now above the grape arbor like a famous acrobat, over and
under the taut fishline that supports him . . . But as I write the
room and its intricacies recede. A problem I shall consider:
spring and autumn are in the room simultaneously (summer too
recently arrived to have a steady seat), the emotions are tugged
oppositely, springward and toward the fatalism of winter
thoughts. The curtains are sails, the hawk tells of wine, an autumn and a spring impression involving the same window; thus
the pleasure one feels has a tristesse. The green mountainous
blanket on the sofa under which Miss Gold dozes, the image

touched with death, brings a brief chill. Now the walls are electric, pieces of artifacts twanging like nerves or harps. Victor saying: If my life was a piece of cloth you' be able to see what I mean without me havin' to do more than hold it up to the light. See, thin as a stretched rubber about to bust, and over here, thick like a welt where a razor cut has healed up. Man, that's ugly, man.

Distance and time: the same if they are anything at all. I had once imagined they were a kind of therapy. In my family, ocean voyages were the cure for all wounds of spirit and body, and the voyages were called Distance and Time. Both (it) lie (lies) between Victor and me, and where is the cure to proclaim passage? I am assailed by an old haunt. I cannot encompass the idea of Time's having any value in the mathmatical sense. It is all illusion as far as I can see. There is the illusion that a week end, for instance, occupies a linear space, beginning here and ending there, and taking — how does one say it? — a measured amount of something to get from here to there. There are events — eating, sleeping, emotional reactions — but after the fact all "events" are seen as simultaneous: anticipation, dread, appetites, emotional valleys and peaks. Everything has already happened, is happening, will be happening. There is a massive illusion that things have not yet come about; the "future" is the hoax. All is within the skull, and "time" is the method whereby we extract it; time is only a tool. We exist simultaneously with ourselves, and there are many, but this thing of numbers — "many" — is itself delusional. There may be only the one, and if there is, then mathematics is hardly needed, and once such subtraction has begun, or elimination, then one could go on eliminating — sciences, arts — until nothing is left. With goals — of becoming scientist, artist, artisan — out of the way, there is no further point at all in the personal self. If one is only an atom comprising with all mankind and animalkind and plantkind THE ONE, then subjectiveness is not possible.

After Victor I worked on an idea based upon man's having a good and bad side at birth, an assumption surely as firmly founded in nature as one could count on. Rather than giving a child one name, so the theory ran, and trying to force that named identity to wrestle in the dark through its life with the unnamed half, if both sides were given names and the battle brought into the open with impartial recognition given to the victories of either side, the two could eventually merge into a workable personality considerably more comprehensive and comprehending than the one resulting from constant suppression of exactly half of itself. (The white race considers its lower half black, and punishes its impulses and deplores its victories, but this "consideration" falls short of "naming," and thus the shadow persists.)

Today I see that this is a highly simplified idea of my old ghost. Take these twin selves and give them each twin selves, and those, twin selves — all with different names. One arrives at all the names there are, coming through the back door, so to speak, to the belief of the basic Oneness, which is, finally, the negation of all but the self, which is seen as pointless: an island entire of itself with no proof of its existence.

If Victor was I, and I was Victor, then one of us ceased, had to, to exist. But which one? Am I, without knowing it, a Puerto Rican delivery boy? Is he, going about his groceries futilely fighting servility and the devastation of his beauty, an aging failed Southerner, perhaps a suicidal cipher, a zero trying to implode like an old star?

Beatrix,

A warning. *Do not couple the dachshund, whatever name she bears, with death images again.* Clearly I cannot, for reasons momentarily beyond me, be master of my fate, but collaboration can take unexpected turns, and to see your edges curl I would endure the fire. Once I paid tribute to your sexuality, but you are, I see now, about as concupiscible as Alecto and her sisters. Even Furies must sleep — and where do you nap, bloody lips in repose, claws sheathed, turbulent brain turned inward upon that triple unconscious, those devastating dreams! I apologize for the outburst. You must be exhausted after writing even my Journal entry! It's a daedel accomplishment, for you have indeed "got inside my skull" while retaining your own style and the flavor of

123

"Chris"— who, you may admit, is so far only an essence in spite of your, as I see it, gallant attempts. But he has no particular background, no roots, no aspirations, no *address*. When I wrote "collaborator" above, I had a specific idea in mind. It occurs to me that between us, even at this admittedly late date, we could

At the age of thirty-eight, Christopher Webster lived in his mind, that last refuge of the old or the sick. To a certain extent he had always been a mind dweller, even when he was young and a probationary member of a circle. He sometimes felt that his address, so to speak, was what had lost him a place in that circle, mainly because, in answer to frequent inquiries about his body — its whereabouts, if you will, since none of the members of the circle succeeded in touching it with any degree of satisfaction — Christopher would refer them to his mind, where, he would tell them, the only important part of him could be found. It had a nice ring and was actually, he now supposed, his bid to the ranks of the exclusive. Consequently he had been more than puzzled when the circle, instead of closing about him, had grown outward until it was as big as the world and he had found himself one day or night merely another anonymous member of mankind.

But not in his mind, which he came to inhabit like an exclusive and active ghost in an old house, rather more like the ghost of a Southern belle than anything else, for two reasons: the subjectivity of his search through the rooms, and the fact that he was no more particularly feminine than he was particularly masculine in the essentials of character and spirit. If the term "neuter" came to mind, or, as it had in the latter days of the circle, to lip, it did not bother Christopher but rather corroborated what he had believed all along: bodies are feminine or masculine, plus or minus; minds are not. Phrases such as "a tough masculine mind," which he came across in the copious reading that was part of his search, were, he felt, projections by the critic of the qualities the critic physically lacked or desired onto a favorite's mind, or the denial of those qualities to the mind of someone he did not like.

Minds were pure, in the sense of being innocent of the taint of gender, and there Christopher chose to live.

His mind was a house of many rooms kept in apple-pie order, or at least those rooms were which he frequented daily in his role as host to Baudelaire, Shakespeare, and others who seemed to share his monomania, which was the compounding of a theory. There were some locked rooms whose keys he held and which he visited often enough; there were some that had no doors but only peepholes through which he looked, when at all, in the dead of night. Though an exclusivist, as a mind dweller he was too knowledgable to believe that his mind, alone, contained those other rooms which had neither doors and keys nor peepholes, but he came to believe that he differed from the run-of-the-mill leaser, at least, in his certainty of the rooms' existence and his feeling, more than suspicion, of what one of the rooms contained, which was Death.

Proposition: Death is something of which everyone is supposedly certain, but of which they can be other than theoretically certain *only* when it has happened to them, and since the revelation dies with them, death must remain, in effect, as pertains to each man's knowledge of it in life, a theory.

Still, life was nothing less than time devoted to the propoundment and refinement of that theory, and the more consciously one worked at it, by somehow opening the rooms of the mind one by one and exploring their contents, until only Death's room remained, the more completely one had fulfilled one's obligations to whatever, or Whomever, had invented the system in the first place, and since the ultimate duties seemed to go to Death, Christopher presumed that Death was the inventor.

The worst possibility was that Death should be the true, nonphotographic negative of Life, which to Christopher was a series of peaks separated by yawning valleys. In life, he occupied the peaks — some of their designations were Social, Racial, Economic — moving from one to the other with ease where emphasis was needed to make a point. But suppose that in death he should be confined to the valleys to labor Sisyphuslike at his misfortune, while from the peaks he was watched derisively by blacks, Puerto Ricans — who had in life worn their puzzling insouciance because they knew the final outcome! The downtrodden harped so much upon Faith, it was as if they referred to someone in the house to whom they gave subsistence in return for something much more definite than Christopher had ever been promised.

Against such a devastating possibility, Christopher came to descend from his peaks and walk about in the valleys as often as he could without openly inviting scandal, returning from his forays with specimens to be studied with increasing feverishness as the years bonged by him (as though he were rushing down a corridor of concealed clocks; he knew he could not stop their bonging, and still he searched for them on his forced journey as if, once face to face with his victim, Time might be moved to suggest some compromise).

Assiduously, even artistically, Christopher picked the locks to the rooms of his "specimens'" minds. His tools were alcohol, a sympathy never overtly contradicted, money given in return for "services."

His most effective and complicated tool was fear. Fear of the specimen; of discovery; of discovery of his motivation. So carefully guarded was his fear that he allowed himself only the smallest glimpse of one corner of it, without suspecting (so careful was his guard) that the bulk of it was hidden below the surface, or in other rooms. He feared fear, feared his possession of it, felt himself to be obsessed by its possession, believed the corner he glimpsed of it to be so vast that he thought of himself as having the Midas touch where fear was concerned. He peered at it through the peephole in the dark of night and shuddered at what he saw, thinking the corner to be the entire room, unable to imagine the labyrinths of it that lay above and below and roundabout the room with the peephole.

He *thought* himself to be reasonably altruistic, or at least liberal, or at very least traditional — his family was known for charity work — as he pursued his chosen task of writing about the poor "discolored," as he thought of them, believing private levity to have therapeutic value in his burdensome career. As he devoted only what he considered a reasonable part of his time to his investigations — the afternoon hours, three days a week — he supposed that he could be categorized as a dilettante, if anyone had known him intimately enough to indulge in categorical epithets. He could have advised that person that the amateur had once been highly respected for, among other things, the purity of his motive, and still was, he supposed, in the field of sports. He admitted, without embarrassment, that his dilettanteism allowed him the aesthetic advantage of interviewing only those minority members with whom he felt it would not be offensive to spend time in protracted sessions, subjects for study handpicked by him for their physical attractiveness and comparative cleanliness. However, he admitted it only to himself, since the dry results of his writings did not attract much notice. Still, to be fair, he pointed out that the ugly and dirty are hardly more deprived, within the ghetto, than the beautiful and comparatively clean. Having done so, and facing up to the fear of the danger inherent in closeting himself with people of more than average criminal potential, he set about his work of observing and recording and compiling with a certain dedication. In observation he approached the sensibilities of the artist, for his fear would not let him overlook or discard as meaningless the slightest change of expression, the subtlest shift in the tone of voice or atmosphere.

In the process of opening the rooms of others, occasionally, with a click, one of his own rooms would swing its closed door ajar. At such times he would find himself in the exhilarating position of sorting the contents of two rooms at one time. He found his profoundest satisfaction in the dissimilarities of the contents, especially (humanly) in those which pointed most clearly to his superiority. When the appointments were too much alike and no examination of the articles in his subject's room could turn up a "Made in Japan" stamp, he suffered afterward from a depression that could not be explained by repeated admissions of snobbism. Then he would come closest to suspecting the true basis of his search and would have to expand his terror in dreams of loss that centered, protective of him, upon his dearest possession, his little dachshund, Miss Gold.

VICTOR

"It's open, Victor. Be with you pronto." There was a pause, then "O.K." came at him from near the floor where he knew the young man was crouching, exchanging caresses with Miss Gold. Their pleasure in each other had given Christopher an answer that seemed both satisfactory and tactful to one of Victor's disquieting questions. During the Puerto Rican's second visit to the apartment, possibly careless because of the vodka and orange juice he had drunk in large quantity, he asked Christopher what made him feel so sure that he would not get jumped and tied up, made helpless to stop Victor from making off with, as he put it vaguely, "things." The dachshund bitch was asleep with her head on Victor's leg when he asked the question; Christopher waited until the other's challenging eyes met his before he gave the answer, which consisted of a nod toward the bitch and a word, "Her."

"You trust her, huh." On his tongue the word "trust" sounded more like thrust. Christopher agreed that he did.

"But not me so much, huh Chris." His smile was lazy; the words were, too, as if they were the smallest small talk. "You don' thrust me so much."

Christopher answered him in a bantering tone he had found to be most effective with Puerto Ricans, the tone serving as well to cover his distaste at the persistent use, despite hints, of the diminutive.

"She trusts you, I trust her. O.K.?"

"O.K., Chris. Shake, amigo." The allusions had continued, however, worse for being indirect, and today Christopher was determined, in spite of a tactical error made earlier in the day, to bring things into the open. Under the circumstances, the "things" he meant to expose were as vague as those Victor had meant to steal: neither man could be sure what the things were until open inventory had been taken and some sense or desire told them "this is it."

Standing in the living room out of sight of his visitor, giving to them both a moment's more grace, Christopher had to admit that the past two hours of analysis of himself and the boy and the progression of their relationship had opened no unopened door. He still stood with Victor in a corridor of many doors, most of them tight shut as they had been before he started the exploration. He was unwilling to admit to fear of the boy (or young man; Victor was nineteen or twenty-six, depending upon which of his answers one chose to believe), for that would have demanded severance. It would of course have to come eventually, for what on earth, in any long-range plan of his life, could he do with an unemployed Puerto Rican erstwhile delivery boy? So he let disquiet serve as the word for what he felt in the charged air between him and his unseen crouching guest, knowing that it could be transformed by word or gesture or even prolonged thought into what lay beyond and above disquiet — visualizing the progression as stairsteps with name plates — one place below horror.

His desire to deny fear a name plate (disquiet was permissible, horror improbable), and to re-establish the old footing where he was the more secure of the two, brought him close to blurting out a question that would have put him at a further disadvantage by causing the other's defensiveness to surface: "Why did you come an hour early today, without at least telephoning?"

He had had the doorman send Victor away. Victor had come at eleven, and Christopher had told the doorman to tell him to come back at one instead of twelve, the usual time. But still the need to know why the rule had been flouted rankled, so that the prolonged silence, adding his sharp displeasure to the charged air that separated them with increasing incisiveness, could be imagined as assuming the shape of a knifeblade which could sever whatever their bond had been.

The thought of the severance of the bond before he was ready to will it, and, far from the least consideration, what asking the question would reveal about him to Victor, caused Christopher to break the silence by going into the kitchen and rattling glasses and ice until he could trust his voice not to give him away. He had learned to fake, for the benefit of these people, an insouciance not native to him. There had been times in the past when, beset by worries, he had longed to do the unburdening, but what he thought to be an accurate sense of his role had restrained him. Holding back his own emotions had paradoxicaly a draining effect upon him. Sometimes when they had left him he felt like an empty husk stretched out on the couch in his study. The facts of their lives — heavy, ugly, valuable to him and his writing — hung somewhere in the room above him like tatters of dehydrated meat, as weightless at those times as he.

He listened to the silence coming in waves from the floor of the entranceway. He imagined the two creatures crouching there, staring in his direction, both gifted with abnormal instinct.

"Drink, Victor?" He counted the beats.

"Sure."

"Hang your jacket in the closet and go on back. I'll be right there."

He listened in vain for the rattle of coat hangers in the foyer closet, but in a moment he heard the squeak of Victor's sneakers on the tiles as he went to the study, apparently carrying Miss Gold as there was no accompanying clack of her claws. Victor's tenderness to the animal reassured him again, and he mixed Victor's drink and poured orange juice for himself. He put the drinks on a tray and turned on the kitchen radio. He had found that distant music — or sound; commercials would do — encouraged the confidences of people who in their own neighborhoods inhabited a continuous stream of sounds composed of rhythms and melodies from an almost infinite variety of sources: radio, T.V., mouths, hands beating bongo drums and garbage cans, sticks on metal railings, feet clicking sharp-toed high-heeled shoes on stoops and pavements. To drive through El Barrio, as Christopher often did under cover of night, was to submerge oneself in an element of the density and fluidity of sea water, beneath which one, as an alien substance, sank, but upon the surface of which the buoyant natives floated. Christopher imagined that if all possible means of creating sound were suddenly cut off, the Puerto Ricans would plummet to the dry bed of their lives and die, blind, deaf, and airless. Sound was their element, and in his apartment he provided it, but on his own terms: distantly.

He let himself into the hall under cover of a nattering commercial for a hair color.

"Hey, Chris, what's this ting here."

Christopher had carefully made no sound; glasses, tray, door had all been swathed in his calculation. Notes appeared, ghost written, in his mind: *Highly developed sensory perceptions — instinct for survival*. "What?" he shouted, creating distance.

"This-a ting, what's it?"

"Minute, Victor. I can't hear you." He opened the kitchen door, stepped partly inside, made an exit, slamming the door on a tide of words.

"Damn the amplified human voice, damn commercials, damn radio. For that matter, damn Marchese Guglielmo Marconi!" Experimentally he stopped where he had stood before. "O.K. now, shoot."

"Hey, man, you know I give that up."

"¿Que dice —" he began, amended it to: "¿Que tu dijistes?"

"Needle — shootin' — comprende? Aw, hell, joke."

"Dios quiera que tu estes relajando."

"¿Que?"

"Not a thing. ¿Qual fue la prequenta?"

"I said what the hell's this-a thing in here — buttons, mirrors —"

"Oh." He spoke carefully over the music. "In my closet. Don't shut Miss Gold in there, please."

"I ask a question, Chris. *Is this goddamn thing a microphone?*" Christopher stepped through the doorway quietly. "That's a sunlamp, Victor, the poor-but-honest man's rebuttal to the pejorative statement of March . . . *Marchen?* No, I guess it doesn't work, after all."

"It don' work. Ssssss." He seemed to be hissing the useless

sunlamp. He closed the closet door with a bang, startling Miss Gold. He knelt, contrite, and fondled her flowing ears, murmuring to her in Puerto Rican which, in quantity, Christopher would never be able to understand.

Christopher's smile was balanced; nothing slid or clinked against anything else. There could be no doubt to an observer that a delivery boy going through his personal closet had not disturbed the balance of his self-assurance. As there was no observer he patiently held the smile until Victor chose to glance upward, then, like a teacher explaining the subtlety of a drawing through slight overemphases, he deepened the lines of self-amusement; it was unthinkable that Victor should be allowed to imagine that Christopher was amused at him because he did not understand the attempted play on words.

"I meant that my pun didn't work." He set the tray on a table; colon or period? He decided upon a semicolon. "The *sunlamp* works fine. I give you myself as proof."

Victor looked him up and down, rising; his attention was filled with critical earnestness, a quality he brought to bear upon any question, however trivial (Christopher imagined) for which his consideration was requested.

"You lookin' good, Chris. Healthy. Sunlamp, huh?" In a series of movements that Christopher thought of as peculiar to the Puerto Ricans, Victor crossed his arms over his chest, hands grasping biceps; his feet straddled, toes turned slightly inward, the more comfortably to support the sagging weight of his pelvis which pushed the loins forward. Head cocked to one side, mouth pursed and lightly indented at the corners, he shifted his bright interested gaze from Christopher to the closet door, as though he might be able to see through to the instrument that could flood a March-dark room with tropical sun on command, and his prolonged, quizzically approving nods affected his whole body.

Christopher found the performance eloquent and somehow sensual, for his own expenditure of gesture was more carefully considered than that of his bank account. Victor smiled as though he could read the thoughts. Christopher fell into a bemused state, habitual though usually unobserved when he was faced with the boy's beauty after a separation.

Victor's teeth were as stainless as good milk. On his beautifully boned, tautly fleshed face there was no token of former dope addiction. Aware of the eyes grown distantly appraising, Christopher continued to gaze as though Victor were the model, he the pupil, in a class of anatomy. He looked at the boy's neck, a perfect unfluted column of dark marble planted on plateau-wide shoulders like a symbol erected on a mountaintop by a cult of phallus worshipers.

"There," he thought, and turned aside to the drinks, handing Victor his without looking at him.

"Sit down."

"You got a hanger for my jacket?" Christopher shot him an unguarded look that asked, "What did you see in my closet if not hangers?" Victor shrugged, smiled slightly.

"I didn't want to mess up you good suits. My jacket's wet. I better hang it in the bat'room, huh, Chris?"

Christopher gave him a hanger from the closet, seeing for the first time that the jacket was indeed sopping wet, as was Victor's hair, both shiny materials: the jacket nylon, the hair slicked with oil in an effort to make "good" hair out of it.

Victor hung the jacket from the showerhead in the bathroom that opened off the study. His voice was flat; to Christopher's ear, the lack of accusation rang as deliberate omission meant to heighten the effect: "I was early today because it was rainin' and I didn't have no place to go." He came into the room, face too brightly lit for the words. "No pesos for the movies. I try to sneak in but they catch. Me, Victor Ramos! 'What you name, *boy*.' 'Up yours, gringo.' I move up Eighty-six Street, RKO, right? Stand under marquee, lookin' at the pichurs, right? Lady in chain' boot' get nervous. Four, fi' gringos standin' there but me, Victor Ramos, she get nervous." He clapped Christopher on the shoulder. "Right, Chris, huh?"

He sat down beside Christopher on the sofa, then jumped up and got a newspaper that he spread carefully on the sofa and sat on, moving his buttocks vigorously. He explained, "My pants wet, man." He shifted back to front, side to side, in a slow circle, watching Christopher. "Somebody say to me, 'Man, what's new?'" He hopped up and bent over. "I say, 'Man, read my ass.'" He had succeeded in transferring a smudge of black to the seat of his faded khakis. When he remained bent over, Christopher indulgently leaned forward as if to read. Softly, straightening and turning, Victor said, "Man, that's not braille." Keeping his eyes on Christopher's face, shifting them from spot to spot as though looking for the hole through which the color might leak out, he stooped to pick up Miss Gold, who had edged up to investigate. She snarled and snapped at the slowly descending hands. On Victor's face Christopher saw understanding for her actions and admiration for her perceptions, and a glimmer of what to Christopher seemed like surprised recognition, the kind that suddenly revealed adversaries give to each other.

Victor held his crouch, arms dangling, lifting his face, which was on a level with Christopher's, and giving him a long, slow look, eyes narrowed, mouth curled at one corner. A trick of vision in the rainy light caused the face to loom, to become disproportionate to the body dwindling away behind. As if to identify the hallucination for Christopher, his tricky vision made the face, from hairline to chin, appear to detach and shift while the ears remained stationary and the glittering eyes achieved an artificial depth; it was the merciless Noh mask of Christopher's dream that had brought him starting sweatily awake last night.

Victor bounced onto the couch beside Christopher, saying gleefully, "Hey, Chris, you gotta watchdog. Ol Pen'house look out for you, man. She don' let no Pota Rican Negro stick his ass in you face!" He laughed with delight and drank, banging the sofa beside him with one hand, a strongly accented rhythm to which Miss Gold responded by standing on her hindlegs, asking to be helped up, her tail lashing in vehement friendship.

Christopher began forming a remark, casual and obvious, about the dog's love for Victor, in which he would make the unemphatic point that dogs (and friends) could be forgiven testiness, and even rudeness, if . . . With coldness, listening to his proposed oblique apology for sending Victor away, he heard, as the boy would have done if the words had been said, the half-hidden plea in the "if." Loathing skittered upon his flesh like insects. He sought imperviousness through inward arrogance that would turn his dislike upon the boy; finding it, feeling it course through him, exultant to be released, he controlled it, arrogance controlling arrogance, and stopped it short at his skin's surface where it ran spirally in whorls like fingerprints, hundreds of whirlpools of identity, and then ran together in a protective coating of blandness. On the wings of accomplishment he began the interview.

"Victor, old boy, I thought today we might veer a bit from the straight and narrow — ah — narrative, as it were, of indignities, discriminations, deprivations, et cetera, and, with your sanction, of course, sort of — ah — dive headlong into a colloquy, though I imagine that word is inapt, really, as well as undesirable for our purposes; you do agree that formality, even as a grace note, would be more of a hindrance than a help?" He bent upon Victor the parodied look of an equal and noticed, with a slight inward sinking, that Victor's outward blandness matched his own.

Victor delicately flicked the ash from his cigarette toward, but not into, the ashtray.

"Boil it down for me, Chris," he said and stretched his legs to the coffee table. The words and gestures conjured perfectly a Madison Avenue conference room, or at least the television version familiar to them both. After his acknowledgment of the boy's power of mimicry, he thought with peculiar relief that it was really only mimicry of an impersonation which children, or even clever monkeys, could do. The thought aided his free-flowing laughter.

When he had finished, unjoined by Victor except for quizzical eyebrows and lifted corner of mouth, he lay back in the cushions in an attitude that he had memorized long ago in college during bull sessions that he had attended but not joined. It was a position of alert relaxation that all the men but he would assume (Christopher was always perched somewhere, preferably on the edge of a desk or table), as if at a signal pitched too high for his ear, when the talk was about to turn to sex. He had thought then, as distasteful as procedure and talk were to him, that the series of movements were like the letters of the perfect word to describe what was to come: the falling-apart legs, the down-thrusting spine that jutted the genitals into prominence, the anticipation, which chose to appear half asleep. His own performance was a modified version, informed by characteristic caution and dislike of calling attention to his body, just as Victor's, following the leader, was typically unrestrained. Even Miss Gold surrendered to the mood and stretched on the floor between them, her rump to Victor, her head to Christopher. At once her eyes filmed over with trusting sleep.

Some brittleness in Christopher melted as he looked at her flowing goldenly on the rug. Often she slept on her back, but that was a gift for him alone. For all her fondness for Victor, she kept her vulnerable belly hidden from him as she slept. With definite longing but with meaning disarranged by a weighty descent of drowsiness as abruptly dismaying as an insult from a friend, Christopher thought that if she ever trustingly exposed her soft underside to Victor in sleep then so would he.

He pushed at the need for sleep with the first weapon at hand, words.

"I thought we might just talk today," he said, "about ourselves" — he stifled a yawn and smiled, "— together and apart. Ambitions, accomplishments, frustrations, even, but not, ah, sociological." He felt no longer godlike; he seemed even to lack purpose beyond prolonging physical sensations that seemed as though they were being brought from his past by the generous hand of an old love. The pattering rain, the warm face only a foot from his own; to accommodate Miss Gold, Victor had slued about until he stretched on a diagonal, his head with its warm secret breath sliding on the cushions nearer Christopher. The coolness of the room, the need to draw together, was pointed up by immobility. Christopher fell a few inches toward Victor, seeking the heat of his body as unthinkingly as Miss Gold might have done.

In Victor's left eye a line of light appeared, standing vertically from rim to rim of the pupil, a thread of gold edging a barely cracked door. It bellied slightly, became a cat's eye, dark-brown and gold chalcedony flecked with christopher. Christopher lay upon the eye and peered into the widening slit like a fly upon a well of light. "Laisse-moi plonger dans tes beaux yeux," he buzzed or droned or sang.

Victor cleared his throat, and Christopher lay upon a flat lightless surface.

"What you wan' to ask me, Chris?" Christopher sat up.

"No, no," he said, hearing rather than feeling the testiness. "It's not that I want to *ask* you anything." Victor spread his hands. Christopher tried briskness. "It occurred to me that we've never had a conversation. We've had interviews, monologues, confessions —" He spoke the last word with distaste and covered it with amplification as Victor muttered, "I don' confess nothin'." "You telling me about the, ah, heroin was a confession, because it was not something I knew about or suspected," though this was not true. Still, Victor's face cleared, and he nodded. Christopher went on, "A conversation can, but needn't, be confessional. What I want for us is simply to talk." He believed himself to be recovering nicely. "As friends." He found that he could not emphasize the last word.

"Amigos," Victor said earnestly. To Christopher the word seemed all at once too warm, too redolent of chili powder and chocolate misused in sauces.

"Friends," he said, and then nodded as if to counter the meant refutation. Victor grinned; it seemed that the grin had an edge of satirical implication. Victor nodded vigorously.

"O.K., Chris, you start." Christopher went as dry as crumbs on a plate. He felt like saying, "No, no," again; "No, no; you don't do it that way," like Miss Havisham telling Pip to *play*. But what was conversation, in the context of himself and Victor? He thought with hardness that the diplomatic meaning was the only one that could apply: representatives of two (opposing) countries exchanging hard-nosed policies in the guise of informality. He had been an idiot to imagine anything else was possible.

"Very well, O.K." he said, smiling thinly. "Aims, ambitions, that would be a topic. Or accomplishments. Do you want to choose, Mr. Ambassador?"

"Yeah, O.K. How about, ah, accomplishments?" Christopher had the unpleasant experience of hearing himself as others heard him, the "others" for whom Victor undoubtedly gave a fuller impersonation. He had learned how clever Victor could be, at showing you a thing you had not seen before. In that particular instance it had been Victor's aping of the old spastic junkie who had turned him on to heroin: knee bent, pigeon-toed, he had flapped around the room with such realism that Christopher had smelled the stench of the bottomless evil that such a man must give off. When, realist, he had asked how such a man could administer the needle to a novice, Victor said, "Oh, that hombre. His han' steady like a rock holdin' a needle. All this stuff —" he staggered around again — "I dunno. To make you sorrow?"

In a bright flash connected with the implied con game, Christopher saw a thing that for all his nosing about it all day he had not seen before: Victor came to him for one reason only, which was the ten dollars he was paid for each "interview." He had come early today because he was broke. Simultaneous with the flash, a practical Christopher was asking himself why else the boy should be expected to come.

Expressionless, Christopher reached into the pocket of his jacket folded on the arm of the sofa and drew out his wallet. As slowly as he dared, deliberate to the edge of insult, he isolated a ten-dollar bill from the company of twenties and fives and turned full face to Victor, expecting some version of the usual byplay: always at this point Victor would have his attention focused somewhere else — upon a book he had taken from the shelves and pretended to read, or, most often, upon Miss Gold, with whom he would instigate a sudden floor-sprawling tussle, realistic in its passion. Once he had bitten her stomach and she had screamed like a human.

Victor had put his glass on the table and bent to Miss Gold, his hands rousing her in what Christopher saw as a purely reflexive action, for although his head was bent to her, his eyes, wide open and staring with strain, were cut upon Christopher's hand

and the money in it that was being rubbed between forefinger and thumb. A vein throbbed in Victor's temple. As though the bill were a small unimaginably depraved creature that threatened all morality with suggestive whispers, Christopher closed his hand upon it with audible, or so it seemed to him, suddenness. He would have sworn that the strangled creature gave a cry that bloomed in the room like an articulate lily. Behind Victor's head, silhouetting it in kinky-haired blackness, was the white flash of the lily's blooming, and the room was streaked with layers of odor as though each door concealed a corpse with a lily growing from it

Through veils of hallucination, Christopher saw that Victor sat stonily gazing at the corner of green pushing from his closed fist.

Victor's head swiveled around, and his eyes rested on Miss Gold, whose chest his right hand cupped. He drew the hand from her chest to her side, ran it up and over her shoulder, along the side of her head, his fingers flicking her ear so that it folded back on itself like a calyx, a ridge of supportive cartilage holding it like the rim of a cup above and around the exposed, sculptured heart. He leaned toward her so slowly, in an echo of Christopher's slow motion handling of the money, that each separate muscular transaction could be seen adding to the disfigurement of the face until it was at last unrecognizable in its cruelty. The skin around the eyes tightened until they lengthened and lay flat; the nostrils flared like those of a terrified horse, and from their outer edges deep-cut lines ran to the corners of the mouth, which, lip-lifted, showed grinding teeth. At the edge of each jawbone a round knob stood out and pulsed, with an indentation in the centers that looked as if a thumb had been pressed into balls of clay.

Miss Gold watched unmoving except for the gradual lifting of hackles. Christopher's hand moved slightly to the left of him until his fingers clung to a surface and then inched inward as though expecting some encounter. At that moment Victor opened his mouth and a great, doglike noise jumped from his throat. In her haste to flee, Miss Gold fell onto her back and lay with threshing feet while Victor roared with pleasure. He fell forward upon her, his knees striking the rug on each side of her swollen belly with no room to spare. Christopher's vision grew dim, and there was a pounding at the base of his skull.

"Gobble, gobble," said Victor, bending over so that Miss Gold's wildly flicking tongue could graze his chin. He got up grinning, his high spirits as shiny as a child's.

"Hey, man, I'm hongry, man," and Christopher got up, thinking dimly of violence as an appetite sharpener.

Victor flung his arm high around Christopher so that his armpit was a socket for the rounded bone of his host's shoulder, a perfect fit. Christopher was repelled and excited by the union of sweaty, acridly virile cavity and linen-clad shoulder faintly scented with the sandalwood he kept among his shirts. They walked down the long hall that way, uniquely joined Siamese twins. Christopher could feel at the jointure a pulsing that belonged to both of them, as though at that meeting of their thinly veiled flesh was where the beat of their life was concentrated, a mutual heart.

At the door to the kitchen Victor released him. Christopher opened the door and gestured the boy through, then secretly felt of his shoulder to see what of himself Victor had left there. Feeling the shirt slightly damp, he had a moment of elation, thinking "blood brothers." Jimmy Weldon stood in his mind, asking Christopher to join him in the ritual. It had been a perfect moment, perfectly destroyed then, as now it was, by the memory of refusal; the fusion had been longed for, but fear of being cut had made him turn away.

He took a long knife from a drawer, Victor pantomiming terror, and opened the refrigerator saying, "There's some kind of loaf here, my housekeeper made it yesterday. Chicken, I think, and veal. Pork, too, probably. I had a sliver." His impulse was right — "some kind of loaf" — but he could not stop himself from giving its name and fame, wondering as he spoke if his purpose was to intimidate Victor. "Pâté en croute, Bourguignonne. It took her most of the day. The puff paste, the crust, has a thousand layers." He set it down on the counter in front of Victor, who started back from it, dramatically dazzled by its fame. It was a rebuke well delivered, and Christopher laughed and relaxed, saying, "Here, help yourself. Or shall I . . . ?" Was there an implication that Victor wouldn't know how to serve himself? Victor nodded. Christopher brought the knife down, indicating a generous slice. "About like this?"

Victor spoke without looking at the food. "You still dietin', huh."

"Same old liquid diet. Vodka, mostly." He managed to conceal the fact that he was not drinking during the sessions by having orange juice, an improvement over the strong cold tea he had had to drink in quantity to mislead the bourbon drinkers of past investigations, during his Negroid phase.

"Imagine that, man."

"Like this, Victor?"

"All."

"All?"

"The whole damn loaf. I don' need no damn diet."

Christopher gave the knife silently, watching the other's fingers close familiarly around the handle. The fingers knew the handle, he thought in deep bemusement, the way his own fingers knew a pen or a typewriter. Thinking "What is he waiting for," he heard with curious anger Miss Gold scratch at the closed door. He turned to open it for her, seeing, as he lifted his eyes from Victor's hand to his face, fleetingly, as he turned, that Victor wore a look of heightened stillness.

Opening the door, Christopher saw the afterimage facing him as if it were Victor entering rather than the bitch; he was thus able to verify the impression that stillness is without color, is only a pale hue, for Victor's organically vibrant bronze had faded until he was the same shade as Christopher, a vague pinky (sunlamp) whitish-grey, the monotone of ashes.

Miss Gold sat up politely at Victor's feet, her paws kneading the air until she found her balance.

"You," Victor addressed her. "You don' get no chicken-veal-pork-t'ousand-layer-somekinda-loaf. You too fat, Pen'house." He cut a two-inch slice of the loaf and balanced it on his palm.

With his toe he nudged Miss Gold's stomach. "Pen'house too fat, amigo, you know?"

"I know. The vet put her on a diet yesterday."

Victor gave Christopher a strange look, his face puckered up as though he would burst into tears. Christopher gazed at him, baffled. Here, in this look, he thought, formulating a thesis as he went along — here in the boy's reaction to the simple remark, which was a commonplace between dog-owners on the elevators Christopher rode and on the sidestreets he haunted in company with the similarly happily servile, was contained the kernal of difference, potentially powerful as an acre of bombs, which separated — more than money, morals, education, the lot — "the classes." Watching Victor turn his frightened look on Miss Gold, seeing the look become a compound of brutality and envy, he thought that it was as if the two were contenders for the same bone. That's it, he thought, with the thrill of discovery: The difference is in our attitudes toward animals, the way in which an animal is seen as an equal: as companion or rival!

As though to bear him out, Victor said, "Dogs. Dogs, even," and tilted his hand, letting the slice of meat and crust fall to the floor. Miss Gold had it before it had quite landed.

Christopher walked abruptly from the kitchen into the many-windowed dining room. He glanced at the rain-pocked reservoir, seething with frustration. Something had gone awry in the past moments, somehow had become obscured, which the dropping of the pâté to the floor had almost recalled, but not quite, like a mechanism set up to trigger memory but which turns out to be faulty in execution.

"Delivery on the way." The doorman, an old man who calculated his privileges as he calculated his tips, upon an assumption of the degree of a sense of noblesse oblige in the person to whom he extended his hand at Christmastime or spoke to throughout the year, was terse almost to insolence, as usual when he spoke to Christopher. His were the bad manners of the old family retainer down home (white; Negroes in Christopher's native South had perfected a much more complex manner of asserting privilege which contained almost no benevolence while seeming to be composed of it entirely), to which was added the special New York ingredient of impudence unalterable by the years. Christopher and this particular doorman did not like each other at all, but understood each other in the matter of attitudes, which included the understanding that the doorman's deference was saved for the dispensers of too-large tips, who provided his luxuries and for whom he felt contempt.

"No delivery expected," Christopher said, patient and distant as if the old man were the gardener's idiot child. "I haven't ordered anything." He took the receiver from his ear, intending to hang up before the doorman could beat him to it, an old game. The doorman's voice squawked demandingly in the air, "Ramos."

Christopher saw that the old man had tricked him again, deliberately putting him in the position of having to break his rule never to see anyone before twelve noon, or else making him side with the doorman by giving the old man the satisfaction of sending Victor away, unreprimanded for pretending not to recognize the boy. Christopher's repeated instructions to him to treat Victor as he would any other guest provided a constant challenge. The doorman's content at the predicament came through the loudspeaker green as laurel. His patient waiting for Christopher's voice was that of a hero lacking only the weight of the crown upon his brow, which even now was suspended above him crowning him truly with its foreshadow that was like the spirit of his heroic act, itself a foreshadowing of the laurel which in turn was its shadow. Thus did Christopher try through intricacy amounting to reductions to naught to calm himself and regain perspective.

The doorman's little victories could not be allowed to count, but his, Christopher's, time did count, as did his instructions to Victor, however tactfully indirect the form they had, in the past, taken. It was not a question of whether or not Christopher, in the sense of being up and dressed, with effects in order, was free to see Victor or anyone earlier; it was a matter of the discipline of civilities being impressed upon those in whom there was a deficiency, and upon Victor in particular, for his own good. Christopher had thought that he had taught Victor this; his punctuality, until today, had been something in which both men could take pride. It had seemed like proof that certain traits thought to be ethnic were nothing more than weeds to be yanked up by the roots by a sympathetic gardener. But the weeds obviously were more deep rooted than the gardener had imagined. Hearing the doorman's impatient snort in the receiver, Christopher told him, visualizing his words as bees entering the old man's ear, "Please ask *Mister* Ramos to come back at one," and he hung up quickly, with a little snap of the receiver on the hook, wondering if the click that preceded his were only in his imagination.

Miss Gold, more seal than dachshund, had taken up a position of waiting by the front door when Christopher had been called to the phone. He hurried out to her and picked her up, one hand on her pouter-pigeon chest, the other cupping her bottom, and carried her, seated in his hand, his lips against the bony ridge of her cranium, down the hallway to his study. He placed her on a leather chaise amorphous with sweaters and woolen ski clothes, which she had fashioned into a deep cavelike retreat, into which she liked to disappear for hours at a time, until he went looking for her, digging her out, impatient for her warmth in his arms.

But the snug dark held no charms for her now. As Christopher watched, annoyed, she threw herself purposefully over the edge of the chaise, grunting when she hit the rug in a splay-legged position, her chest and stomach taking the brunt of the fall. With hardly a pause to assume a reasonable walking stance she took herself from the room with a dignity that should have been ludicrous but was not, to Christopher, who took his cues from her. Sometimes she clowned deliberately, and then he laughed, unable not to in view of her considerable artistry. Her dignity was as genuine and unassailable; he would not have dreamed of laughing; she was as sensitive as he to the nuances of ridicule.

He lay down on the couch after removing his jacket and folding it over the arm for a headrest, and listened to the clicking of Miss Gold's claws against the tiles as she made her way back to her vigil by the door. It seemed to Christopher to go on and on, the clicking, as if without him his darling found halls without boundaries to wander along; as if, without his presence in it, with his sense of fitness and order, the hall itself reverted to the native state of its materials and grew and grew, pushing out walls, lifting ceilings, until no barriers remained between what was *here*, this safe place, and *there*, where all the unknown elements were.

He sat up, his fantasy having carried him into disquiet. His discovery that it was rain pattering on the terrace that had given rise to the fantasy of her journeying did not allow him to relax. He was first compelled, all logic to the contrary, to go to the door and peer down the hall to reassure himself that Miss Gold had not somehow contrived with her tricky intelligence to let herself into the public hallway where she could, and he was despairingly convinced, would, if she ever got out, be stolen by the first passing delivery boy. Her loss would be so mortal a wound — his imagination knew about the gradations in mortality — that all else beside it, all possible maimings, came to resemble remembered desire. ("In *life*, there is other sleep, other closing, compared to which, death's dozing!")

For the moment Miss Gold rested her tender burden on the cool tiles, tilted upward as though pausing midway in one of a series of pushups prescribed for overweight dachshunds. Christopher's heart slowed with love. He blew a grateful kiss, and Miss Gold's left ear twitched as if the kiss had landed upon it.

He went back to the couch and lay down facing the windows, as though hopeful of finding answers or clues written on the sky. When he lay down the sky was all he could see. He could imagine into being whatever he wished below his windows, as he had done as a child. A trim garden had been his prospect then, intended by its seasonal blooming to instill in him an awareness of natural order, and into this garden he had summoned a nightly procession of disordered exotica. Below his window there had been Pyrenees and deserts, Petra, the Dead Sea. The muezzin had called there, jackals had fought, and ancient carp had swum in his garden.

146

Today he imagined the surge of the ocean, and the traffic obligingly metamorphosed itself into the distant roar of tides agitated by the pull of storm clouds. He felt safe, but knew it to be temporary. Anxiety hovered without, in the clouds, over the ocean, like a bird that would soon come tapping its beak upon his windows. But why did it wait for him, snug in his eyrie? Did it imagine that he would actually come and fling the casements wide, inviting it in?

His mind spoke to the bird: City apartments such as this one, owned pieces of the sky, are islands, separated from the mainland by an elaborate system of security. Even the wing-borne are eventually buffeted away, or if they hover too long, will find their pinions weighted by the sky-dweller's weapon, the formidable incinerator, and will plummet to earth to crawl dirty and miserable with the rest of the earth-bound.

The bird told him: Despite elaborate security systems and public weapons, sky-islands are frequently connected by bridges of scandal and crime to the mainland, over which the dirty, miserable, earth-bound pour in a stream, to gawk, to touch, to destroy by their envy and malice what is left, and it serves the islanders right for inviting outsiders to cross over.

As I have done, you mean, Christopher said. Scandal, crime — are these things usually preceded by premonitory dreams, such as the one I dreamed last night involving Victor Ramos?

In the dream Victor moved within a shadowy layer of odor. It was as though his shadow had been projected onto a surface some distance behind him, the shadow six inches fatter all around than the boy. This shadow was cut out and somehow imbued with the odors of oil, hot spices, armpits, rut, until it was malleable, something like silly putty, then it was reshaped around Victor, made somehow invisible and impermeable to water, soap, rainfall. In the dream Christopher had seen it as a plain definition of Victor's unchanging, unchangeable difference and his attraction for Chris and others like him.

But "definition" meant nothing. Only the ingredients of the difference were known but not their proportions, nor how they were administered, nor why the knowledge was vitally essential to Christopher. He knew with certainty that his life depended upon obtaining the formula. As though his desperation forced the issue, in immense close-up he saw huge needles like those with which the livers, kidneys, and hearts of embryonic sheep are imparted to decaying human bodies in Switzerland. He saw phalanxes of white-swathed doctors and nurses at work making Victor's shadow pungent nearly beyond endurance. He cried out at the deepening of the mystery, cried with rage, demanded something in words that had no meaning. "Rut!" barked the doctor. Nurse and intern fell to a frenzy of fornication on the floor at the doctor's feet until Christopher ground them to white powder beneath the heel of his shoe, handing, the meanwhile, the hypodermic to the doctor, for Victor's shadow had begun to neutralize in the moments of neglect, and without the acridity Christopher would never have known him, and could not bear to think of that. It was then, as though Victor had read his mind, that the cruel Noh mask replaced the boy's features. Looming over Christopher, the mask produced words from behind itself, clearly enunciated and yet not understood, though Christopher had seen them written out as they were spoken: ¿Quiere que te lo ponga en le roto? Brutal, vulgar beyond comprehension, preceding the rest, the violence —

But Christopher had tried too hard to look at the dream direct, and like a star it faded and was gone under his concentration.

Coldly, to counteract the thoughts that beaded his forehead with sweat, he took himself through another door, back to the night he had first met — no, picked up; euphemism now could serve no purpose — the young Puerto Rican.

Unaccustomedly, Christopher had walked from the house where he had dined to his apartment house, a distance of fifteen blocks. Fear of violence on the New York streets had long since settled into the subconscious, where it controlled routine. Once, in balmy weather, it had been necessary to invent reasons for not walking, but now the reverse was true, and Christopher told the doorman, who was automatically whistling for a cab, that he was heading for a bar not two blocks distant, on Madison. The man put up an argument to which Christopher was, in his vulnerable state, a grateful listener, until he saw that it was not concern for his safety but loss of a tip that brought the opposition, and the partial return to normality gave him the impetus to wave the cab away and cut across the street to the Park side, leaving the doorman to dislike him as much as he wanted, which was no change at all in the night's status quo.

The recklessness that let him walk along the Park, past figures on the benches and several of the Park's gaping black mouths, was due to his having been for an entire evening the setup for a game whose denouement he had not allowed. He knew that no speculation now would ever unriddle it, and so he was frustrated as well as reckless, and fear, too, was pushing to the surface and eventually would have to be looked at.

His host had been a man to whom he had been presented some years before at the opera by a reprobate cousin, but a willing forgetfulness, based upon what he had felt to be mutual antipathy, had all but erased the meeting from time's record of occasions. And yet when he received the summons to dine — the man was famous and old and issued summonses — Chris recognized the voice before it identified itself, and he had gotten the clear impression that his own voice had been recognized by its "hello."

He had assumed that he would find his cousin, whom he hardly ever saw, in the company that filled the drawing room, if for no other reason than that Christopher's telephone was unlisted, and from whom else could his host have gotten the number? But his cousin was not there, and when Christopher mentioned his expectation — though, he implied politely, certainly not his disappointment — he had received a blank stare from the ancient yellowing eyes which denied the cousin's acquaintanceship and managed to reprove Christopher for the gaucherie of forgetting through whom they actually had met. As if to make sure by paradox that the evening would be memorable for him through the early onset of total confusion, his host had introduced him into a group as the especial friend of someone of whom Christopher had never heard; he thought the name was "Miriam."

From his bluff height the host bent upon Christopher a look

of conspicuous dislike and left instantly, a departure so abrupt that its rudeness could be called breathtaking. Finding himself in the double jeopardy of false pretenses and his host's challenge to him to reveal himself if he dared, Christopher's disorientation was compounded by the strange effect upon the group of his introduction as a friend of the unknown woman's. It was as though the statement were both repellent and anticipated. The sound they made collectively was like the soughing of a copse in which the fox has hidden before the onslaught of hunters.

No effort was made to resume their conversation, and Christopher, whose opening wedge, "Do you know my cousin?" had been taken from him along with his identity, gulped martinis from passing trays and played his part as well as he could. It seemed to him, upon whom alcohol had the instant effect of heightening prescience, that their eyes melted together, preparatory to forming a weapon, and he waited for the attack on whomever it was he was thought to be. When he did not run, for he imagined he could not, they reacted with a display of teamwork which bespoke an old alliance and probable masses of blue ribbons affixed to black velvet in shadowboxes on bathroom walls. Veiled, hostile remarks flew his way, to which, finding his footing, he reacted characteristically; then the veiling became latent and the hostility manifest. It was as though the point were to fix his outline, bristling with arrows, in space, to be used for their private purposes at some later time.

During the remarkably bad dinner, which he made no pretense of eating beyond the initial forkful of each course, it came to him that the gathering was archetypal, for a certain stratum of New York, in its composition, which was: cleverness, money, malice, estrangement, a sexuality so unsensual as to have the sharpness of weapons or acid. For him, the scapegoat that such gatherings demanded, or, barring the fortuitous stranger, created out of their own matter, there was deliberately fostered confusion which had been fed like an already obese animal all evening. In his deepening drunkenness he relived in lightning glimpses other such occasions to which he had been witness, or at which he had been the baiter or the victim. Tonight he played the game as he always did, as he had learned or perhaps been born to do, he did not care which. He insulted the food by refusing to eat it and degraded the wine by drinking it in large quantity without comment, as earlier he had inspected the pictures and objets in the drawing room with, not amusement, which would have been naïve, but with an artless, open indulgence. It was intrinsical to the players of such games that the illness produced by the adrenal glands in overactivity should be concealed; the stance of "cool" was a strict, necessary discipline to hold in the vomit of fear and aloneness until one *was* alone. In the clarity of his alcoholic vision he saw that such parties were the roots from which the urge to violence seeped upward and out to undermine the city. Any literary gathering, he knew from long experience, was the equivalent of a bomb factory.

He also knew that the denouement, whatever it was — which the players at that juncture might not have agreed upon — would occur when the coffee cooled untouched beside the sticky liqueurs, when the token splash of Perrier in the Scotch was abandoned like a final veil. When that time came he would know it by a fraction of a second before it was set in motion. In such timing lay the art of survival.

Even while the frisson of recognition of the moment coursed his skin, he was bidding his host good night, bending swiftly and up and gone toward the door before Claudo could respond or try to hold him back. Leaving the room, he watched in a mirror both his approach and that of the hastily assigned huntress who was propelled from a group by a frantic push that caused her to stumble. She called after him, her voice strident, "We've just discovered who you are!" He admired the tactic, for ordinarily who would resist it? but he felt the acuteness of the danger when even a pause would be his undoing. Without stopping he turned his head only enough to project his voice toward the silence, "Oh? But I don't know who *you* are," and made it without honor out of the room and into the elevator.

Once on the street and out of sight of the doorman's contempt, he gave way to the thought that had been pushing up: his knowledge of death had been somehow increased, as if a thinning of the wall of death's room had occurred, against which he had been pressing his ear and listening to unimaginable preparations for a visit.

It was during the failure of his imagination that he saw Victor Ramos, standing with one leg encircling a fire hydrant, light from a distant streetlamp picking his bones clean. He was ostentatiously waiting for a bus; a sign around his neck could not have proclaimed it more clearly, especially to cruising police cars, than did his stance which, despite its leg-looped casualness, wore transience in every line as does a bird's on a telephone wire, with awareness of the hazards of high tension.

The image that reached Christopher's brain was multiple, a straticulate cross section of an emotion, spheroidal by virtue of its two poles, ultimately static (it was Christopher who circled the emotion, its restless satellite) because both poles were named "delivery boy": a delivery boy; a dark gold young man of ideal beauty; a skull; a statue of phallic symbolism (the hydrant between the legs) both lewd and desexed by antiquity, like a temple carving; a person hunted, without explanation, as Christopher had just been; the embodiment of the type through whom Christopher could restore his superiority and toward whom he could, therefore, be benevolent: a delivery boy.

Miss Gold was spending the night with Christopher's housekeeper, the practice when he went out for the evening. Fear slept.

He caught the boy's eye, unsmiling, the game too serious for that. Then, apparently forgetting the exchange, he paused and took a cigarette case from the pocket of his dinner jacket, extracted a cigarette, tapped it on the case (recalling, he saw the movement as calculated to draw attention to the case, which was platinum with a jeweled monogram and a concealed lighter which did not work), and futilely flicked the lighter with the exact degree of impatience to seem to remain entirely private: no drop of self-amusement, with which the knowingly observed indicate the basic good humor of their natures.

Back bent over the lighter, Christopher watched with a resurgence of foreboding a shadow advance on the pavement and cover his shoes and mount his ankles like dark secret water. When a lighter snapped under his nose he jumped without pretense at the flame leaping in the dark hand. He drew on the cigarette, loathing its staleness (he carried the case for others, in all senses, and had last filled it in the fall), and expelled a cloud of flat smoke before he again looked at the other's face, finding deep shadow in which two hazy luminosities seemed no more committal nor unbenevolent than a moon divided into twins by capriciously unfocused binoculars.

It was soon clear that, by lighting Christopher's cigarette, the other had exhausted his part in the pickup, or the part he was willing to play. It was equally plain, because he did not move away, or speak, that he knew there was more to come, and the quality of his waiting bespoke experience at such encounters, which depressed Christopher in some undefined way.

Reliving the night, depression took the form of Then and Now, for two reasons: the unresolved and the all-too-plain. He had always kept a special reserve of dislike for those relentless trackers of the virgin experience. Seeing himself among them, he could not find the courage of hypocrisy to make the distinction between their purely physical intent and his own. Chilled by hindsight, the most he could do for himself was to press on, knowing that the door to that room was now permanently ajar and that, sooner or later, he would have to go back to it, and enter, and take inventory.

He moved, the boy following, until the light was on the other's face. Watching him closely, Christopher said, "Yo estoy muy agradecido," and ease settled over him at the expected reaction: the quick reappraisal of his clothes, skin color, and hair (the latter a repeated mystery until Victor explained about "good" and "bad" hair) by eyes in which a certain deference had been replaced by a like amount of familiarity dimly tinged with tentative contempt. To exorcise the contempt while retaining enough of the familiarity, which was a kind of trust, to make the rest possible: this was the delicate task, differing from case to case, which Christopher felt lifted the moment above the potentially sordid.

It had been his belief, until the past few hours had placed it in escrow, that in that moment of assessment and decision by and through sensibilities heightened to the supranormal, he came to know more about the "subject" as pertained to degree of trustworthiness and similar basic concerns than at any time that followed. That it was *his* decision, arrived at without help, had preoccupied him at the time: he had wondered how closely, under the circumstances, decision resembled invention, and therefore how much of what the subject subsequently said and did, apart from the seldom varying facts of life in the ghetto, was seen through the frame of that decision-invention, which he called the d.i. He imagined that the d.i. was like a picture frame, blocking out the nonconforming bits around the edges which otherwise spoiled the composition. But this line of questioning frequently led to the posterior thesis that the subjects *knowingly* conformed, an act of sophisticated duplicity which Christopher could not concede them, as it gave them the clear advantage of anticipation and even led to the further question of who had invented whom. The thought that unriddling the maze of mirror images could bring him to a place where he functioned as the reflecting device — empty, unless a socially deprived, inferior person chose to stand before him — was enough to make him abandon the concept of the d.i., but his former preoccupation with it assumed negative coloration and hid out in his mind, another link in the chain of submerged fear.

He told the boy, "Yo he bevido un poco," met the now hostile eyes and said, concealing his distaste for the corrupted language which he had had to learn, "Yo estoy fuquiao." Hostility was replaced by astounded merriment at his admission to being fucked up, for the phrase, in street argot, was infinite, open-ended. It expanded his first admission to being a little drunk into a universe of implication, hinting, on a dark street past midnight, of the knowledge that drunkenness is but a station on the way and not the destination. The words were a clear invitation to camaraderie. Observing the facets of the statement, Christopher rested.

The boy divined easily that the next step was up to him. He spoke with enough exaggerated humor to be able to point to the joke in case Christopher should turn out to be a cop. "Wha' you wan' me to do, walk you home?"

The surprises of the night prevailed. Christopher did not know how to answer the question that cut so quickly to the bone of the matter. He had not thought beyond the game in any immediate sense and supposed that it was due to his real drunkenness that he had not. Staring blankly at the boy, he supposed that he had had in mind giving his address and telephone number after some sort of exchange of credentials, a practice that was only a token, as their "credentials" generally would not bear investigation. Also, the fact that he had been answered in English was like having a curtain behind which one was partially concealed pulled suddenly aside. He had been denied the cover of the argot before he was ready to relinquish it, and was being commanded to step forth as himself. Momentum had been lost through hesitation, and the boy was turning away to the curb. Christopher sighed, hearing the released airbrakes of an approaching bus as a gigantic echo of his signal of defeat — defeat, because the decision had been made for the first time by another person.

He said, a bit briskly for someone in his avowed condition, "Why not? We can have a drink, if you like, and I'll send you home in a taxi."

The boy raised his eyebrows, and it amused Christopher to imagine that he could hear the other's mind emphasizing the pride-offending word: "SEND?" He turned back to the bus, which was pulling into the stop, but the quality of the movement was so unaggressive, even coquettish, that Christopher knew one more word from him would be all that was needed. "Please" or "por favor" would not do: simply saying amigo, which had worked for him once in a difficult situation, would be worse in the present one, for any note of pleading would revive the contempt, and rightly so.

Things were so far out of hand, as it was, that winning the game now consisted merely and entirely of keeping the boy from boarding the bus. After that, as far as Christopher was concerned, he could go hang.

But the word? It was given to him. The bus opened its doors, the few people inside gazed at the unlikely pair in the street without curiosity. The boy put one foot on the step, turned, and asked loudly, "You still wan' me to come wit' you?"

Christopher increased the price he had been asked to pay in public. "Yes," he said, and then, "What's your name?" leaving no room for doubt for the audience about the nature of the scene.

Recollecting, he saw again the amusement return to Victor's face as they exchanged identities, and with it a measure of admiration. Something in the look had made him feel his earlier drunkenness, which he had forgotten in the minutes that were emotionally hours, so that when he turned to lead the way he staggered and Victor rushed to take his elbow and steady him.

They walked in silence for a block. Opposite his apartment house Christopher said, "There," and they crossed the street under the watchful eyes of the old doorman to whom his activities were never less than suspect. He thought, "Let it all come down," and smiled at Victor, who was taking in the building, expressionless.

Victor said, "Where you learn Espanish so good? You got Espanish wive?"

"No."

The doorman was holding the door open with mocking deference, his eyes on Victor.

"Girl fren'?"

"Nope. No boy friend, either." He ushered Victor in ahead of him, saying to the doorman, "This is —" but Victor beat him to it, with a certain élan, "*Mister* Ramos," and the two of them proceeded to the elevator united in triumph.

And there it was, or the worst part of it, with no clue in the reliving to help Christopher in his present quandary.

The remainder of the evening had been predictable. Christopher had once again been in control. He had explained over drinks about his "job," giving the title of his novel, *Minority Report*, as though it were a needed sociological document. He had watched Victor's adjustment to the fact that this was an encounter different from others that Christopher was sure he had experienced, for he had been told about such pickups and their aftermaths by similar young men who looked upon sex with other males purely — in an odd way the word was precise — as a source of income. That night Christopher had thought he could detect disappointment in Victor's behavior, smooth as the readjustment had been, that seemed to go beyond the idea of the money he might have been given, or stolen.

Today, not entirely because of the reflected light of Victor's subsequently revealed antipathy to homosexuality which was like, in a complex way, Christopher's own, Christopher half believed, or half remembered, that what he had witnessed had been disillusionment. The idea fluttered in his mind, tantalizingly like a clue, but there was no place for it to alight. He hurried on in his mind, looking for some basis for the really odd thought.

From the time of their arrival in the apartment until the revelation that what Christopher wanted of him was his hard-luck story, Victor had continuously assessed the apartment and its contents as if he were a prospective tenant. Following Christopher's explanation, he had been silent for a while and then asked, "Why me?" He had laughed, unamused, and answered himself, "Because I was *there*, huh." He seemed willing to settle for it but he was not allowed to.

"Why did you come?"

"Man, everybody got a story. I never heard no rich man's story before. Me I go along wit' *live*. ¿Vida si? You wan' my story —" He shrugged. "May' I wan' *you* story. May' I writin' a book." He had seemed to laugh out of one side of his defiance, and Christopher had laughed with him, relieved that Victor had not repeated his question of "Why me?" Christopher could not have answered it, and could not do so now.

Victor's beauty, certainly. He had never lied to himself, at least, about that. And yet, having had it to gaze at for long afternoons, he could not find wherein his satisfaction of it should lie. In frustration and what he feared might be honesty, he let himself imagine that it lay somewhere in destruction, in the destruction of the source, perhaps of beauty's source. Victor's death could not accomplish it; he would be equally as beautiful in im-

157

mobility, the cold unmarred marble of his skin no more remote, no less beautiful, than when warmed by blood. And beyond that, beyond the marble's ultimate destruction by time, and beneath the marble and below time, the hard clean white bones, which were the broad preliminary but strong strokes over which the marvelous coloration and texture of his most overt beauty had been laid, hidden guarantees of the beauty's indestructibility. Even broken and crushed with a mallet, the bones still would sing in their dust and fragments, like pulverized jewels.

Christopher's forehead burned his hand. It took effort to lift his arm, as if in reality that arm had wielded the mallet that crushed Victor's bones to an everlasting white powder. Everlasting. The source of beauty, then, lay in the opposite direction from the only one in which he could travel, in the country of death's antithesis, where he had never been and could not go.

"Nonsense." He sat up and mopped his hot dry face with a handkerchief as if his insanity had congealed on his face like a beauty mask. A corner of the handkerchief slid beneath an eyelid causing the eye to burn and stream water. Obscurely he said, "Beauty is in the eye of the beholder," and then understood his use of the cliché. He examined the handkerchief as though to find Victor there, safely, at last, removed from his body.

Leaving Victor and Miss Gold in the kitchen, on his way back to the study he reviewed his review, feeling that this time, unlike the mysterious baiting at the party the night he met Victor, there must be a denouement. He must, if necessary, force it, for Victor not only held the position that Christopher had had assigned to him by the host that evening, but had held it — and "scapegoat," he saw, was the only word — since their meeting. Christopher had paid him to play the damned role and, fascinated, had kept him on long past his right to demand tenure. He saw that, infinitely more than the others, Victor had been meant to give him some key to himself. By his every action he had repeatedly asked Victor both "Who am I?" and "What am I?" There was subservience in the thought, and it rankled even more than he had imagined earlier, when he had let the supposition touch his mind: that until someone like Victor stood before him, he was an empty frame. The image he had used then was of a picture, but it was of a mirror he was forced now to think, for in Victor, somewhere, was the quicksilver that could throw back to Christopher's eyes an accurate self-image.

At the study door he paused; Victor was not following him. Of the minutiae of sounds from behind the closed door of the kitchen he composed an acceptable picture of explanation: Victor, who really had been hungry but too proud after his outburst to go on and eat, was now eating the crucial loaf; apologetically, he was feeding small bits of meat and crust to Miss Gold.

Stepping into the study, it was as though he had tarried for an unmeasurable length of time in the hallway, for the sun was now out and glittered on the reservoir. A boat moved slowly along the submerged causeway that connected the pumping stations, sending up flights of gulls or ducks, he had never learned which, just as he had never learned the function of the boats. With cold distaste he thought how little he knew about his own surroundings. Even the facts given him by Victor over many a long afternoon had been distorted by his imagination.

He stood at the window and watched the boat, saw that on each side of the turbulence of its wake there floated large circles of flat water to the edges of which the wake extended and nudged but did not break through. The reflected sun in the exact center of the largest gave it the aspect of one bespectacled eye, but it occurred to him that it and all the other rounds of water — he determined that they were not oil by minute inspection through the binoculars — were like the circle of which once he had been a part: self-contained, oblivious to other circles and the agitated, uncommitted swirling about it; and that the reflected sun in the center was the nucleus that each circle, of water or people, had to have to be autonomous. He thought it was like the finger that was needed to keep a ring from rolling away. For the first time without revulsion, he wondered if he and Victor and Miss Gold comprised a sort of circle.

As he watched, a weakness in the wall of the largest, sun-centered circle of water allowed a sharp little wave to skip through, and then another and yet another, each individually observed by him as they made their way to the sun-eye and sat upon it. Revulsion came then, because the effect was that of an eye covered with gold scales, and though the intruders did not retain their alien sharpness, but leveled out into glassy anonymity, he could not forget that they had been intruders, and he imagined that they affected the sun-eye's perception as though they were a rheum laid there by time and other excesses. The eye was lulled by its weight of gold beauty into an unwatchfulness through which a needle could pierce; perception would return a moment after blindness.

He stood at his bookshelves holding da Vinci's *Notebooks*.

THE LEAP OF WATER IS HIGHER IN A BUCKET THAN IN A GREAT LAKE. This is because (confined) water when struck by a blow cannot make its impetus pass from circle to circle as it would in a great lake; and since the water when struck finds near to itself the edges of the bucket, which are harder and more resisting than the other water, it cannot expand itself, and consequently it comes about that the whole of its impetus is turned upwards; and therefore water struck by a stone throws its drops up higher when its waves are confined than when they have a wide space.

"Yes" he said, and turned back a few pages and found what he had come to find:

No part of the watery element will raise itself or make itself more distant from the common centre except by violence.

He raised his eyes from the book and saw Victor, Miss Gold in his arms, quietly regarding him from the doorway. His face was troubled. Miss Gold struggled to get down with such determination that Christopher wondered how Victor had offended her. The doorway framing them was like a page retaining the afterimage of what had just been read; Christopher read the final sentence on the air: *No violence is lasting.*

Without a trace of friendliness he said, "Can't you see she wants down? Put her down."

Victor set Miss Gold carefully on the chaise, apologizing in a gravely polite voice, though the words were too softly spoken for Christopher to hear. When Victor picked up his glass, Christopher turned away deliberately. After a pause Victor asked, "Drink?"

"No, thank you."

"I mean for me." Christopher let the silence deepen, staring at the reservoir, the circles, seeing the little high-ceilinged study as the bucket da Vinci had written about. He turned to Victor suddenly, as though to catch him at some misbehavior.

"I imagine you know where everything is by now." The subtle emphases, carefully placed, were as daring as he had ever been with someone like Victor, for they had almost the intimacy of equality. He was exhilarated and depressed. Victor's eyes slitted for a moment as though to improve vision.

"Not everting."

"*Thing*," Christopher, said, "Ev-er-*y-thing*."

Victor said, "Everting," flat as a slap, moved to the sofa, and sat in a series of gestures meant to be, and taken as, insulting. Ordinarily he edged his way in between sofa and coffee table, a space to which only the thin-legged should aspire; Christopher had said that it was his housekeeper's way of trying to dictate the size if not the gender of his guests; but now the table was impatiently brushed aside with foot and calf and an aisle cleared by Victor. Then he turned and assumed a squat over the sofa. To emphasize his meaning he first looked back over his shoulder, then ducked his head and peered between his legs; finding something on the seat not to his liking, he straightened up, turned, brushed with vigorous scorn at the material, then turned again and fell back, legs thrown wide apart.

Christopher snatched up a glass, feeling fury at the pantomime and needing to get out of the room. Victor told him levelly, "Leave it," and when Christopher stared at him, repeated, "Leave it." Christopher set the glass down quietly and waited for directions, which Victor gave him in the same level tone.

"Sit down." Christopher moved to skirt the table and sit on the sofa; Victor told him, "There. Opposite." Christopher sat down in the opposite chair in which he sometimes read in the soft north light of morning, terrace door at his back.

Victor's movements continued in deliberateness which said,

"Here is the end to pretenses." When he had thrown himself on the sofa he had flung his arms up and back, clasping his hands over his head, resting them against the unprotected surface of a painting. Christopher had thought of the hands sticky with food on the white-lit street of the Chirico; it had been a corner of his fury. Victor opened his hands, palms backward as though to smear the painting, then brought them slowly down to rest, equal partners, precisely sharing, on the perfect hemisphere that swelled at his crotch. His curved palms rode the swell, tightened only enough to reveal how thoroughly his manhood filled his big hands.

"Now," he said, and Christopher felt his heart jolted by fear. There was a vacancy between him and Victor that was like the space beteeen quotation marks set in the air; he expected the space to be momentarily filled by the words of the dream that he had not understood and yet understood. ¿Quiere que te lo ponga en el roto? Frantically he felt certain, he had to be certain, that if Victor looked at him, really *looked* at him, he would be able to read in his eyes without error his mistake about Christopher. There had been what could be called flirtation between them, there had been sexual nuances, but in a sense that Christopher had always known was Lawrentian: that male antagonism has a sexual base, and the more submerged, the more sexual, but . . .

Victor's sigh, loud and disgusted, saved him from what for all he knew might have been some overtness. With relief he saw that Victor's hands were moving, moving away, and then lay at his sides. As though demonstrating the wide possibilities of drama within the "Now," he said it again, "Now." He proceeded onward without the frightening pauses. "You ever had a fren' like me, Chris?" His enunciation retreated before his earnestness, consonants dropping by the way. "Like" was "li'," or as Christopher saw it, inevitably, "lie." "You ever had a fren' li' me? I mean, no money exchain hans, liddle loan between fren's, but no pay for talkin'?"

"No." He hoped Victor would not say, "Well, *could* you?" for the answer—what was the answer? Miss Gold snored loudly.

Christopher gestured toward her —"There —" but Victor did not pursue the question by asking what he meant. Christopher's "no" had contained whatever he looked for, which could have been vindication. Instead, with softness more brutal than a shout he asked, "What do you *know*, Chris? You all the time correctin' me. Tell me what *you know*. What you learn in all these years about livin'. You not such a young man, Chris. You live a lon' time, you ou' to know plenny. Say what you learn that make goin' on livin' you right, man."

Christopher felt dismay, but sensed that it was not only the inherent threat in the words that was the cause. He gazed at Victor, looking for the scintillae of reflected light to identify him. Victor was in no hurry; indeed, now that he had asked for something his face was suddenly anxious, like a good teacher's, that Christopher should acquit himself well. Christopher felt a dreaminess like an echo of the response to some other sound, someone else's need for him to bring off a situation well if not nobly. He thought, "Well, what do I know?" and spoke not as an answer but in response to an inner voice.

"—Je vois ma femme en esprit. Son regard, Comme le tien, aimable bête, Profond et froid, coupe et fend comme un dard; Et, des pieds jusque à la tête, Un air subtil, un dangereux parfum, Nagent autour de son corps brun."

"*Beautiful*, Chris. You wri' tha', man?" Victor's enthusiasm promised amnesty. Christopher shook his head. Victor slammed his palm hard onto the sofa. "Dammit, Chris, tha' wha' the *man* learn from live, not you, Chris. A parrot, a stupido bird! can do what you do, Chris!" He shook his head, making a sound of disgust, "Chee!" He looked around as though for something to do with his hands, an exaggerated search, perhaps, but its franticness was plainly not all show. He grabbed his glass from the table and started up, violence in all his movements, in his restraint. At the door he turned and gave Christopher a head-lowered long glance, and said in an orgy of discarded consonants, "I go' to thin' abou' this, man," and made the sound "Chee!" again, and left.

For a comedian acquaintance Christopher had once written a

series of ideas of things people do immediately they think they are alone and unobserved, or, turning away in a crowded room, safely facing an unmirrored wall, the facial expressions they might register to relieve tensions. He was reminded so forcefully of these by his own actions when Victor was out of sight that he went about the grim business shaking with giggles. He moved the heavy cigarette lighter to the ledge of the bookcase nearest his chair, took the immense ash tray, a real murder weapon, and placed it on the windowsill where a lunge might send him in time. Quietly, with a stealth he felt to be awful, he shifted the chaise so gently, moving it out of Victor's reach from the sofa, that Miss Gold hardly noticed. When he had done these things he could not have told under oath exactly what had made him do them. Listening for Victor's return he sat down and reflected upon his predicament. If Victor came back and said, "Two things you've learned, Chris, in exchange for your life," what could he offer?

He was smiling, rueful in self-knowledge, over the two answers that came out a lifetime of experience when Victor returned: "Paranoiacs at bullfights identify with the bulls." "Left-handed people cannot tie a decent bow tie."

Victor came into the room wearily like a man moving under duress. He leaned over the table to set his drink down, and Christopher saw the weight inside his shirt, narrowness above thinness was the way he mentally described it, and though he arrived quickly at what the weight was, when Victor pulled the butcher knife from his shirt the suddenness of the reality brought instant release. A torrent of sounds sluiced through the room. In shocked amazement, the heavy lighter in his hand, eyes fixed on the target between Victor's eyes, Christopher first heard and and then felt that the sounds were made by him. There was so much movement in the room, the scuttlings of dreams; and odors; and so much for the eye to encompass; and there was the sound jumping in his throat like a fish and the taste as it passed his tongue; and there was the gathering weight in his hand and the translation of it into arm movements. Victor came at him slowly, but his face remained his own; there was no Noh mask at which to aim. Distinctly and simultaneously, like two musical voices of equal value, he thought, "I have never been so fully occupied" and "I'll have to destroy his beauty." With no further thought he pulled the lighter back and brought it forward with such force that, hanging onto it, he followed it to Victor. Victor threw the knife into a corner where it clattered on the floor, then Christopher felt Victor's arms around him, keeping him from falling onto the coffee table as he followed the trajectile of the lighter.

"Now," Victor was saying. "Now now now now." And "O.K, Chris? Come on, Chris." And "Amigos, sí." And "Now I can be you fren'." He murmured away, soothing and patting, "Frens, amigos, sí. O.K?" until Christopher managed to shove him away. Without looking at him again, Christopher found two tens and pushed them out toward the man, his eyes rising no higher than the beltless loops on the khaki trousers.

After a while the money was taken from him. He watched the hands fold the bills carefully and aim them toward a pocket before he turned away toward the reservoir. Thinking, "Oh, get out," he waited out the long pause before he was obeyed.

He stood by the bookshelves, wondering about anger, about innocence, about essence. All of it was here to be studied, here in books, without ever going out again into the world. What wealth of real experience was here between book covers, tasted and tested by others, by others who knew how to translate and condense and present experience, knew how to account for their lives.

His hand touched a volume of Shakespeare's histories. He said, smiling for no reason he could have named, "Brief summers lightly have forward springs." Heavily, he said, "Likely, in this case; in his case," but it was not really appropriate. It was Victor who had acted Richard, and Christopher who had been the young, inexperienced, noble York. No, not noble; nor young; nor inexperienced. Dangerously stupid, stupidly dangerous, for he had come within an inch of smashing Victor's skull with the lighter. He could feel the desire and disappointment in his right hand, twitching on, as snakes are said to do after death.

Victor would get his, too, and soon. "Brief summers —" *Likely* was more hopeful than lightly. Yes, he would get his: an overdose, a knife in the belly; he would get his and soon. The vulgarism bothered him not at all; it was as though he were thinking in argot. Having suffered the ultimate indignity, the vulgarism nonpareil of seeing his own death before him, he could hardly be squeamish about slang, for all his old hatred of it, and thoughts of Victor getting his was a comfort as cold as ether on his skin.

He made himself stop it. He plumped pillows, emptied ash trays. Did the dead move so? Did dead minds twitch on remembering poetry? "Vien, ma belle chienne," was the way he always said it to Miss Gold, "Profond et chaud —" His bowels melted with the heat of horror. Where was she. A statue, he stood with the silent butler in one hand, Victor's glass in the other. In his stone head a memory tried to stir like a rock striving to create from itself a living worm: her claws clicking on the tiles beside Victor when he went to the door. And out. Both of them.

He crashed to the table the vessel that held Victor's breath imprisoned in alcohol as if it were the boy's body. The violence released his voice as the sight of the knife had done. Keening, he started for the door, discovered, by barely avoiding falling, that the only way he could walk was to place one knee-bent leg, foot pigeon-toed, laboriously before the other like a spastic.

He nearly stepped on Miss Gold as she emerged trembling from under the chaise. His hands reached for her, two points of life at the tips of his dangling arms. She bared her fangs and backed away, under the chaise, a rumbling in her throat. Christopher's spastic legs gave way, and he fell to the floor. The furious pain at the base of his spine was simultaneous with the intelligence that Miss Gold had moved her bowels under the chaise; he could smell and see the loose results, and this broke another obstruction in him. He crawled toward her, mumbling until the words he wanted formed themselves.

"You troublesome little bitch." Her ears lifted and folded back, and as his hand darted for her she snapped and caught in her teeth the fleshy pad that formed the base of his thumb, the part of the hand known as "the mound of Venus." The sick fear in her eyes and the sharp stab of her teeth revived, like summer rain, the parched part of his brain where pity grew.

"Don't be afraid, darling. Please. I won't hurt you." Soothing, cajoling, reassuring, he kept repeating the words until she was nestled in his lap and her trembling was subsiding. "Now, now, now," he told her.

He caught a glimpse, then, of himself in the mirror he had set up, and called Victor, and tried to shatter. Though he did not like it, hated the recognition and the implications of it, he paid it what respect he could. He told Miss Gold, making the mimicry as exact as his talents, slenderer than he would have thought, would allow: "Now I can be you' fren'."

That summer he kills in perpetual frenzy moths, all moths, every moth he can find. Later he feels that he has been driven virtually insane by the insects' death drive. It is as though he can not escape from his own suicidal fantasies and urges long enough to get a holding grip on his life, for with the dusk the moths arrive and batter at screens and doors until they find entrance and throw themselves at living and glassed-in flames, rattling with the sounds of death within the parchment lampshades. At first he sees the moths as symbolical, finding always his truest reflection in a natural glass, but as he watches and hears their agonies the barriers between himself and them are let down. He lies on the bed in his summer house like the gisant atop his own tomb and the light lures around him, the hurricane lamps and naked candles are like heraldic blazonings, the facts of accomplished death. He watches himself in the persons of the moths enter, fight his way to destruction through screens (he comes in the latter days to make the task difficult and more difficult by stuffing up all the holes he can find with cotton, rags, paper; his windows resemble some modern canvases), and flirt-flirt-flirt with burning, keeping a nearly safe, odorous distance, which he finds he cannot tolerate. Thus he becomes murderer and self-murderer, killing and dying hundreds of times in a few days. He keeps the crushed insect-selves in a felt-lined writing box. At the end, looking at the velvet dust between thumb and forefinger — prime killers, money-holders — and at the particles of wing on the white wall, all that is left of the lovers, he remembers with all his senses something not even noticed during the orgy: his left hand gloved in the fabric of dead moths, a hand smoothly, lightly clothed as though it had been dipped up to the waist in the finest talc. Just so felicitously garbed does his hand feel when

it is wrapped, in play or in the somberness of reflection, about
with his bitch's beautiful ear. Just so had it longed to be thrust
into some fabric of Victor's life: guts, or the snug mitt of the
heart valve.

April

Beatrix?

Thank you for letting me escape the knife . . . I am weak with
the closeness, the narrowness, of that passage, as I was once when
the rope released me and let me fall into the light I had relin-
quished. That was before the black ox had trod upon my foot.
This was an expression of my mother's, a link with antiquity, as
she would say, for it is older than Rome and also means, among
other things, old age, which she never achieved except in her
mind. Compared to the escape(s), the loss of pride, excess bag-
gage, I agree with you, is nothing, or little. This is the closest
you have come to my "real" life, which I read as an indication
of some increasing weakness in me.

Is Claudo a fate narrowly escaped, too, or a character in some
book I am not to see until, spying your name among those on the
remainder tables, I buy it (49¢) and read a life that I never
knew I had lived? Is that how you felt, reading yourself? But I
gave you the advantage of toughness.

Still, are you accurate — by which I mean, are minorities (including, I gather from you, women) always endowed with superior moral strength? Why then do they remain minorities?
What lesson am I to learn from that? I ask this, for me, humbly.
It is a "large" idea, even in a democracy, especially in a democracy, that the servant class should be the natural teachers. And,
Beatrix, these "islands": if they are all, exemplified by Christopher, composed of such infertile soil, such rank undergrowth,
then why should others like Victor join them in their efforts to
become peninsulas, building from their loamy and healthily
treed sides their own portions of the causeways? One deduction

would be that moral superiority drains off mental strength, and here, with certain deletions, we find ourselves joining the camp of a Shockley, which can't have been your point. I admit that you have made me think thoughts not native to me, and I admit some gratitude, but with it I acknowledge weariness. I never suspected that perversity could be such a drain on the spirit. If this were common knowledge do you suppose it could bring about change? But pity is condescension and to me the saddest part of your story is Victor's pity. And yet if I were Christopher, I would – almost – gladly swap places with Victor, swap permanently the "peaks" on which you have ironically placed me for the evenness of the valley floor, and, if need be, servitude. Is that the way, dictated by you, the only way I could defeat you? I appreciate the punctilio of the predicament, when defeat equals triumph: your defeat, your triumph.

How could I petition you, without fear? I asked, once, for a Wasp and was given Low (lapsed Catholic, but we are probably all the same to you). What he needed was Christian Science, an invisible poultice for the removal of warts and other blemishes. I said that Chris had no address and was given a fearful one, a mind nearly destroyed by terror. If I should ask – this is only theoretical! – for levity, for a world in which GAMES are once again possible, should I find myself a child, perhaps a retarded child; or a night-bound croupier, or a hunter? There are games from which no one emerges. If I should ask you for an absence of sexual perversity, the world would be narrowed, not expanded. Unlike soap, purity in sex is not desirable. The missionary position, even for the length of a story, may develop the thighs but it deadens the imagination. How would my appeal be misread?

Perhaps no appeal is better than the humiliation of refusal or distortion, of being sent to bed like a bad child. Perhaps failure is better than the risk of unimaginable success. If this were poker, I could try to convince you to take your earnings, or let me take mine, and go. But it is not poker. It is close to a life, or lives – so much is underlying by now, all the growth extending downward – and when we "take" those we are simply dead.

QUESTION

Because you are a poet
Do you really think
It is incumbent upon you
To kill *yourself?*

Your amanuensis,

Chris

YOU WERE TEN YEARS OLD when your father took an off-islander for your second mother. She was in all ways oppo-site to the dead woman whom smallpox had marked for its own before you were old enough to learn that a face like that of the moon's revealed by winter was not the epitome of earthly delight.

Your mother, you learned, had been as smooth as camel-lias when your father won her. She had held down the rep-utation as the island's most beautiful girl until you were a few months old. At that time, as though for belated pay-ment—because she had wanted a son above all else and had so stated in meetinghouse where such beseechments are binding — Mr. Pox fell in step with her. In painful sessions of re-education she would tell you how Pox stole bits and patches of beauty, mining her face like a man fallen onto a diamond field. Re-education, because it was learned that you were afraid of the reptile-smooth island women and that your fear of them was capable of making you physical-ly ill. Hence you did not come naturally by the Anglo-Sax-on's measuring device of beauty; it was not laid upon your pillow at birth.

Unlearning is a scarring process; the loss of beauty is an unlearning; but the marks of your loss of your mother's beauty were inward and set you apart without announcing, as did your mother's pockmarks, the reasons. A child thus re-educated carries anomaly beneath the skin and in later times of stress, such as drunkenness, the anomaly blooms from the secret pocks of the pores like masses of invisible flowers whose perfume, aberrant to the average nose, can terrorize with strangeness.

It was said of your mother by those who knew, that your father's turning from her in revulsion had hurt her almost purely as an aspect of his hurt; and that her dying was objective up to the point where only total subjectivity could accomplish the final breath.

Your father's second wife moved within a cloak of self that bore a hood like a cobra's. It remained a moot point as to which was the more terrifying: to have her concealed by the hood, motive hid; or revealed, motive bare as a gnawed bone.

But when she was first brought into the house and presented as your mother, you thought, having learnt what standards to apply, that she was pretty, with a skin like the dusty pink to be found within the cup of a field mushroom. Small, where your mother had been tall; rounded, where your mother had sloped; and two hands that never touched you without seeding your marrow with ice.

As others carry in their pockets vials of scent or a kerchief, very small women carry the possibility of evil; malcontent like a poisonous root cocooned in tissue; a sense, in common with abnormally small men, of both deprivation and omnipotence: small enough (they seem to say) to slip through keyholes, or into the socket of an eye to reach the brain.

The day she was brought with her alienness into the house, you and the bondmaid, Julie, made a bustle of welcome, a scurry of warm doings, with hospitable hummings of kettle and fire and half-musical throat sounds precluding the intrusion of thoughts of their expendability. For Julie was bonded by silver and you by blood to the household, but man and new wife are bonded by lust, which, if the wife is grasping and virgin, encompasses both silver and blood; if she is grasping enough she need not be virgin. So your role and Julie's were seen as possibly supernumerary and subject to momentary notice.

You wooed her with dustless curtains and shined copper; with vases of bittersweet, bowls of apples; with a punch-bowl based on hard cider; nut casings and picks burnished in a wooden trencher; the smells of beeswax and lemon oil applied like a honeyed poultice to the old vaguely camphorous wound of bereavement. The document, the seal of the first marriage and consequently the testament of your birthright, was first flensed by you of woodfat gathered as patina above the chimney piece, and then, with what Cassandra visions no one could have told, snatched from you by Julie and hidden in a drawer in a cold room, as though against the eventuality of spoilage.

As the new mistress of the house watched from a chair by the fire, her hands twined in folds of a red-fringed shawl, her smile seemingly too careful to show its teeth, Julie and you bumped each other fore and aft, trod each in turn upon the other's toes, made elaborate apology replete with bow and semicurtsy, as you flew about in needless industry. You fetched and carried, carried and fetched and circled like the weather figures on an alpine barometer, grinning sunnily in the face of storm predictions (the man of the house growing more restive and cloudy as error piled onto miscalculation) until the new wife broke into a laugh so like a bark that you and Julie hurtled toward each other for safety.

"Come here. Let me see what I've got myself into," and she drew you by the wrist to the edges of her knees. For the first time you looked into the abyss of a woman, and your face froze as though from an east wind, as, in the gesture of women who seem to push the mask from a boy's face, she placed her hands on your temples, her thumbs nearly covering your eyelids, and smoothed backward, temples, hair, skull. Her hands were hard and tight, leaving no chance of mask between you; some inward mechanism akin to hands smoothed her own face of custom and artifice. You saw, and knew without understanding, that she would possess you if she could. She saw your withdrawal and loathing, for proximity and stress had delved beneath your unlearning and tapped the old well, the waters of your ancientness and atavism, so that her tight sleek skin bore the mark of the beast that such beauty had worn when your mother's cratered face had been your touchstone.

At such moments life can be seen as a film laid over a thing dimensionless, if without dimension a thing is a thing. The film can be seen as a film because such moments tear it. If you listen the rip can be heard. Looking back, the boy become man was to realize that he had sensed the underlying — what? matter? series? — of your life following that moment with your stepmother, and had fought attendant fear with real sinew and tendon pulling and a willingness toward chipped bone if necessary. Though you never found a word that was mildly suggestive of what it was that inspired fear and fight, frequently words figured in the idea of the tearing process.

For example:

You, quiet by the fire, your beloved bitch sleeping on the settle, her head on your knee; a noise; she awakens, looks inquiringly at you, ears perked; you imagine yourself saying to her, a question, "Old Clootie" . . . and rage takes her. Her ears lay back, her fangs are exposed length and breadth, her eyes glare devoid of reason, from her throat there breaks a baying that you know is the *underlying*.

Example: House shut for the night, doors between rooms closed to contain what heat there is; bed warm, sleep nigh; remembrance that a lamp burns upstairs, used to light your repairs to a window sash in a closed-off room, placed on the floor and left when you came downstairs to supper. You slide out of bed, quiet for your wife's sake, open the door suddenly, for if snatched open it does not grumble; facing the stair, you see the shadows cast by figures moving before the lamp. Ghosts are no tearing of the film, we know our ghosts here; you whisper, to show no ill-feelings and to forestall same, "Sorry." Chaos. Blackness. Winds that suck and pull without sound. The needles of night at the eye.

But the *underlying* is not all drama, rage, soundless winds. Some of it is in finding yourself being quietly watched by a bird. The scrutiny of a neighbor whose eyes look different than your remembrance of them. A handshake that bears the threat of permanence. A pebble lying too precisely in the center of the doormat for chance. A stillness in the barn loft (you avoid asking "Swallows?" for if you do they will not return). The corner of the eye glimpses you have had all of your farmer's life, high noon or dusk in summertime, of the black man in the hedgerow: crumpled, feet askew in the way that proclaims broken legs, surrounded by the drone of flies that requiems death in summer hedgerows. Groups around a table in yellow light, tall straight chairs, straight tall people, right through the wall at which you might be staring in dull-eyed reverie; once you had seen them hanging over the sea like a chandelier of figures; you had wanted to call to them, "Don't," with all of your voice. Therefore you knew something about them, in the underlying place, which meant that you existed there, too; perhaps you were someone else's phantom to whom they shouted "Don't."

Such visions of the *underlying* could be manavelins from other lives, but you did not think so because they were never dull, and once theology gets into anything it becomes so dull that you would change it back for your old fear any day.

You were restrained from words or amends to your naked-faced stepmother by the dread of what words would draw from her — perhaps streams of blood from her hidden pores, like the dripping fringe of her shawl. Perhaps a greenish pallor shaped to your head with the smell of cucumbers about it.

You saw that she was relieved, even amused, as she consigned you to your place in the kitchen with a small push in Julie's direction. You turned to your father's ignorance and indifference to danger, and were drawn by a trembling Julie from the room.

"He will do," your stepmother said as the door was closing, "quite nicely. We understand each other, I think." Julie, rough-faced enough for your eyes' comfort, began what seemed a headshake then thought better of it and took you to the kitchen: buttermilk and gingerbread, a wedding feast.

Winter stood on the roof and shouted the banns all night, for repeated reminders of legality were necessary to condone the passion and terror that you imagined were transpiring from the room below into your attic.

She was the third woman you had known, and it was to counter her that you rushed, runaway sailor, suspected murderer, fourteen-year-old passing for sixteen, headlong into the bosom of your Spanish Jew. Her flesh was like a muskmelon gathered in and split at noon and served salted and peppered. Her flesh was hot, salty, sugared. Of all you lovered or were lovered by — girls, women, hags; boys, too, but it was them fed on you, licking you into quiet — of all who variously fed you, she was the one most turned you cannibal. Ripeness made her stink, and what's rank to the nose can ravish the tongue.

Still April

When the flickering of the child's lamp of tinware by whose light I was writing began to fade and assumed the outlines of my study lamp, it seemed that I held for the few moments of passage an old piece of newspaper.

ISLANDER ACCUSES MURDERED WIFE OF WITCHCRAFT

But denies killing her. Bondmaid and absent son accused of complicity in the awful deed. Bondmaid to stand trial but whereabouts of son unknown.

The effort now would be to cut off the past with its parallels grown dangerously close, but the wish is not father to the deed. I am caught in velleity, as my poor mother was until she found — can one make a pun at such a time? — legal aid.

UP *AT CLAUDO'S* / *A Remembrance*

I met Miriam Wiseman on a night just like this one. Maybe it
was this night, or is; maybe we have just said how-do-you-do
and she has gone from the room to repair her ravaged face and
will soon return and we will smile (maybe) across the room,
vaguely, at each other, and will not speak again, and maybe the
things I am about to write about us — all of us — never happened
at all.

It is entirely possible that this is true because anything is, but
in Miriam's case, as in my own, it is more probable than not that
they did happen because of one nicety: as we are essentially un-
imaginative people, we are open to all experience simply because
we can't imagine it *not* happening to us. Anyway, if this is not
the actual night, it is surely the same place and the people are
the same, or similar. It is extremely difficult to tell one group of
people from another in Manhattan, especially up at Claudo's,
which, in a way, is Manhattan to most of us here. We each have
our distinguishing characteristics, if you look closely enough,
but we dress alike, drink alike (heavily), and say more or less
the same things. This has the effect of seeming to make life here
easier for us — this sameness, and the fact that we all have a little
money, and enough malice in the bank to allow us to get by on
the interest. Our host is rich in both money and malice, and we
feel at home here, among his souvenirs, and his souvenirs feel at
home among us because we are souvenirs, too. He has collected
us randomly, this old, old man — Claude Darius by name — much
in the manner of a tourist gone mad in the junk shops of Europe,
and some of us are kept crated a lot of the time, in various ware-
houses and ateliers scattered throughout Manhattan and Brook-

lyn, and are brought forth when he thinks a change in climate might keep us from cracking.

He is quite a character, Mr. Claude Darius, big as a mountain, lecherous as a goat, and some say so evil that he is like a little child in the purity of his condition. We have all learned so much in his school for perfidy that we never, no matter the circumstances, turn our backs on each other. We walk backward from rooms after making sure that the path to the john is clear.

This, and our malice, and our attentiveness when he speaks, gives to his levees the air of the Louvre in the time of Louis XIII. Claude, or as we call him, Claudo, has his Richelieu, too. His name is Cy Solomon. He lives in Brooklyn, where he makes women's hats, jabbing the pins in and muttering in Yiddish. He, you see, is waiting for the old man to die, knowing himself to be the sole beneficiary of what can only be a remarkable fortune. He, alone of all of us, does not know, or will not believe, that Claudo will never die. In many ways, and in this one in particular, he is naïve. In the meantime, between waiting, and muttered incantations over démodées toques, and the long trips from Brooklyn to Fifth Avenue and back again, he plays, in Claudo's drawing room, the role of admirable jester.

We all admire him, we all wish him luck, we all laugh freely at his slanderous, improvised jokes about us, which he delivers to our faces, because we know it to be a case of quid pro quo: the futility of his waiting for Claudo to die is the tat for which we are willing to give him the tit of our indulgence. We pet him, actually, on the lower back where, to our knowledge, there are no teeth.

Claudo smiles at his jester, his yellow incisors gleaming topaz-like beneath the slightly drooling, lifted lip. His jester smiles at Claudo and mentally ups the asking price on the chandelier beneath which he stands, feeling the tingle of its worth in his toenails. We all smile at each other, knowing how fortunate we are to be here. All of us smile, that is, except Miriam Wiseman, who is crying. Having just arrived, I do not know her name until I ask someone.

"Who is that ugly woman?" This is the proper way to frame

an inquiry up at Claudo's. To have asked who the *crying* woman was would have been too obvious. She was certainly the only crying woman there but far from the only ugly one, so that by putting it that way I conferred upon all the others beauty, managing therefore, in the opening question, to lie, to flatter, and to give to my interrogatee the chance to exercise the subtlety of her divining powers.

The woman I questioned could have been a tragic figure if she had allowed it. In the Twenties her screen career was cut short by a disfiguring bout with smallpox, and those who knew, or remembered — most of us were too young — said it was a pity because she could really act, almost alone of all the people out there at the time. She was a pet of Elinor Glyn's, who was then trying to make Hollywood over in her own image, and it amused Agnes (she pronounced her name An-yea-si, the other half being, God help us, Delicious) to go along with the gag by playing the part of dedicated disciple until the time came when it amused her more to reveal which disciple she was playing. Poor Miss Glyn should have known, because Agnes was red-headed, too.

Agnes was born to rich parents whose name, of course, was not Delicious; in addition to these endowments and good looks she was possessed, from birth, of a perfectly formed contempt that was embedded in the middle of her forehead like a third eye, and this contempt — all-seeing, all-rejecting — set her apart in such a way that nothing that happened to her could ever be considered tragic because it could not reach that core of her where the deep-noted, tightly stretched string waits to be plucked. Her contempt, set in the front of her brain, was a sort of sending station, and what it sent was something like an endless roll of barbed wire that rasped out and wound about her in fangy coils, but here the Laocoön resemblance ends; the fangs were turned outward, toward the world, and nothing could reach her through them with, as I have said, the exception of disease. Agnes had a flair for diseases, sporting always at least the remnants of a new one. Viruses adored her; someone said it was quite narcissistic of them.

At any rate, my question about Miriam Wiseman made Agnes

happy. She licked her purplish lips, savoring for a moment the little unloosed deposits of venom.

"*That*," she said, "is Gabriel Wiseman's wife." My in-drawn breath gratified her no end. I believe she squeezed my arm. It isn't often that one of us can draw a gasp from anyone else up at Claudo's. I'll say this for Agnes: her sense of timing is not something that can be learned. The pause following her identification of the crying woman was, down to the semidemihemisemiquaver, musically perfect. I must admit, musician (poet) that I am, or was, that I handled my own little solo passage very well, sight reading Mrs. Wiseman as I would a score: her hair was a frightwig of the color mouse, of the texture horsetail. I was sure that spread on the pillow beside one in the morning, taking one unawares, it could give one quite a turn. Her eyes peered dimly at the world through what seemed to be mullioned panes, this effect given to her glasses by the tatters of veiling that fell from her really sad hat like occupied cobwebs from an old rafter; the veiling was rent from, I imagined, catching on the harlequin frames that swept upward in a sharp attempt at escape and her dress looked not so much as if it were kept in mothballs as that mothballs were kept in it, for protection against moths. Her legs were pretty and her feet small and, as they say, well shod. Noting these details in Agnes's eight-bar rest, I thought Mrs. Wiseman's crying was understandable. She touched me, and I wanted to meet her, but first noblesse oblige dictated that I hear Agnes's interpretation of what I was seeing.

"She's shocking, and I don't know why anybody asks her anywhere. I really don't think she washes, Chris. I would be terrified to lift up that hair, wouldn't you? for fear of what might run out, squeaking. I knew her before Gabriel – Gabriel! honestly! – before he got to be a World Power. She was never pretty – oh no, impossible – but back then she was at least clean. I think. Tell me now, Chris –" her Covermarked face close to mine, her slightly dizzy eyes surfboarding the voice with the gathering undertow – "tell me now, knowing what *he* looks like, can you picture them in bed together without asking for the vomitorium?"

I said that I had never seen the famous Mr. Wiseman, pointing out that his constant publicity was of the written, rather than the photographed, variety. Which was only fitting, I added, since theatrical producers are not, as a rule, handsome, distinguished, or even particularly human looking. Once again I had said the right thing; so right, in fact, that I felt in some danger of becoming Agnes's favorite, and that would never do. Favorites should not have favorites, but more about that later.

By this time a little crowd had formed around us, and Agnes played to us as though we were a battery of cameras. Somebody, safely anonymous on the outskirts of the group, even said "Roll 'em." I say "safely anonymous" because Agnes always directed her own scenes; her monologues were peppered with such professional terms as "roll 'em," "cut," "quiet on the set" (though she had never made a talkie), and so on. I looked a bit nervously in Claudo's direction because he hated us to form groups of which he was not the center, but he was taking one of his upright naps, leaning into the curve of the piano, surrounded by photographs of himself. Cy Solomon hovered nearby to catch him if he started to fall, or to push him; I don't know which.

Agnes:

"Well, dear, Mr. Wiseman is, if possible, even worse than she is. He's terribly slick. If you fell against him you'd keep sliding, chances are, all down the length of those natty black suits he affects, doubtless from a Hamlet complex, though God knows his own mother —" an eloquent shrug, the unmarred shoulders lifting and falling with attractive but abrupt angularity so that some grains of powder, or dandruff, find themselves in momentary free fall. Her speech becomes cadenced, as though she were reading poetry:

"His hair gleams like a polished saddle; in fact, his head is saddle-shaped, ending in the pommel of his enormous nose," and she sketches it for us on the air with both hands, tweaking, when she gets to it, the nose. "His mustache, I think, clips itself whenever he turns his head: click, you know, click. Somebody said he has the face of an Armenian rug salesman." She becomes judiciously doubtful, fair to the end —"Weeell, maaaybee. But there *is* something about him, an emanation, that makes one think of a

Yorkshire pudding—" Smiling about at us with a turning of the head like radar apparatus—"You know: damp and low lying." We applaud her with our silence, waiting for more. She looks at Mrs. Wiseman sorrowfully, knowing that the time for the coda has come because she sees, as I do, that Claudo is jerking awake like an old marionette.

"She, Miriam, is an heiress; horse manure, from some place in the Southwest, wherever they've got the most horses. I mean she *was* an heiress; Gabriel spent all her money getting ahead, and now he won't give her the time of night, and that's why she cries." Her speech becomes rapid. Claudo has seen us. "Rumor has it that she's an incredible virtuoso in the sack, but nobody will trace the rumor to its source because who would admit to having got that close to her? Frankly, I think Wiseman started it himself for obvious reasons. I mean, he can't divorce her without proof of adultery, and so he has baited the trap with that old lure—ssssex," and she hisses the word like a firecracker at the end of its fuse. She gives us a look that we know well as she adds, "That's typical cunning, isn't it, for a Yid?"

Agnes specializes in some words. In Claudo's court, where a fair percentage of the habitués are black, her sharp clever voice gives contour to the appellation "nigger" and bounces it off the walls with the brittle but resilient sound of a ping-pong ball. She eschews the monotone and climax of homosexual, preferring the unoiled squeak of "queeeeer" or the puncturing sound of "ffffruit." Next to Cy, she is Claudo's favorite. (He is gathering himself together to descend upon us now.) At the time of my meeting with Miriam, I was third in line of favor. We were very conscious of our positions in the hierarchy, and in another time we would have worn bands of fur on our costumes to make it plain just what our rank was. To explain my earlier statement about the inadvisability of favorites having favorites, it was Claudo's fancy and conceit that we, the fair-haired ones, should be—not always discreetly—at each other's throats, vying with tongue and physical deed for first place.

And here he comes, tottering over—no, that will never do. The truth of Claudo's walk lies somewhere within the following: the lurch of a spastic, the lunge of a dying bull, the shuffle of a syphilitic. He leads with his large bent head, peering upward and out at his target with eyes that seem to be straining to see through the thickened lids. The stubby white lashes, because of the reddened rims they cover, look pink, and the large irises set in veined yellow marble are like dishes of cloudy milk left out for the cat who has run away.

He has arrived, displeasure puckering his face like a birthmark. Without a word to anyone else, giving to Agnes the lion's share of his boycott, he says to me "Come," and his cottony hands seem to stanch the flow of blood from my wounded arm as he leads me away toward the crying woman.

When we stood before her, Claudo presented me and then, putting the english on the long-nailed index finger of his left hand, he goosed me viciously. This is something he does a lot of, irrespective of the sex of the person, and it is always performed viciously, though I doubt if anything so violating could ever be done with anything but. Suffice it to say that that left index finger knows intimately many behinds. It is one of the indignities we put up with for the pleasure of his company. The effect of the operation is to make one appear to start violently at the sound of a name, and this is undoubtedly gratifying to the person to whom one is being presented. To quote Claudo on the subject — and the only stab I will make at trying to identify his voice for you is to recommend a visit to an old-style Chinese family on a feast day when there are many guests classically expressing admiration for the food in unison — Claudo says, on the subject of the goose — well, I won't even quote him exactly because I can't, but in effect it's something about the element of gallantry, which he somehow equates with a proper show of surprise, being lacking in today's social intercourse: everybody, he says, more or less, has not only heard of everybody nowadays, which is fine and dandy, but everybody acts as if he has had everybody, too, and is just too bored to react in a gratifying manner to a famous, or infamous, name. In his youth people got up on chairs to look at other people. I never asked him what this did to upholstery, or if they took off their shoes first, or if ranks of un-upholstered chairs were kept around just for that purpose.

Whatever the answer, it's bound to be complicated, and Claudo likes simplicity. Anyway, he can surely speak with authority about the famous and the infamous; being both, himself, he naturally knows everybody of consequence — his word — in this world, and a large percentage of those in the next world, or worlds, too, because he is so very old and they were so mortal. He has never said he knew poor Yorick well (I think Yorick is one of the few exceptions), but if he did say so, we would believe him simply because Claudo does not lie. Lying, for Claudo, would be a virtue compared to what he can and does do with the truth.

I am very fond of Claudo tonight as we stand before the woman who is to become my mistress. I am twenty-five years old, and how old she is is anybody's guess, but standing there I see the line of her breasts — flawless, unaided — beneath the sleazy material, and the slope of her shoulders, in their dejection as disarming as a child's. I see, also, that her skin is of the thick cream variety that bemuses me. The hair is much worse than it appeared to be from across the room. All that I can think, looking at it from this proximity, is that somebody exploded it in a faraway desert and observed the result through smoked glass and then went home. I think of Beau Brummell painstakingly plucking forth each hair of his face with tweezers, and it is my impulse to do this to Miriam's scalp. It is the last unkind thought, if it is unkind, that I ever have about her. Even now, thinking it, I am half in love with her, my half love matching the half moon of her peeping through the riven clouds of her veiling.

Within a week we will have waxed full, and how did Claudo know, for surely it is by his design that she sits and I stand here in this crowded, murmurous room under his eyes that harrow us, furrow us, plant and reap us? How ... but there. His motivations and plots are things we have no traffick with, except passively. Then, at least, the night Miriam and I met, I felt as most of us felt: that to be a pawn was a comforting state; the small everyday affairs we accomplished for ourselves, but for the important ones, the ones with repercussive connotation, we waited for Claudo's direction. None of us sought the larger design, the ultimate purpose of the moves required of us. It was enough to be singled out for special attention by this man who had been so many kinds of lion — literary, musical, critical, social, to name four — that in himself he composed a pride. I have said, not unfairly but perhaps in the wrong order, that he conducted a school for perfidy. I should have told you first that at the time I met this extraordinary man he was nationally known for his interest in, and help to, the talented young. But if I had begun with telling you that about him I would have had to tell you that there exists that faction which believes his interest in the young is identical with Gilles de Rais's. This, of course, is calumny, because Claudo is a vegetarian. His impressive bulk is made up of that pride and liquor. But the young of the land do come to him in a steady stream and not all of them disappear. He is, and admits it as though asked, to New York what Gertrude Stein was to Paris.

Miriam. Claudo left us and I sat beside her and we talked. She was interesting, eager, funny and the ceaseless rain of her tears soon became like autumn leaves to me: after a time of looking the eye becomes sated and stops registering. One cannot will the leaves to be green again, and I could not cause Miriam's tears to dry up.

I began by feeling that she was justified, then I felt sorry, then her crying became the natural thing and the dry-eyed women around us looked freakish, and then I stopped noticing even when she talked about the cause of her tears — according to the Gospel of St. Agnes; that is, Miriam talked about her husband, The Producer.

"Gabe and I grew up together, I guess you'd say, secretly. His family didn't have a pot, and if there is one thing that made Momma mad it was people who didn't have pots and windows. She couldn't understand poor people at all; I guess that's because when she was growing up her family was so poor they had meat only once a month. The rest of the time they lived on noodles. If Momma couldn't understand their being so poor, how could she understand Gabe and other poor people? Well, Momma hated them, and so Gabe and I had to sneak around, and that made us closer. My Poppa died when I was sixteen, and Momma died when I was twenty. We don't last long in my family. Anyway, Gabe and I got married a year after Momma died, to the day. I won't say we were happy, because I don't, I guess I can't, believe in that word. Not since I found out it means, or used to mean, or was connected with, *chance*. Just thinking that word brings back all those race tracks where Gabe and I used to sit and peel in the sun and lose money. Taking chances. I had the damndest feeling of being always on the job at those race tracks, because my Poppa made his out of horses, you know, in a different way. Everytime we'd lose, which was everytime we went, I'd tell Gabe I thought I ought to go around to the stables with a broom and a pan and recoup our losses. He didn't think that was funny. He had a system, you see, and it almost worked: his system was to lose every goddamn penny I had and get back at Momma that way. I don't mean I was surprised to find out that he didn't love me; I never thought he did. I just thought we were close in, I guess you'd say, spirit, or something, and that was enough. I mean, people don't love people that look like me. Miss Ethical Culture of 19— whatever it was. Jesus. I bet you won't believe this, but I was worse looking then than I am now. Fat. Green-looking. My God, I used to wander around in the woods reading *The Prophet* out loud and scaring hell out of hunters. They thought I was some kind of talking bush, I guess, all green-looking and sappy. I don't know why green — because of all those goddamn spinach noodles Momma used to eat? Anyway, I guess Mr. Darius has told you all about me?"

I didn't say anything. She shook her head sympathetically. "That bad, huh?" Shyly, "He said some nice things about you; how promising you are, and all. I didn't want to come, I'll tell you that much; I told him if you had all that on the ball, what the hell would you want with me? But he, well, you know, he said come on, so here I am."

She sat up straight, clutching her glass, as though someone in her head had told her not to slouch.

"Look, he's not God Almighty. There's nothing that says we've got to do something just because he planned it. I thought he was an old kook when I met him, and I still think so. So if you want to get up and walk away from here, you go on and do it. I wish I could say something grand like, 'I never thought I'd stoop to even considering this kind of thing,' but I can't because I know damn well that you can't stoop from a prone position. Supine? Whichever, I'm down there and there's nowhere to go but up, so I guess I do need the old pimp. But not you. You I can do without."

She waited and I did too. In the center of the room the others were beginning a game involving a broomstick. One at a time they would grasp the stick, arms spread wide, and through the triangle formed by the stick and arms, they would place one leg, which put them in a straddling position. I think it began that way. Ask Claudo. He thought it up. Whatever the formal first position, the rest was chaos, involving pride, determination, hidden fears and so on. I don't know how long Miriam and I sat watching, uncommitted to each other or to the spectacle, but in what seemed a short span of time we saw people reduced to shattered and trembling animals by the things they found in the corners of themselves. Obviously, pride forced each one, despite the failure of those before him, to undertake what appeared to be merely a tricky physical exercise, the point being to bring the broomstick entirely around and over their bodies without letting go of the stick, but once caught within the confines of their own arms, disorientation set in: which was the stick and which their limbs? The brain's commands, directed by mistake toward the inanimate object, elicited no response. Feeling what seemed to be their bodies' failure, they experienced the terror of paralysis. The paralysis approached their brains, and their most important thought, desire, fear, submerged until now, was released, and the game became a rehearsal of their own deaths.

The sounds they made and the words they said were deathbed words and sounds. Their immutable loneliness was shown to them, and their impotence: that stick that they could not command became the base of their lives, which was, after all, they realized then and fully, death. That's how it looked to me.

I turned to Miriam and lifted her soppy veil back from her face and kissed her. It was the only antidote to the poison in the room, and it worked for both of us. We left quickly without speaking to each other, and though I was sure that Claudo knew we were leaving, despite his narrow-eyed concentration on the sweating pretzel at his feet, I couldn't have spoken to him because for the first time I was afraid of him.

I don't know how it's possible for a love affair triggered by fear to be anything other than macabre but ours was, completely other, excluding the end. True enough, there were grotesqueries, mainly of the comical kind revolving around my Pygmalion stirrings toward Miriam, surely common to all men with tatty mistresses. For the idly curious, the serious researchers, and the dirty-minded, those rumors about Miriam in the sack are fully justified.

A week after we met we had an understanding that we would spend all of our nights together except Saturday and Sunday, which Miriam said she would like to keep open for Gabriel in case he should require anything of her, making it plain that all he had required of her for over five years was her occasional, preferably silent, presence. The morning after our decision to become almost full-time lovers, Miriam went back to their hotel apartment and carefully segregated the closets, making certain that no tie of his or belt of hers should contaminate the other's separateness. It was a difficult thing for her to do, more so than taking a lover, because she said — much later; I didn't know at the time what she had done — that separate closets and not separate beds spell out the real end of a marriage.

I spent the daytime working on my folk play. Miriam, typically, kept busy gathering clothes for Cuban exiles against the coming winter. She was amazingly good at this, managing somehow to shame otherwise penurious people into giving not their second-best but their first-best clothes. We still spent most of our time up at Claudo's, and Miriam would go up to people there, compliment them on their clothes, and follow through with a request for the dress or suit, saying, "How do you like my late-blooming *chutzpah?*" As I said, she usually got a promise for the clothes, and at these times Claudo's cloudy gaze would sharpen into splinters of extraordinary love or hate, I couldn't tell which, as it lingered on her. Maybe hunger comes closest.

Along about this time Miriam replaced Agnes in the line-up of favor, and as I retained my old place and there was no question of anyone's supplanting Cy, this made Agnes fourth and furious; quietly, slumberously, crusted-over furious. Her fury was driven deeper by Miriam's obliviousness, which looked like indifference.

One night as I stood with my reluctant Galatea bidding good night to dear sweet Claudo, I heard Miriam give a muffled squeak, and when I looked at her I saw tides of red washing her face and neck. When we got outside the apartment door she let her stole drop to the floor, and twisting her left arm to an angle impossible for anyone but Miriam, who didn't know it was impossible, she exposed the innermost flesh of the arm on which a frightful bruise was growing.

"Agnes—" she said, pronouncing it the way it is spelled, accenting the first syllable so strongly that it sounded as if she was retching, which she probably felt like doing because of the pain. I hadn't noticed the Lady Agnes near us when we said good night to our benefactor, and though I felt that Miriam was right, I asked her how she could be sure.

"I smelled her goddamned perfume at my elbow," she said, "and then I saw her in that old man's eyes after she pinched me. She was *in* there," she said, patting the bruise consolingly, "in his eyes, and he *wasn't*. Where in hell was he, Chris?" As soon as she said it her eyes widened with some insight, but the elevator arrived and I pushed her into it, draping her stole around her shoulders. I was afraid she would tell me what her insight had been, but she didn't. While we waited for the doorman to whistle us a taxi down the windy street, I reflected that I, at least, was leaving Claudo's more and more frequently with a sense of fear between Miriam and me like a third person. I hoped that she did not feel the fear. I was so content with her, and pleased with the progress of my work because of her, that I thought contentment and pleasure themselves might be responsible: when you're that happy you're also fearful that something will come and take it all away.

In the taxi Miriam ascertained, by peering nearsightedly at the posted license, that the driver was Jewish. She did this often, and when the driver *was*, she relaxed, feeling herself in good hands and freer to talk. This had a clamming up effect on me; I felt somehow that she and the driver were allied against me, but I never told her so. Leaning back, she unsnapped and snapped her purse, an emphatic gesture that set a crisp tone for her voice to follow.

"That broad hates me because I'm Jewish," she said, and waited for the driver's response — a stiffening of the spine, a forward-thrust, belligerent jaw, an acceleration of the taxi — before going on. "She hates all Jews, Negroes, and liberals. You know who her best friend in this world was before he died? *William Randolph Hearst.*"

"No," I murmured as I had done many times before. The taxi perceptibly picked up speed. The park by now was only a gauzy blur.

"Yes. She told me so herself. She used to spend all kinds of time at that place, San Whatever it was Simeon. Oh, I've known that babe for years. The first time we met she pretended she didn't know I was Jewish so she could sidle up like a goddamned crab and say she wasn't staying long because there were too damn many kikes."

The driver was batting us down to Gramercy Park as though Fifth Avenue was the track at Indianapolis. He was crouched low over the wheel, so that he could have used his chin to blow the horn, which might have helped: I was certain he could see nothing but the upper rim of the steering wheel.

"She hates me, too," I said quickly, hoping to divert the driver from what appeared to be an unspoken suicide pact with Miriam, but his only response was something that sounded like "har." Miriam the Immortal was, as usual, oblivious. I didn't want to disturb her by pointing out that we no longer observed traffic lights — well, we *observed* them, and saw that they were red, and passed through — but I strongly hoped that she would say something, if not soothing, then nonethnic. She patted my hand.

"Sure she hates you," she said. The driver pricked up his ears, or picked up his head. I held my breath. "She hates you because you're a — uh — liberal." It was comforting, if surprising, to discover that I held views that could cause the taxi to slow up. I blessed Miriam's myopic perception.

I settled for a shadowy "Yes" that I hoped would convey to the driver, through its reticence, a feeling of all sorts of liberal derring-done on my part. Anyway, I have a short memory for danger, and as our pace was now funereal, if I had said anything more it would have been a request that he go faster. In keeping with the general feeling, Miriam said pensively, "A Jew is —" and paused.

The driver tensed, ready to crush the accelerator beneath his foot like a beetle.

"A Jew is like an artichoke — layers and layers of leaves that hide the heart and protect it." The driver relaxed sadly, thinking of his heart. "People say that Jews go around with their hearts on their sleeves, but that's just a dummy for people like Agnes to stab at and think they've made a direct hit." I felt melancholy, all surface, as I always did when she spoke that way.

"Or they can tear away at those leaves — customs, acquired things — and just come up with more leaves. The Jew has learned to bury his heart deep, his *Jewish* heart, I mean. But sometimes somebody like that broad AGnes can get through in spite of — well, us." The driver nodded. "She can make herself into a kind of hatpin and stick right through all those leaves to the heart. A bunch of Agneses together are like Germany under Hitler." I'd been waiting for it. It always comes. "By themselves — individually, I mean, they can't kill you or hurt you very much, but they can touch you."

We all fell silent, most of us hating Agnes. I thought of the bruise on Miriam's arm and wanted to touch it, but I didn't because of a feeling of resentment that pushed past potential good will: was I rabble to be roused by mention of Hitler, a rat rising to the cheese on the string, flailing front feet triggering the trap, day in and night out? Why in hell shouldn't a Jew be *touched* like everybody else!

I grabbed her arm and bore down with my thumb on the bruise. She found love in the gesture and gave me a sweet smile, though abstracted: she was thinking, a sometimes ponderous process. I kissed her arm and gave up, my Red Sea parting before her faith.

"Are you superstitious?" she said out of a silence.

"Yes."

"Me too. It's a kind of religion, I guess." The driver and I waited.

"One day," she said after a time, "I was walking to the river on 79th Street, the East River. There's one of those crossovers at 78th, and I was going to walk up along the river, past Gracie Mansion, to my Tante's house on 90th. I walked on 79th because it's more of a city street than 78th, not so many trees, I mean. Trees still make me nervous; you know why, Chris. So I got to the corner and turned to walk down a block to the crossover. It was spring and the river had some flowering things floating on it. I think. I mean, I'd like to think it did. For some reason. Anyway, just as I was getting to the crossover, an old man, oh, he was so old, old as Mr. Darius, this old man made a dash for it across the street and a taxi got him. I saw it happening out of the corner of my eye, but by the time I could turn around he was already dead, his old blood all over the place. A package was still sailing through the air when I turned, and it landed at my feet. A little package. I opened it up, and it was a bagel with cream cheese and lox. It was like his heart, his Jewish heart, landing at my feet, another Jew."

"Christ, lady, was that you? Jeez, I didn't know he was Jewish until I'd got him a'ready!" cried the driver. (I'm making this up. The driver didn't say a word.)

"So I walked over the crosswalk to the river and picked out a bench I thought he'd like, and I sat down and ate his lunch."

I have thought about this a lot: her taking his Jewishness into herself and sprouting more protective leaves to hide their two

hearts, but my thinking about it bears no fruit. I cannot understand it. But there's no need to go into that beyond saying that
I know what I have — I was about to say "have become," which
would be lying. I know what I've always been, with the exception, perhaps, of my time with Miriam. Almost a year. I know
that neither chance nor bad luck led me to Claudo and others
like me. I flowed, a provincial tributary, into New York, and
out of all possible levels (euphemism, go home) found my own.
Obviously, since I am still here. But Miriam isn't because, just as
obviously, she did not belong here. For a brief time her lostness
allowed her to be diverted to this place, but she didn't stay long
enough to be sullied by us. It is sometimes my fancy that she
couldn't have been, anyhow, but might have, given the time,
cleansed us instead. That is my fancy, which may be, as usual, at
some remove from fact. She couldn't, after all, cleanse *me*, but
on the other hand, I didn't soil her. It was a pleasant June to January draw. And even in February and March she held her own
remarkably well; damn well, if you ask me.

In February, when Miriam and I had been together over eight
months, my folk play, *Little Maggie*, went into rehearsal. There
was a certain amount of jubilation up at Claudo's, mainly, I
think, because they all felt that I would be too busy with the
production to read the play again in Claudo's drawing room.

There was an undue amount of publicity about the production
and about me, because it was known that I was a protégé of
Claudo's. It was his custom to attend the first rehearsal of anything involving one of his people, and that first day, as I read
through the work for the cast, who were seated in a semicircle
around me following scripts, I occasionally glanced up to see,
in the middle of the darkened theater, Claudo's huge bulk
flanked by Cy and Miriam. Other forms, bent and scuttling,
which could have been reporters or, assuming there is a basic
difference, large rats, came and went. I chose to think that they
were reporters because it was Claudo's practice to give interviews at such times. But later, when I mentioned the ceaseless activity around them to Miriam, she said, puzzled, that there had
been no one.

By that time I had gone slightly deaf, the key symptom in the Failure Syndrome, and may have misheard her. For it was apparent, from the reactions of cast and director, that my labors had been misdirected. Of all those present that day, only Claudo seemed genuinely, if frighteningly, satisfied. The force of authority in the statements he made saved the day.

It was the only day that was saved. From then on, above the sound of wrong cues and complaints that the words were unsayable, could be heard the clangor of plowshares being hammered into swords and the high squeak that bats and I could hear of ribboned egos as the swords were put to use. Bronx voices attempting Kentucky accents (issuing from mouths that would require Red Devil paint-remover and bushels of steel wool to scrape off the layers of old Kiss-Pruf — proven, God knows, proven; removing all of their makeup would have been, to those girls, the same as deliberately cutting their fingernails to the quick) gave to the work a feeling of parody that made me wonder whether I shouldn't suggest we play it for laughs.

I will try to keep that sort of thing to the minimum; this story is not about the rehearsals of a New York flop except where its failure touched the characters I have already introduced, touched them oppositely from the way they had been touched by the broomstick game. Miriam and I had been only spectators at the first cruel game, though I suspect, as I have indicated, that we became lovers *because* of the game, because of what it suggested to us, through the participants, about ourselves. In the same way, we were spectators at the second exercise in futility, and if it brought about our parting, it is not for the following reason: Miriam did not like my play, and from the beginning could not hide this, but she wished to be proved wrong about it; I think I have never known anyone to *wish* so hard for anything. At times I could almost see a horse materializing — how nicely the adage fits the case — from her wish: a horse for me, the beggar, to mount and ride to triumph.

Once, when she sat staring at the floor in our apartment, after I had told her the latest story concerning rehearsals, I asked her if she was trying to reverse her father's footsteps. As deliberately obscure as the remark was meant to be — that out of shit she was trying to make a horse for me to ride — she found its source and burst out crying. I left her in the apartment, without love, and walked in the streets and up and down the earth wishing that I was in it. When it came to me that she was crying for me, and that I had treated her tears with absence, the way her husband had done, I went back to her, but little jigsaw pieces of the end were there in the room with us, waiting to be gathered together and made into the familiar picture: Miriam Bereft, because left. I felt, even as I saw it pieced together, lying on some table in the future, that the interpretation was wrong. Her stance: lowered head, curved-in shoulders, helpless, lax hands — is also the way some women receive their lover, Laughter. Laughter, the physician (my lover the doctor). Twice — first with her husband and then with me — she had asked for a strong shoulder to cry on, a knee to lean against, and had wound up with a heel. Her inner balance should make the repetition with me as funny as the initial mistake with Gabriel had been tragic. Women like Miriam need only two lessons in perspective to learn the underlying principle, unlike the majority of us whose eye-motes perpetually distort our visions of the future and our memory drawings of the past.

I like to think of Miriam and Laughter tumbling each other with the naturalness of children and the passion of experience. I like, indeed, to think of Miriam on any pretext whatever. That is not as romantic as it sounds. Sometimes I think of her — not meanly, but coldly. Scientifically, if you prefer. I'd like to know how she effected alchemy with some of the base metal of me without having to share the result with me. Whatever was transmuted, she took with her, slyly or before my eyes? I don't know. I do know that I am missing part of myself, so I must dub her thief. Scientifically. Without emotion.

Claudo had told me many times that I must cultivate an attitude of detachment toward the rehearsals of my play, to serve as counterbalance to the hysteria of the others. He said there was something compelling about a creator who maintained equanimity before the fact of all those slit throats. And so I tried. But I was not very compelling. They paid no attention to me at all.

I took to staying away from the dirty, splintery rehearsal halls for days on end, living in bars, going into whatever body presented itself next to me at the bar. The story of this, I guess, desperate promiscuity got to Miriam via poor old poxed Agnes, who knew that the shortest (upper) cut to Miriam was through me. I was not secretive about what I was doing, because drunks can't manage that very well, but I did not flaunt my catholic tastes or tell anyone at all about my fairly late discovery of the partouze. Therefore I have to assume that Agnes had me watched.

I write this without rancor because if there had been anything at the time that I needed to use against Agnes to effect a change profitable to me in our relations with Claudo, I would have set spies on her, too. Anyway, Agnes did find out, and her next step was to get terribly chummy with Miriam, lunches, shopping sprees, girlish confidences, paving the way toward that goal of telling my lover what her best friend alone could tell her. Miriam, poor trusting sap, fell for the act, and though she was puzzled at the change in Agnes, she came to refer to that delicious creature as her best friend.

It amuses me still to think of Agnes's frustration, when she finally got around to spilling the beans, at Miriam's reaction. (Miriam told me about the exchange when I was making a clean breast of things, having no other choice and rather enjoying it, especially in the number-of-times department.) Miriam assured Agnes that she was grateful to her for setting her mind at rest; she had been on the edge of being hurt by my diminished ardor, thinking it was a reflection on her beddy-bye abilities. Perhaps Agnes loosened some teeth in the gnashing, and swallowed them, and they took root on the periphery of one of her stomachs where they chew busily at the old cabbage leaves she lives on when she is not stuffing at Claudo's. It is pleasant to think of Agnes having dental work done on her stomach teeth — all those suction cups and gurgling tubes hooked over the edge of her tum-tum, and the drills — all those marvelous inventions applied to her because, indirectly, of me. I dislike Agnes, but I love her deeply, to the height and breadth and depth of her stomach teeth.

The last words, as far as I know, that the ladies exchanged were these:

AGNES [*with the indignation one woman feels when another has said what she wishes she had said*]: Really, Miriam, I didn't know you had such a *tiny* mind.

MIRIAM [*blandly; she has learned a thing or two*]: I used to call you my best friend; didn't that give you a clue?

One late March afternoon — one afternoon when March was vouchsafed a clearcut preview of its whimpering end and in retaliation swapped its playful bluster for dead earnest sadism — one afternoon late in March when it snowed, rained, hailed, and blew all at the same time, Miriam went to Claudo's an hour before she was expected and found no one there. She rang the bell, knocked on the door, questioned the elevator operator and the doorman. No, Mr. Darius had not gone out; in this weather? No, ma'am. She tried the knob and found the door unlocked. She went in and wandered through the apartment, checking all the rooms, calling Claudo's name, feeling guilty as hell for looking upon things of a strange and intimate nature. I don't know what things; just that they were strange, intimate, and puzzling. Apology and explanation (the dreadful weather suddenly unleashed as she walked in the park) lay on her tongue like unsavory food waiting to be deposited on a napkin: Claudo, especially from favorites, demanded formality; one did not arrive early any more than one dared to arrive late. The third time through the apartment, feeling sick at the thought of a scene, she looked, half hopefully, in all the closets in case a burglar-murderer had strung Claudo from a clothesbar like an old suit.

Steam hissed and pounded in the ancient radiators, the windows were misted, a low fire burned in the library, but these energies, heat and cold in untiring competition, and her own eerily chilled progress through the many rooms, were the only evidences of life. Miriam grew too warm to keep her coat on and still her flesh rippled with temperatureless cold. Finding bourbon in the kitchen, she poured half a waterglassful and took it into the drawing room where she sat down, her back to the wall and all of the room available to her gaze, to wait for Claudo.

She had been told to come at four; without knowing why she did so, as that hour neared she found herself gazing concentratedly at the chair nobody but Claudo ever sat on. She sat and sipped and stared, hearing the dozens of clocks mark three-thirty, then a quarter to four. After sounding the three quarters signal, and *signal* was the word Miriam latched onto to describe to herself what the clocks were doing, those ruthless mechanisms of which Claudo was inordinately fond joined their ticking in a Hallelujah Chorus that battered and shook the walls of the apartment. Miriam felt as though she were composed of steel filings and the sofa on which she sat was a powerful magnet. The storm, the emptiness, the signaling clocks, her dizziness from the bourbon, the feeling of being riveted to the sofa, all brought her close to gibbering.

Feeling that the clocks were taking a long time to strike the hour and release her, she brought her left wrist with the watch on it to the level of her nose and darted one quick look at it, expecting it to present evidence for the prosecution. It was still eight minutes to four. The look was such a quick one, and the watch was so close to her eyes, that it could hardly be said that her eyes had left Claudo's chair at all, but in that split second a change took place: on the floor, pressing lightly back against the brocade skirt of Claudo's chair, there sat, stood, or lay a foot. It wore one of Claudo's favorite carpet slippers, a needle-point affair worked in shades of green. As Miriam watched, there grew from this pedestal a column of leg wearing lounging pajama silk, also green. When this fleshy plant reached the height of the knee, it made an abrupt inward turning, as though to espalier itself. Some movement, copy-cat and parallel, though tardy, was beginning on the floor where the other foot should rest, as if that as yet unformed foot and the leg to follow were inferior, as they actually were: Claudo was lame in the right leg.

Her mind jolting like a cart over the rough, new-laid cobblestones of her thoughts, Miriam cried out his name once, then flung her glass toward the chair, ripped herself from the power-ful sofa and fled. Wrestling with the doorknob, she heard a ten-tative clatter in the kitchen where the maid should have been all along, and as she got the door open and all but fell into the hall, she heard the clocks' preliminary whirr as they cleared their throats to sing out the hour.

Coatless, with only her rapidly circulating blood to keep her from freezing, she stumbled into the chaos of March and walked, or ran, from 88th and Fifth to her aunt's house at 90th and East End Avenue, where she spent the night tossing and muttering about people who live only *on schedule;* who, like the theoreti-cal tree that makes no falling sound when there is no ear upon which to vibrate, vanished when there were no eyes to attest to their existence. She muttered about old men who could, in the middle of crowded rooms, take into themselves, and install be-hind their eyes, other, younger people, prolonging, by the para-dox of ceasing during those periods to *be* — at least themselves — their own lives indefinitely (the reverse of what Miriam had managed to do with the old murdered man, but this did not, of course, occur to her.) She muttered, finally, about experiments with mirrors and reflections, people who invented people who reinvented *them*, which was another way of prolonging life, and she spoke clearly of sacrifices and of finding the mark upon herself of the sacrificial victim.

Her aunt, a Russian lady for whom dibbuks had more reality than non-Jews, managed to locate a rabbi with similar beliefs, but though they took turns at the telephone and standing on the corner of 90th and York importuning passers-by, they were not able to round up the necessary number of believers for the ex-orcism of dibbuks.

In the dawn hours, on account of her fatigue and the many glasses of rum-laced tea that her aunt and the rabbi poured down her, Miriam fell asleep and woke up sane, none the wiser for the events of the day before. That is, she had no memory of them.

Which explains why Miriam did not tell me about the fore-going. I know it by, I guess you'd say, assumption, but on im-peccable evidence: for one thing, she did stay the night at her aunt's; for another, her fur coat disappeared, and where else would she have left it, if not at Claudo's under those precise circumstances? Easier to part Miriam from her skin than from her fur, which she carried on her arm like a life preserver against the humid seas of a New York July. However, the real proof, if you are not yet convinced, is that when Miriam threw her glass at the chair containing, or about to contain, the materialized Claudo, the glass dented the air where the head should be, and when the head appeared it struck against the bruised air and got for its pains a lump on the forehead. Claudo said he ran into a door. Naturally, he would *think* that.

Soon after this Agnes swam back into favor, having proved, through brief exile, her superior worth as a pilot fish. What, after all — I'm sure she said, logically — had Miriam done for Claudo besides deprive him of some of his most favored and ancient clothes, which she had then bestowed on spicks? She had brought him no new prey, nor had she divulged to him the "why" of what he longingly, repetitively, referred to as the "mystique" of the Jew — impelled, I suppose, by the idea of massive survival sans magic; what T. E. Lawrence, whom Claudo quoted profusely, called "the everlasting miracle of Jewry." Whether Miriam's sudden status as flotsam not worth storage charges and therefore about to become jetsam was because of her discovery about Claudo, or her failure to unriddle herself to him, or both, I do not know. All I can do is present evidence. You must weight it, or may; I hate imperatives and liars like sin.

My own adventure of that late March afternoon runs as follows.

I was lolling about the apartment drinking, imagining ways to dispose of the director's body permanently once I had stabbed, shot, strangled, poisoned it and pushed it under the river ice, when the doorbell rang. I thought indulgently that Miriam had lost her keys again, and went to the door laughing, thinking of the way she walked down the street scattering belongings as though she were feeding birds. Her confidence as she strewed herself over the landscape, her absent-mindedness — once she had walked two limping blocks wondering how she had crippled herself before she discovered that she had put on one high heel and one flat — were two of the things about her that melted me down to a malleable lump of sentimentality.

I should tell you that when I loll, especially with intent to kill, I do so in the raw. I have found nothing so distracting at these times as clothing binding the crotch, like a too-tight headband restricting thought, because I believe that murder and other such acts are formulated in the regions bounded on the north by the stomach pit.

I opened the door and there stood Gabriel Wiseman. I would have known him anywhere from Agnes's description and from his self-importance. Some Selves are admixtures of which Importance is but one ingredient of varying degree; there was, in Mr. G. Wiseman, no admixture; he was all upper-case *I*, Simon, Pure and purely, allowing of no impersonation. If there was the suggestion that the oil of his manner concealed troubled waters, the oil, too, was purely his, manufactured by some interior press from the fruit of high-grade trees rooted in his own private dirt.

At what a disadvantage is a naked man faced with one whose very bones must wear frilly little pants like those on festive lamb chops! Especially when the bone-clothed gentleman wears also a cloak of such loftiness that it was certainly woven of the high air of Olympus by the Parcae themselves. His voice, however, when he finally spoke with *it*, reminded me that the gods' sense of comedy was their most beguiling quality: Gabriel Wiseman spoke with a — I'm not trying to be unkind; I don't have to — ratty squeak with a whistle in it. Of course, as one of the master puppeteers of our time, he must have swallowed the swozzle more than once.

As I scrabbled through the closet looking for a robe, pulling out first a negligee of Miriam's and exposing other garments of hers, unmistakable in their extreme tackiness, Wiseman sat, fingertips together, playing "Here's the church and here's the steeple," humming the hit tune from one of his early successes that was distinctly derrière-oriented — highly appropriate in view of his view of my fanny. I found myself hoping that his choice of tune betrayed a sense of humor about which I had not heard. Alas, not so. He hummed the tune because it was, in a sense, his; and because it employed the diatonic scale with no impossible arty little excursions into the chromatic. He and his audiences did not believe in musical miscegenation; they wanted those little black notes to have equal facilities, but, you understand, separate, and no little half-white, half-black songs running around their stages. The man who wrote Wiseman's musical shows knew where middle C was, and could play it with virtuosity, and could go backward and forward from and to it in a nice white line, but woe and WHOA to crossing that colored barrier!

Nervous in monogrammed flannel, I offered Wiseman a drink, which he refused. I sat opposite him and we stared at each other. He smiled; I wished he wouldn't. That his smile was intended to convey a sort of camaraderie was evident. He was like a rattlesnake across one's path who tries to defang itself to prove good intent. Just as I wouldn't move under the eye of a rattler, so I was damned if I'd open the conversation with Wiseman. He was unperturbed and certainly curious. I posed and he photographed me many times, the shutter, or his teeth, clicking softly. When he had used up his plates, or developing fluid, or something, he said, squeaking like an old door, "Are you Irish?"

"Scotch."

"Ah. That's quite U, isn't it?"

"To be Scotch?"

His laugh was arming. "I meant your saying Scotch rather than Scottish. Nancy Mitford tells me —"

I forget what she told him, but I should have known he'd know her. She doesn't despise Americans for no reason at all, surely. But he knew some other people, too. He told me. Great names. (Ephron comes to mind.) Names with which to conjure — well, I'm not sure what. Awe mounted in the room, mostly his. I itched.

"I'm glad," he said, harking back to my ancestry, "that you are not Irish. I, of course, hold the Scottish (Hon. Nancy, where are U?) race in the highest esteem."

I took my bow, hearing his voice, over the bagpipes, exhorting:

> Onward, esteeméd Scottish race
> And wipe that smile from the Irish face.

He leaned forward, and if I involuntarily threw up my hand, it is a time-honored gesture of which not even a Scot need be ashamed under some circumstances.

"Mr.— uh — a few years back, when I found my time increasingly taken up with and by the Immortals of the Theater, I strove most earnestly to — would *wean* carry an unpleasant connotation?— then to divert Mrs. Wiseman's interests from me into more — shall we say?— self-gratifying channels: haute couture, Cordon Bleu cookery, extensive travel, fast cars, sky-diving, shark-hunting, Latin American revolutions, uptown riots, leukemia —" He may have stopped with "extensive travel," but so little is certain in these conversations. Also, his extreme unction brought on a fever that gave me the sensation of sinking fast. He continued:

"But Mrs. Wiseman is, as doubtless you have discovered, a most dependent woman. Perhaps it is permissible to say that she is — uh — incomplete." He wanted my permission. The weather balloon that I keep handy pointed the direction of the wind, nervously. "However, I am not here to criticize Mrs. Wiseman. As a man of the world, certain facts cannot have eluded you concerning my former . . . my wife." Something snapped nearby, traplike. Former . . . Agnes's voice: *Can't divorce without proof of adultery* . . . I grimaced widely, exposing my teeth in a man-of-the-world grin. He gave me a penetrating look, without Novocain, darting his head forward until his jowls reverted momentarily to neck. "You gotta chipped molar. I can get you a brand-new tooth wholesale," and he brought forth a card that he extended to me between index and middle fingers. "Bes' goddam' dentis' in Nee-ork." His basic Neeorkeese gave me permission to relax a little. Up to that point he had made me think of a preacher paying a week-day call on a delinquent member of the flock.

Emboldened, I got up and poured myself a drink (Miriam and I drinking at the same time, for similar reasons, trapped, the fingers clutching our glasses unconsciously making the sign of horns to ward off evil: *Are you superstitious? Yes. Me, too. It's a kind of religion, I guess*). As I poured, Wiseman nodded approval; he was no puritan. I believe he also said, "Smoke if you like," and I gratefully lit up. As I took a drag and a belt he observed me benevolently.

"I hear that you write things." I nodded with quickening heart. Here in my living room sat the master pimp for whom all, or nearly all, hungry, variously accomplished theater talents worked The Street. Why, did you ask, if he is that creature of legend, a true abomination — why the quickening heart? Because he would, and did, take the spawn of one's consorting with a diseased muse and dress it so gorgeously that few suspected the sores beneath. Least of all the critics, to whom the smell of pollution had grown as sweet as the musks of a sixteenth-century French court, which also disguised the smell of sores.

Not least important, when these—oh, productions—died, their epitaphs were the epitaphs of kings. Even when they died aborting, Wiseman's personal force of will, motivating a complex of publicity machinery more secret than (and possibly including) certain rooms in the Pentagon, changed, as it were, the past course of history. Simply: everything he produced, stillborn or not, was pronounced an unqualified, artistic, smash hit.

Before Wiseman's shows opened on this spectered isle, columnists grown accustomed to the taste of butter on their bread were writing about Miss Cushy Hills, "now starring in Gabe Wiseman's latest Broadway smash." If the show closed out of town the same columnists — undaunted, still hungry — made reference to the lady, now stripping in New Jersey, as "lately starred in Gabe Wiseman's long-running hit." To say that its long run was from here to New Haven where it died of heart failure would be to flood the presses with extraneous wordage. No. . . . satire, irony, cynicism, truth, are futile in the context of Gabriel Wiseman and Co. What he managed in the loose name of Art, at the expense of talent, was, as they say in Harlem, something else. Therefore it followed naturally that this hyperthyroid, unclean, idiot-savant was the most sought-after man in the English-speaking theater world. Was I an unseeker? An exception? Have I ever been, I wonder?

I sat in his presence salivating like a rabid dog at the idea that he knew of my existence, not as his wife's lover, but as somebody who "writes things." He himself had written (the words have already, in some elementary school textbooks, replaced the Gettysburg Address): In this world, the Law is nine points of Possession; I, Gabriel Wiseman, American, intend to Possess; I am a lawyer; Ergo —

Since he wrote this credo for Everyman, pointing the way, Everyman, echoing the foreign word as Everyman is wont to do, has caused to spring up Ergo cults. Ergo has become the most fashionable name for little boys and girls. There is a new automobile named The Ergo, as well as a detergent, a chewing gum, and a philosophy. There is talk of renaming East Hampton, Long Island, East Ergo because Wiseman wound up there once on an overshot attempt at Levittown. New editions of famous quotations include, under *Wiseman, Gabriel,* the one word, ERGO. He is modest enough not to mind that this word, rather than his name, has been adopted by humanity. He is, after all, inseparable from the word: Therefore Gabriel Wiseman. They are synonymous.

In *Commentary* it was written that the Greeks would have approved of Wiseman's attitude toward Art: Menander broke an old mold and cast a new one with his New Comedy; Garbage (sorry, Gabriel) Wiseman simplified the Greek's idea and smashed all molds. In any revolution (Mr. Podhart continued) *to break* is the important act. What follows—substitution? Anticlimax. Replacement? Secondhand. But he has caused statues to be erected in the name of the theater in Central Park. And surely old theater posters in Shubert Alley commemorating expired shows are the modern version of the stele? Et cetera.

My eyes told Wiseman of my admiration, my desire, my willing subjection. Seeing the obvious, in spite of his Heraklean soul and his legend, he was, in his fashion, human. His lip curled, one withered petal of scorn. It could be that he had not expected it to be so easy. A lesser man would have been regretful, possibly, at foregoing a match of wills, but I don't believe he was. First of all, his stomach must have been bothering him because he kept smothering, not always successfully, belches, and when he saw that I was in the bag he stopped trying to hide them. Coincidental with, or as an extension of, the curling lip, he aimed at me an eructation that lifted him out of his chair.

I was rather anxious lest one wind entice another, as water primes a pump: farts make me laugh. To his wife, laughter was lover and child, morning orange juice, first martini, presleep yawn. Not so, I felt, to Mr. Wiseman. In fact, though the idea did not come to me at the time, so busy was I swallowing the legend of myself as headlined in *Variety*, if this man could be destroyed at all, laughter would be the one instrument to use. But I could not, then, with everything unspoken and therefore possible, think of his destruction.

I knew quite suddenly, with the most casual tug at what might have been, under Miriam's tutelage, a heart, why Gabriel Wiseman had come to see me, emerging from March's cold eye like a squeezed-out cinder: possessors may hold their possessions in contempt (witness Claudo), but the point is, they *hold* them. He, I was convinced, had come to me with a proposition: give up his wife and he would cover my sores with rich embroidery. I felt it in my bones, which I cast before him to reassemble as he liked. I was not impatient for him to speak. I knew.

With a gentleness somehow shocking he said, "They tell me you are good to her." I nodded eagerly: for you, Gabe, anything. At once I was in doubt about the wisdom of agreeing: his painted-on, disdainful features shaped into life, shifted about, searched for something.

"And she —" He seemed to be asking if she was good to me.

"Oh, yes," I said, and then, because I hate success along with liars and imperatives and foolish hurts, I told him, "*You* know Miriam," and contorted my face with a lewd wink.

He and the look on his face were alone in the room, two separate embattled entities, representatives of opposing, mutually destructive ideas — obsessions, I guess. For the length of time that they could endure the moment of truth without withering they did so, and there was no place for me. The look? Maybe dark, maybe fierce, maybe despairing, though I doubt it; it was too feral for that. If you know any falcons you may have seen it. It didn't last very long; you couldn't have photographed it with a high-speed camera. But when his disdain returned without knowing it had been away, it was damaged. In fact, returning myself, I felt sure that Wiseman's high-flying career was due for a crash, and I had no intention of allying myself with the doomed man. Which was just as well because he didn't make me that kind of an offer.

What he did offer, like a dispirited afterthought, was a sizable amount of money, in the form of an annuity payable jointly to Miriam and me, if I would persuade her to divorce him and marry me — or live with me; he didn't care.

Nobody can really write about rage, at least in any current earthly language, so I won't bother to tell you about mine. We parted amiably, but not before I had extracted his promise that he would allow me to take him to Claudo's two nights later.

I forgot to mention that *Little Maggie* was opening two nights later, and it was to the opening-night party at Claudo's that I invited Wiseman. My own producers had displayed uncommon sense when they decided to forego the out-of-town tour for economic reasons. That decision accounts for my continued presence in New York throughout this period.

On Thursday, the night before the opening, Miriam and I dined at home, quietly and well (I remember strawberries and Chateau Y'quem: the taste of them on her lips).

For me, to honor me on my opening night, she had bought a new dress, a sea-green Grecian column of pleats, that she modeled for me. I don't think I have ever seen a prettier dress. She made one or two mysterious allusions to spending the entire following day at the hairdresser; it would have taken more than nerve for me to have discouraged her, for her voice suggested belief in a most specific miracle.

She talked about our going somewhere warm and unfashionable for a month, leaving the following week, a trip long planned. Unfashionable, because faded spas that once had known greatness were one of the two rather peculiarly somber things for which we shared love. The other was amusement parks covered with snow. As she talked enthusiastically, our hands touching, I looked around the room, and wherever I looked I saw Miriam in the things she had given me: a stuffed tiger, a globe of the world that lit up, a weather-vane horse of corroded copper, some terrible books, including *The Prophet*, which she had read to me with exaggerated voice and gestures, draped in a bedsheet, expecting me to laugh, puzzled when I couldn't: Miriam everywhere, everywhere Miriam — except beside me; I could not look at her.

Her presence no longer had meaning. Only the Miriam of her gifts existed for me. What I sought, and found, was alcoholic poignancy, something I still understood. The evening that began with the air of an elegant picnic under blossoming trees ended, for me, in a frost-struck garden.

I lay beside Miriam in the dark, love tried and acquitted for lack of evidence, feeling her absence and hearing, faint as a wind-moved dry leaf, the whisper of the gown her ghost wore as it moved from window to window in the faded spa by the sea, gazing out at the snow-hung Ferris wheel with its feet in the surf. I borrowed her wide eyes and saw what she should never see: in the swinging baskets of the icy wheel, separated from each other by other empty baskets, sat Claudo, Agnes, Cy, Gabriel, me. As we reached the pinnacle in turn and paused there on the upper rim of the circle, each of us reached up and tore a star from the sky and ate it so greedily that pieces fell between our fingers into the dead sea and sank.

Someone cried out in sleep and woke us both. With early morning earnestness each of us insisted that the blame was his, as though it were terribly important. Neither would give in. Groggy, dogged, we argued until Miriam said that I woke her and she woke me, and so shut up, for Christ's sake, baby. We fell asleep face to face, our arms clasping each other loosely like the strings on a carelessly wrapped package.

When I woke she had gone. Around noon a box arrived, but

as the handwriting on the envelope tucked under the ribbon was hers, I didn't open the card or the gift.

The day scratched along like a letter written with a quill pen, blotted and punctuated by the doorbell and the arrival of telegrams and bottles of stuff. Claudo called at two; his voice was vigorous and cheerful, almost childishly gleeful. He said he had a surprise for me, told me I was a good boy, and rang off. Agnes and Cy called, following Claudo and each other so promptly that I imagined they were all calling from the same phone.

I dressed around four and left. From the corner I saw Miriam drive up in a taxi, her head bound mammy fashion in a bandanna. I went to a bar on Irving Place where I drank draft beer.

I walked into the theater as Little Maggie came before the curtain and sang:

> Once I had thyme of my own
> And in my own garden it grew
> I used to know the place
> Where my thyme did grow
> But now it is covered with rue.
>
> Time is an annual, it's said
> So blackbird and lover, take heed
> For time cannot flourish
> On its own, alone
> The provident swain saves a seed.

The curtain opened on the cabin with its curl of blue smoke and the talking blackbird in a cage by the well, and in the light-spill I saw Claudo's bald head, Cy's pompadour, Agnes's Judas wig — and Miriam. It had to be Miriam. I had chosen her seat myself and paid for it and the empty one next to it. But the illusion that it was not Miriam was persistent; I could not tell why until, straining my eyes, I understood: her high-held head was crowned by a miracle, a captive miracle, pushing at the bars of the golden fillet that bound it. Somehow, between them, she and her hairdresser had threatened, twisted, beaten into submission and caged her hair, the plague of her life. It smoldered and pouted, like a child who has been told to sit there until given permission to move; there was an air of "Just you wait!" about it, and I imagined it springing free, when the chance came, and rubbing dirt on its dress in sheer spite. I imagined that because I needed to, because I had thought, for a moment, as Claudo, Agnes, and Cy must have done when they saw her transformed, that now she was just like everybody else.

On stage, in the middle of the duet with Little Maggie, the blackbird stepped through the unfastened door of its cage and flew away over the audience, cawing and letting down the contents of its bowel on the wife of the *Post* critic, while the taped voice of the bird went on and on. The audience, no doubt keyed up by advance warning for screaming, screamed. Claudo, Agnes, and Cy huddled together, cheek by jowl, for all the world, from my point of view, like a sister act quivering in song, but I suppose they were screaming, too. I heard the noise from the street as I caught a taxi and gave Claudo's address.

The maid, mute, small, and eroded in appearance as the meat of a walnut, or a brain — Agnes swore that she was Claudo's wife — led me proudly to the dining room that bespoke, through its formidable, fanciful display of food and drink, Claudo's generosity. There she left me where, in solitary appreciation of my joke, I helped myself to some cold turkey.

Afterward, full of food, bored, I went directly to the library and looked through Claudo's desk drawers. In the middle drawer, on the top of a stack of papers, I found what was unambiguously my curriculum vitae. The major portion, because of my youth, was cast in advance like a horoscope, but the main events of my New York past were there, nail-headed, die-true. The present occurrence of the dying play downtown was there, too, but unimportantly notated. Around Miriam, alone, was there ambiguity: lines of crossed-out writing, question marks, the iteration of the word "idein," which I looked up and discovered was Greek for "to see"; the dictionary further informed me that this word was akin to another Greek word, "eidolon," which stood variously for idol, image, phantom — the phantom of her, last night peering from the windows of that forsaken spa? Bullshit. Claudo was the spook around this place (read New York), haunting even his own house. Idein: Miriam: "She (Agnes) was in there, in his eyes, and he wasn't. Where on earth was he, Chris?" In back of her eyes, darling, seeing how it felt when she hurt you. Prolonging his life with the adrenalin of Agnes's anger at something she couldn't understand or use. But I looked through your eyes last night. That makes me a spook, too.

I was hungry again and went back to the dining room and supped on black bread and butter. When I returned to the library to take a look at my future, which I had neglected to do beyond a cursory glance, the drawer was locked, with me in it. So that was that. Luce — the maid, or wife, or mother — had not stirred, to my certain knowledge, from the kitchen corner where she sat on a high three-legged stool and napped when nothing was demanded of her. So that *was* that.

The doorbell rang. When Luce did not go to answer it, I looked in the kitchen and found her gone, the door of the servants' entrance standing ajar. Missing, too, was her old black coat that always hung on a nail beside the broom closet. I went to the door and admitted the first arrivals, knowing that congratulations to the cast would detain Claudo backstage for awhile.

These first comers were the seven gentlemen of the press. I learned, as I took their hats and coats, that they were to write their reviews here and phone them in to their papers, a refreshing innovation, they agreed. I made them comfortable around the long library table — scratch pads, sharpened pencils — and took their orders for drinks.

Perhaps because of the refreshing innovation of place, service, and so forth, the critics relaxed, chuckled as they wrote, and occasionally read bits of their reviews aloud. I stood by in case they should require anything. One of them kindly pointed out that having a towel or napkin at the ready for mopping up might be feasible, as I had failed to provide them with coasters for their glasses. I remedied both oversights, earning distracted smiles, though another of them inquired if I was not new, and I said I was.

The gentleman who finished first addressed me politely as "boy" and asked if I would like to be the first to hear what he had written. Naturally, I was only among the first because his colleagues stopped and listened appreciatively. It was very funny: he reviewed the audience, which he called the smartest of the year *sartorially*, but begging the forgiveness of his many friends who had been there, he questioned their mental acuteness for staying without pay. He, having no choice, had equipped himself with Lethe pills so that now, fortunately, he could not remember the name of the theater, the name of the piece, nor could he recall whether it was an opening or a closing night, though he suspected the latter was the case. Undoubtedly because of the Lethe pills, he did not mention what the blackbird had done on his wife's head.

The doorbell began to sound repeatedly, and I let the guests in, some of whom I knew but who did not seem to recognize me (the napkin over my arm) as they gave me wraps, hats, sticks, and drink orders. If I must say so myself, I was a neat and efficient bartender, not spilling the champagne, not giving the bourbon to the Scotch man.

Sometime later, Claudo, Agnes, and Cy came in with linked arms, carrying, I thought, the sister act a bit far, and greeted me profusely. Saying wasn't it a divine party? they disappeared into the throng.

I am sorry to say that although the party was noisy, it did not develop into an orgy with rampant passion and people being trampled to death. It was, if anything at all, more like the aftermath of an orgy, everything over but the boasting. There was a lot of that.

The last time I went to the door it was to admit Gabriel and Miriam Wiseman. Wiseman's eyes were strained as if he had been looking too long into smoke or some other substance as dense and obscuring. He focused on me with difficulty. As though he could not help it, as if it were a reflexive action rooted in the most basic need for survival, his hands sought his wife's arm and clung there like two pentafoliate parasites to a vital tree. I wanted to reassure him that he had not lost her; that I would not have her for love or money, but I gazed silently at his hands on her arm, holding hard. Last night I had held her so loosely; I could not recall if I had ever needed anyone badly enough to hold on hard. I thought I remembered wanting, various wantings, and loving, various lovings, but *need?* Semantics, like drama, has never been my strong point.

I walked away from them, leaving them in the foyer.

Sometime later I saw the two of them step through wind-billowed curtains onto the small corner terrace where, in the summertime, Luce had cajoled with her knotty little hands a few scraggly plants to stand almost upright. All I saw, really, was Gabriel standing blackly aside to allow Miriam to precede him, and the glimmer of her skirt and a few sparks of gold struck by the chandelier from the fillet binding her hair; his blackness and her glimmer — that is what I saw.

I don't know, nor did I think about it, how long the Wisemans were on the terrace; only that, at some time either later or simultaneous, Gabriel rushed into the room and ran from group to group, person to person, shouting at pictures and china cats that Miriam was gone. Gone. Gone. People smiled at him, drew him into groups, pressed refreshments into his hands. The cats smirked, the paintings stared. Gone. Gone. Not fallen. Gone. One moment, standing there, and then —

My duties called. I was needed to carve meat at the buffet. Passing the door of the dining room, from which I could look into the foyer, I think I saw Wiseman running from the place, into the hallway, looking as small and wizened as Luce, bent, scuttling, the shoulders curved inward with something old enough to be primitive. I think. Later, from the street, there was the cry of sirens. In the apartment phones rang. Doors were opened, people came and went.

Before I retired, in a room that now contained all my things, I caught a glimpse of Wiseman sitting on a seventeenth-century sofa, drink in hand, arguing, voice raised to make a point, about the economics of the theater.

These things happened in a calmer time in New York, halcyon in comparison to now, fourteen or fifteen years ago, perhaps, or thereabouts, if, as I said at the beginning, they happened at all. I am not one to fool around with morals or allegories, so when I say that I believe something happened to bring about change, it is because I was brought up to believe that a life, like a river, has a course, and tides that are affected by the other elements; that, like a river, a life can be polluted or purified, can change its own course or allow its course to be changed. Sometimes it is only the scenery along its banks that appears to alter: where there was a tree, none; where grass grew, stones. Where people grew, stones, too — and where there was a Rock, none. And so forth.

In our case, up here at Claudo's, the scenery has an imperturbable sameness with merely the slightest shifts in perspective. For instance, I used to see dinner guests pretty much on a line level with my eyes, depending on seated height. I noticed such things as eyebrows, thin lips made full by art, whether or not ears had been washed. Nowadays my focal points are toupees, cleavages and the like — the bird's-eye view. Just the other night as I was serving Agnes the rissole potatoes I noticed that she had crumbs in her cleavage, whether of bread or skin I couldn't tell. I was distracted by something she was saying about having seen Miriam . . . I did hear the name, but then I had a sudden spell of deafness that lasted for surely a full minute. After dinner I screwed up my courage and asked her what she had said about Miriam. Her look was one of her justly famous enigmatic ones; when one receives it, one has been answered.

Luce, I have reason to think, is living in my old apartment in Gramercy Park. Once a month a check goes from Claudo to that address, although I must say that the name on the envelope is not a familiar one. In any case, she is not missed here. Claudo says that I am much more efficient than she was and adds, twinkling, that my only drawback, a slight one, is that I am not mute, as she was. But, he says, laughing outright, there are remedies for all things, and he gooses me playfully as he says that light was not always silent. It pleases him to speak in conundrums.

Gabriel Wiseman has received the Ergo Peace Award and another citation for having eliminated the necessity for drama critics: he now reviews his shows himself. His one millionth opened last week, a smasheroo. He spends a lot of time here at Claudo's, where he occupies an honorary position of favor recently created. He is very big here at Claudo's.

Claudo? Big as a mountain, lecherous as a goat — you know. We're all here tonight, all of us up at Claudo's. Over there by the open window they are beginning to play a new game called "Trust Me." It involves hanging out the window, ankle-held. It should be interesting to watch.

ET {
He
~~Chris~~ believes that Beatrix means Claudo to be a portrait of him in his old age. That even now he prolongs his life by taking other, younger people into him and ceasing, at those times, to expend his own life (as he took her into him etc.). This leads to the "poem"; "And now she wants his life."

NOVELLA

(For Beatrix)

And now she wants his life.

I

She took the good Island
name
Then swiftly, as though it
Were a festering,
She lanced from his future
The sea
Promising on land rarer salt
For his savor.

She took children from his
loins,
Though not before she took
His hot hope
And spent it in rubber
Spelled it for a while
In french letters
(Her term; the only real french word
She knew was capeau;
Merci — non; she knew it not
Nor its English homonym)

But he was a fountain
Recirculating,
In the moist Island air reconden-
sing into himself with small
loss
Though some essential dryness in her
Did suck at the basin with
Occasional pain.

He caught her, finally,
As his confidence said he should,
And in swells of manhood,
Again and again:
Three children,
Before she and Progress dealt
The cancer possibilities to her womb.

II

Then: Enough, she said,
Meaning: of motherhood, of him;
And turned inward, she said,
For a rest, for contemplation,
To regain her Selfness
(She talked that way)
And hordes of dark-blond
Island men
Flocked to her implosion
Like scientists to a Black Hole
in space.

Her lovers suffered her
Reputation at his
Hands, which were seldom
Unfurled.
Looking at the colors and
Shapes of his handiwork,
The darker side of the spectrum,
Asymmetry,
He was seen to look
With compassion, and some lust,
And a rumor like black rot
Spread over the Island
That he was a queer.

And I was there when she set
It going.

III

Astounded, he floundered,
Clapped his ear for the reassurance
of sound,
Countered red-eyed, raging
Under neon, with nightly
Public apostasy:
All the names women have taught
Men to call them.
But he was like a man
Dead of self-betrayal
Yelling into his own coffin.

She said he drank to drown
His violets
(Some heard "violence"
 But she was Jewish and could turn
A floral phrase)

Then, attested to by a winter
Widow, and some summer girls
On grass,
Impotence occurred
And she said he had taken the
Final Cure for Queers
And laughed down the gutter
Of her glass
Like rain in a cistern,
A private storing.

IV

They awarded her the drunkard's children
And the house he had built for her
With the good chimney
Founded deep in the earth
On old iron bedsteads from the
Island dump.

He was taken to stay with his
Mother.
She tended him in his old room,
Small, rain-reverberant,
Giving him what he mumbled for,
Mainly fluid.

Footnote
Islanders are mortise and tenon;
Scarcity breeds versatility;
The organist in the loft on Sundays
Though too apt an example
May the other six days
Pull the levers and punch the
Stoppers in the Tavern;
And the tree surgeon, botany in
His blood
May slaughter the warm-blooded
Biota.
Fireman and Promethean dealer
In furnaces—
Constable and Connection—
These couplings flare up like
Hermaphroditic love
On Islands.

In all their tightness of fit,
Seen from the air,
Islanders are like parquet
And one buckled tile
Imperils the floored-over
Common roots.

V

Some inquiry—
(In one of my Island capacities
I must ask these questions)—
An inquiry revealed
The fatal hoard,
Fused stockpile,
The insurance:
A dogged sanity against
His life.

And she sent for me.

I have seldom gone
With less relish
To accept a job.

MEMORY MAY YET UNDO YOU, will assuredly lead you soon
enough to the edge; its course is set, its profluence need not
be rushed, upstream, to make the fall showy when the precipice is reached. The violence of the fall is within the first
drop that bubbles from the fountainhead. Times of shallows, eddies near the shore — ride them like a leaf; the illusion of time wasted on the way to death is industrious
man's saddest invention, leading him to "make up for lost
time": lost time, on the way to death?

A man accused of murder is like water blocked by ice
from the sea. What cannot be submerged must be thawed a
bit at a time.

That first time of meeting with her, when she smoothed
your face: if your lifting hand had met hers? In the sudden
warmth a thaw and a binding pact: we will not freeze and
tilt our ice upon each other, nor block each other from the
sea? Can you be sure that behind her face of conciliation
there lay deformity?

In the village they would ask after your father's Winter
Bride. After a time your father was omitted from the question; the inquiry would be for Mistress, or Dame, Winter:
how does she fare? The solicitors were in the main females
at some remove from youth, who spoke in archaisms; their
age was contained in somberness like a vessel of bronze, incapable of showing a chip of levity, or malice. And yet you
came to imagine that deep in the vessel, plunged like a spice
into the dried petals of a potpourri, there was an element at
odds with solicitude.

That your stepmother was an off-islander would account in part for what you came to hear in their voices as suspicion. Another large area of her foreignness was chalked out by her shunning of the Meetinghouse, though charity and neighborliness were extended to a family of agnostics and to the lone Jew who attended the islanders' tailoring wants. Even a runaway slave, blue-gummed, incomprehensible of speech, had been set up by collective island endeavor as a tanner and given equal voice in civic affairs and the freedom, though not so unanimously granted, to sue for a bride among the island girls.

Therefore, regrettable foreignness was balanced by rigid adherence to the democratic ideals that were being violated, according to report, in the country at large. Work, religion, the right to seek moral happiness, were a stern music to which the islanders marched, and if duty precluded joy, this too was seen as traditional.

One clew that you had to the submerged attitudes toward your stepmother was the appellation, Winter. You found out by asking that it was not her maiden name; nor had your father taken her in old age. Consequently, to call her so was to imply loathing, from which your father (and, the gift extended, yourself) was excluded, for if there was a citizen who less than loathed fog-girt, ice-riven, wind-slammed Winter, he had yet to come forth and declare himself. Further, wasn't there an implication that she would have her season and leave, or that it was hoped she would?

You would practice synonyms, head-plunged in wind to and from the schoolhouse, or lying in bed at night, mocking the eighteenth-century speech of the old island ladies: Mistress Adverse; Dame Drear; Madame Decline. To balance them and allow for study and sleep you would name your mother: Lady Spring. You would see her emerging from the sea at the Water Gate twined with anemones, bearing lilies, advancing up the mossy stairs in clouds of soft-colored birds, chains of whelks at waist and wrist, the marks on her cheeks as though tiny shells adhered there. At the

head of the flight she would take your hand and lead you to
the home of her maidenhood, a tall house with parapets of
skewed brick stepped, terminating in kneelers; elegant
flashing windows; a motto in molded plaster.

You sat bolt upright in bed hearing the smack of wind's
assault on the walls, a great flat hand that both violated
and laid claim. Had not your father's house from the beginning invited the woman downstairs, anticipating her existence, waiting for her like a map of fate inscribed: Come...
Winter ... ?

Your mother, then, had been an error of choice, corrected
by the house itself, so that Mistress Winter could come and
stay. Spring would never come again to the house. Was confined to the sea below the Water Gate. To find your mother
(Spring) it would be necessary to go to the water. Your
mother was of the composition of the sea, fluid and salt,
born to it by decree, for the motto of her own house — not
morbid, she had told you, if seen in the light of temporal
brevity and Christ's promise to the spirit, as her ancestor
had intended it to be seen — her motto was:

```
            l
            a
    h a e c   s u n t
            r
            i
            m
            a
            e

            r
            e
            r
            u
            m
```

You abandoned the word "spring" as applied to the season, seeing that it could not leap high enough to transcend
Winter.

When the year turned and crops were planted, you heeded the alien decay upon which such renewal was based: mainly dead fish. Regeneration was not an upspringing of kind from kind; wheat did not grow involuntarily from fallen stalks. In the bringing of the sea to seed the land you suspected mysteries profounder than the known properties of fertilizer; you guessed at immortality itself.

In the parable of loaves and fishes, was it the presence of fish that expanded the wheat to such proportions, a secret to which a leader of fishers would have been privy?

Dead sailors walked upon the island; most of the houses claimed at least one ghost from the sea. What was the connection between the sea and their ability to return?

If your mother lay actually as well as metaphorically in the sea rather than beneath a stone in the earth, would she be able to come to you and take your hand once more?

You became fixed upon the idea that the flow of your mother's spring was blocked by the stone; that she was kept from attaining the sea and palpable immortality by the granite chiseled with her name. The deep carved identification was like insistence: Here You *Must* Lie. The branches of a carven willow tree with tear-shaped leaves were a canopy above the names and dates of her life, a pictorial echo of the motto "haec sunt lacrimae rerum" that had doomed her to lie thus even before she was born. *In The Twenty-Ninth Year Of Her Age On Earth* the inscription ran.

On Earth. You understood. The stone was thin, its bulk of no consequence in the face of your understanding. It was moved, and broken for its arrogant directive that she should lie rooted in earth, removed from the sea's redemption, without the measure of grace accorded a stalk of wheat. Whether or not a visible spring was expected cannot be recalled, but as the season ground on like a waterwheel the thought that she should have further outlet became grist to your mill. Bright nights, two in a row, you went with a spade to the grave and dug there a runnel for the course of your mother's spirit.

The second night the woman followed you, watched you, caught and held you when you would have run.

What did she say? Do?

There were questions, horror attempting to hide behind concern. There was trembling; a try at tears. There was the touch of her face to mine, so awful that I spewed my supper onto her nightdress.

Nightdress?

Of thin stuff, for winter; bridal material. A cloak thrown over, but insufficient. She planted freezing hands about my head, fingers like the shoots of tubers grown in darkness pressing, attempting to sow my intelligence between her breasts. My head pushed back until her wrists cracked with stress. How she hated me. It was close to holiness. She let me go and crouched over the grave; moved only when she heard me lift the spade.

Lift . . . . ?

The movements of lifting, many separate sounds, cloth creaking across shoulder blades as arms strained downward, sleeves sighing along the arms; cloth and flesh; metal from earth, through air.

But . . . lifting . . . ?

Above the head, the spade turned sideways better to cleave air, skin, bone, to carve there too a runnel.

May Day

He has gone for good. It was as though he could share with me, by whatever method, his life only up until the point of the killing. I walk through the rooms at all hours half longing for, half dreading, the beginning flickering of some lamp, but in the two weeks past there has been a cessation of hauntings, by him or by Beatrix. If I am on my own, I do not know where they have left me, nor *as what*. I share with my lady a lucidity that still fails me when she is not present, or is sleeping. In a curious way, it is as though my ghosts have told me that it is now *up to me*. It is the *it* which gives me most trouble.

Before he left I was able, by intuition and something like pictures thrown upon an inner screen from a stereopticon, if that is possible, to make out some of the events that followed. It seems that eventually he did not know if the night had happened. The only proof was the missing woman, who was not found, to the Islanders' satisfaction and his father's grief. He believed that he had recounted the adventure to Julie, upon his return, waking her by hisses at the chinkhole, whispering the tale over and over until dawn. But after his recovery, from a fever lasting some weeks which caused all of his hair to fall out and during which his face was stenciled with red marks as though by tracery from another's face, it came to seem as though he had spun his yarn to another bobbin. He saw his words as a red skein wound round and about an object of notched ivory, which was then tossed to the fire to the accompaniment of a muttering. Set behind the fire were trees and a moon. It was as though the walls of a room had dissolved, or were in a state of flux, for now it was a parlor and now a wood. A hooded crouching woman was the source of the muttering; it was she who tossed the bobbin to the fire.

During convalescence when his bendable bones would not serve him, Julie was often by his side. If he had indeed told her the story, nothing in her attitude confirmed her knowledge. Many times he came to the edge of an outright question but feared her innocence. In time the neutral position of the household, whether or not it was officious to his recovery, restored his own innocence. When he was able to get about again and perform his chores he did not include among them the completion of the channel from his mother's grave to the sea. He went to sea himself. When he returned, it was as an adult and Julie had been tried and condemned to death and hanged for a murder without a corpse. Only the bloodstains in the attic and the twice-widowered man's insistence of foul play: this is all there was.

THE SENTENCE

Memorial Day

People. I must see people. I feel Else's subliminal influence here. Daily calls, rented house on the Mainland. Besiegement after long quiet. I have resisted as she must have expected. Her masculine voice ripe with sympathy and concern for my work, her understanding a carefully erected barrier to my work so that I must think of her waiting there, wanting to be with me, each time I slip a piece of paper into the typewriter. It is an interesting technique, witchy: to manage to have herself identified with my work — her first question on the telephone was, "How's the work going?"— and thus, finally, to replace it. Did I say "subliminal"? It is blatant. Even here, in my subconscious, she exists, usurps, sprawls withering across the door of my instinct. Why don't I tell her, "There is no work now except my Journals, which other eyes, especially yours, shall never see!"

JOURNALS: They are the way the secret, instinctive, intuitive, are given form. Journals are interior photographs using the Karilian method. In the hands of a scrupulous keeper, journals are candid photographs preserving mysteriously perfect likenesses. In other hands they are like attempts at witchcraft, or at worst like murder by God or a godlike hubristic creature.

One of the reasons that an author may keep a journal, aside from what Else monotonously called DATA, DATA, DATA, is based on a kind of sophisticated superstition: IF there should be retributive forces to which or whom someday we must display our works, hoping for forgiveness or a show of mercy for our assumption of imagination, God's own mantle from whose folds emerge worlds without end — we can, pointing humbly to the lowly journals, prove that all the seeds were THERE, taken, involuntary donor system notwithstanding, from God's, or the gods', own creatures. Our journals are proof that we only played variations but did not presume to invent or create the theme.

Why can't I say to Else: You are the world I came out here to get away from? Because I don't want to fascinate her further.

Here is a Journal portrait of Else, untouched by me save as observer:

A red-haired woman, capable of voluptuousness, capable of kindness, of generosity, of a degree of selflessness in extreme situations but generally showing an overweening self-esteem based, one presumes, on her remarkable ability to make money. From this springs a confidence sometimes shattering. I hate the word "literally" because of its misuse as an interjection, like "hopefully," like "seriously"; but Else's confidence in the supremacy of her pronouncements can literally shatter because she not only pronounces, but follows through, with crippling sometimes if not always the result. Her decision to take a house "to be near" me was a pronouncement which a more sensitive person could have been subtly dissuaded from doing, but her follow-through was swift, and now she is inexorably ensconced "near me," and the result is or will be shattering. The daily phone calls have a ballistic power; the bones give as I write. In vain have I tried to exorcise her through vindictive sketches, giving her other personas, sexes, colorations, faiths. At some juncture the enormity of the task flattens me, the enormity of the thought that she may be indestructible. Yet the desire to finish her off, however privately, persists, and to my distress I find, counting the man-hours represented by the pages written about her and thoughts thought about her, that she has "literally" contributed to the wastefulness of my life, to my shallowness, to the narrowing of my ability. She is homeless in a way I can't define, but slithery as an eel. I feel that first I must force bones upon her, within her, before I can

Under the blanket amnesty of Independence Day Else came, unasked, unannounced, unwelcome, bearing the Ransoms to mollify him. She had a way of presenting people that gave the impression that she held them on a tray or a shield. The accompanying thought was that she had shot them, cooked them, and dressed them in their own plumage. Throughout the first samplings after presentation she held herself aloof, concentrating as it were from a distance, the chef lingering discreetly by the kitchen door. When the dish was approved, as it usually was, for her taste in people was modishly eccentric, she came forth and joined the feast.

The Ransoms seemed not only her shield; they were as well her credentials. She had not dared to take a house on the Island "to be near" him; he knew even she was afraid of that degree of unsubtlety; but in the Ransoms she had found a perfect excuse to visit as often as she liked. He imagined that "to be near" him had become a directive as compelling as "to make money." Viewing him as a market to be cornered simplified her tactics to a level of familiarity where thought was not necessary.

The Ransoms were, he supposed the word was, prepossessing. They were both members of that crowd of academics who were also in the arts, or that crowd of artists who were also in academe; he himself was part of an increasingly small group of exceptions. It bemused him to think that they had made an early decision about it; he saw them small and solemn, consulting relatives and advisers about the wisdom of dividing their attentions and abilities.

The Ransoms were as small as children, and ageless. He had met them — in New York, one would add "of course" — at Claude Darius's. In the inevitable side-taking that had occurred in those baroque rooms, the Ransoms had sided with Chris and Miriam, and shortly afterward had disappeared, both on sabbatical, to this very Island, it had been rumored. When they returned, as he supposed they had to, he was no longer welcome in Claudo's drawing room.

Since his own time as an Islander he had not seen them, owing perhaps to their discretion having to do with his advertised need for privacy, though it might have been from cowardice based on the open gossip about him since Low's year with him. In any case, Else did not know that they had known each other in other lives, and it amused the three of them to let the secret lie.

Those years of not seeing the Ransoms, which had clawed and chewed at him, had not even snarled in passing at their curious youngness. They reminded him of Gerald and Sara Murphy, if one could think of the Ransoms as somehow one self, which was how — not having known them but after reading far too much about them — he thought of the Murphys. The Ransoms were equally self-contained, but if there was smugness because of it, he had not caught a glimpse of it.

But they were not really alike. He — critic and teacher — was acerbic, curious, candid; she was diplomatic, remarkably untouched by the nastiness through which she had to wade in her twin capacities of professor-painter. In any case it was not their virtues that made him happy to see them. He told himself, charmed, that it was because they made him GLAD, which was not analyzable, though for him gladness had seldom sprung from plot or pot heavy in virtue.

He was borne away to the beach for sun and wine and shrimp marinated and chilly in polystyrene (the sun too was encased in an ice bucket of a sky, white and blue-flecked and synthetic appearing).

Else, burbling through a full mouth: "You do such fascinating things with marinade. What is this black stuff in the shrimp? Too large to be pepper, I think." He waited for the answer, knowing that the stuff was shrimp intestine: he had seen Miss Gold fastidiously disgorge it. Obviously the Ransoms shelled

234

but did not devein. Hella Ransom did not let him down. She named the stuff; the name was exotic, Indian-sounding, extempore, not having existed before Else's question. He looked on Hella with such gratitude that she was startled and spilled some wine. She stood up, flapping her beach caftan for the chilly air to dry. The cold white glare around her refracted as though she were a prism. Squinting, he put her with difficulty into focus and saw that what he had taken to be a long ray of light was her arm waving. He saw a person at the water's edge, a slender darkness that divided and became two people wading toward him in the gentle surf of the Sound. As though they were in silhouette he saw their features plainly. He saw Beatrix and Jeremiah Dresden.

He did not know if the sickly sweetness in his mouth was because of them or the Chateau d'Yquem. Beatrix's long legs were aureoled; Jeremiah's breast was ratite; he intimately knew the formation of their parts hidden by clothing, each detail lovingly sculpted by his imagination: Beatrix's mound was, for such a slender woman, an Etna, prominent in its promise of rich lava; Jeremiah's pendulum was long and fat and thick veined, inadequately cradled on prepubertal balls. His thought had been to place the balls high up on the base of the staff as though Jeremiah were in a constant state of climax: the poet incarnate.

Hella sat, stretching the still-wet caftan over spread knees. He looked at her for some further reaction to the couple, then looked back to the Dresdens. They had either dived into the waves or had metamorphosed into a split spiling bared by low tide.

Had he seen the gull diving at Hella? The picnic must be spread near the exposed eggs. It seemed the gulls dive-bombed you, actually nipping at your hair if you did not fight them off. He wondered why the attack had been so belated, so brief. Hella shrugged pleasantly (Beatrix's shrugs had been tortured, like a woman in combat with her brassiere); Hella's gesture was the amiable punchline to an old joke: It's your fantasy.

Else was saying, "It took them twenty years to promote what's his name, darling, but now he's universally admired." Catching his attention she gave him a bright, bitter look. The two books she had published for him had both flopped. "Your new publishers, baby, as I was telling Randy." He knew her pauses, her timing was often good, and counted the beats. She said, "How long do you think it will take them, with your stuff?"

"Oh, I can't guess." He lit a cigarette, felt her counting. "Maybe I'll be consigned to obscurity, like you . . . Like *with* you, I meant." He smiled. "Of course."

They all relaxed. With the small exchange the wild chilly beach had been transformed into a familiar corner of Manhattan Island — Claudo's, for Chris and the Ransoms. There was no longer a need to loiter on the cold proving ground, sand in the crotch, gooseflesh and stinging salt worrying the skin. They had brought him here to test, in effect, his worthiness of their continuing consideration. He was surprised to have earned it. Else, for a dummy, an artifact — old publisher, old lover — was palpably gratified; even in sex her ecstasies had had about them an air of response to string-pulls, so her present gratification could be read by him as an ecstasy.

They drove him home to his car but waited, not entirely lulled, until he was safely on their tail, winding up to the pinnacle of the Island. He had thought that Else's appetite had been directing all their moves but found that his own matched and probably outstripped hers. Watching in the Ransoms' rear window her despotic red head (she always occupied the middle of the back seat so as to be seen from all angles by admirers), the sharpness of his gaze was matched by a prickling in his tastebuds which filled his mouth with winey saliva. A vintage brew of invective seethed in his skull.

Refugees from all the beaches pitched camp at the Ransoms' as sunset fell and broke, tumbled to the sea and sank, like a cold fishy gull egg crushed by tourist indifference. The myth of the need and search for fresh air was expended in the smoke-cloudy rooms, in the small tight hissing breaths of pot smokers. On the Island during the season high windy houses were nightly squeezed and scaled down to the narrow dimensions of Elaine's or some other claustral abattoir.

"He's not even a first-rate shit. He's like the shit you have after too much Mexican food."

"Sure, she's ugly, but she has a lot of potential for getting uglier."

"I know they own the Divina Costiera, but they're still just a bunch of Wops."

"One thing I won't call you, and that's on the telephone. One thing I will call you is a cab."

"Her snout makes Barbra Streisand look like No Nose Nanette."

"You belong to the world; don't let me keep you."

"I've been saving up rope to send critics to hang themselves with; I'm sending *him* a piece of thread."

"When she was six months old she lost the Ivory Snow Softness Test on T.V. She was the baby in the rough diaper. From then on everything in life was downhill for her."

An image and its reflection arrived clanking with precious metal. To emerge from them would be like leaving a mine. Like cave-growths, hair sprouted from them; both had mammaries of unusual size and sag. He shrank from them: would he have to experience *them*, have to know them intimately from blocked colons to the sourness between expensive teeth? Was there to be no mercy until he had lived behind those pendulous bosoms? They were truckled to, fawned on. New York was their sugar tit. "Ah-hhhhhh," went the assemblage at their pronouncements, mouths open for the scattered drops.

She sat upon Chris, engaged him as though she were a leech on his flesh. Her mouth was like a sponge used at a particularly morbid surgery. Talk, to her, was to face her antagonist and squeeze the sponge, repeatedly throwing into his face gouts of foul matter. The face approached his in vehemence, mouth stretched open in the throes of some glee. Far back in the cave he saw the uvula erect and explosive.

Behind him, a girl's fresh impudent voice: "If I'm going to take up pot, I might as well make up for lost time and start dropping acid, too."

The answer was in a voice as rusty as charity, as though it had been unused for a like time. At first he could not make out the words, heard them as an echo:

"Is tha' killin' one bird with two stones, man?"

Victor?

He swiveled from the vibrating uvula on the verge of erupting, found himself facing a wall hung with votive offerings: a bowel, a pancreas, a heart.

The weight on him lifted as suddenly as though it had been snatched away by furious hands. He was to be spared another time. Feeling his legs plump up with life, he lay spent, unable to look for and thank his benefactor. If benefactress, he did not want to know. Else could extract so much in return for an ostensible act of mercy; she was worse than Portia and equally self-righteous. How often, when she had had the ill-paid-for right to tamper with his words, had she made him play Shylock, imposing penalties that it was not possible to counter, bolstering her argument with worn or made-up allies.

"One proof of Else's self-esteen is her bestowal upon rather a large share of her observations the rank of Axiom."

Is he speaking? Is anyone listening? The words emerge slowly, worked over in the skull before committing them to air; he speaks as though he were typing.

" 'It is axiomatic that,' she will begin, and while the succeeding utterances are seldom of a strict banality, they are almost never honed to pungency or tinged with universality. People new enough to be dazzled by her reputation — a response that could be equated with being struck blind by the light from, say, Mars — may either ignore the face value of such remarks and look for deeper meanings, or attribute the confusion and anticlimax of such statements to Else's claustrophobia within the confines of the English language. The latter group would argue, perhaps, that mastery of a language, down to and including the exactitude of its axioms, is a science; that, despite the dictionary definition of an axiom as something of universal application, they are frequently built upon untranslatable figures of speech. To which I would reply, seeing her confidence in her expanding girth, that to expect scientific proficiency of a woman who has

238

achieved *so much Else* would be to be a greedy guts." Applause. Jeremiah's smile is ironically admiring. Victor, lifting an eyebrow, claps vigorously as though to kill the words' reverberations. Chris sees with sorrow the deep lines around the once-unparenthetical mouth: has Victor become an oracle? Efraim crosses the room quickly, escaping. Are Sabra and Beatrix on a deep sofa somewhere, discovering links, as though examining each other's jewelry?

A Mr. Moss, steep and slick as the sides of a cistern, sat across the room gathering stones. Leaving, he said, "Consider yourself no longer present."

When Else came and sat beside him it seemed to him that her eyes, wide and flat, were those of a corpse. A partial impression gained from her eyes was that she had been dead long enough for a lily to grow through her body and bloom, and this sickening odor seemed to come primarily from her mouth. It was as though the mouth were a lily bloom. When he gazed at her lips he noticed for the first time that her teeth were small as a child's. Had they become that way since the affair? Had extreme dental work made them so pointed, as though filed? It seemed that their bulk had been destroyed by corruption of dying. Her lips were set in a grimace, too cold to be predatory or amoral. The sweetish breath was part carrion. When at close quarters she slowly looked over his body and implied that she remembered its power, he became aware of the unfamiliarity of hers: he knew nothing about the formations underneath her clothing, and it seemed as though those parts had not yet been given flesh. What of her flesh that showed had a tentative look, like curds forming into cheese, or like an embryo.

She got up to leave, perhaps embarrassed by his lack of response. He saw evidence of *neglect* and felt responsible, as though her only partial formation was due to him: the small teeth, the unsettled hide.

In the games that followed supper, among them the broomstick game, he was reminded of Miriam's simplicity and cried, inwardly, he supposed, for no one asked him why, nor offered to soothe him. He concentrated on their mouths from which the lily smell came increasingly, even from Victor's, whose breath astoundingly had always smelled of health, which cigarettes and drink had never marred; now it was as though his youth were festering for being so long cooped up.

All eyes, Victor's too, and Low's, seemed like Else's to be flat: beyond predacity. He saw all of them feeding on a sleeping body. He looked through the rooms for the body, then escaped for a walk with Miss Gold and tramped along the beach until she rebelled and sat small and adamant in the moonlight, though he longed to reach the stand of reeds. It was as though he had expected to find Anubis there, to lead them all away to death.

Else met him on the veranda, and her grasp on his arm felt the way Wiseman's had looked on Miriam's arm, the last night he saw her. He wrenched away from the present succubus, feeling blood being drawn up by her fingers. He told her, "In such a night of smoking and drinking and eating strong cheese, I would like to scrape my tongue and make you an omelet."

"I've always loved your cooking."

When his turn came around to tell a story he saw in terror the wattage of their concentration upon him. Claudo, Agnes, and Cy were locked together in their famous pose, an enormous bulk against the firelight. Low and Victor sat separated by the group on the rug, eying each other across the bodies like antitheses. Efraim had found a hand to cradle between his legs, and Sabra sat behind the pair, leaning forward a bit to catch any word that, inspired, might rise from the hand's owner.

The ponderous hairy couple had gone, their roles played out, taking the Ransoms with them. Miriam was missing, and Beatrix, though he could feel the latter like electricity around him, and it was as though he were one of her limbs and she the filaments crackling responses to the synthetic.

He had not listened to any of the other narratives, preferring to recall Chaucer over the drone of other voices, and to stroke Miss Gold and cut off the part of his mind that should divine what lay beneath their words. But, spotlighted, he wished for the return of his intuition. Instinct alone, he found, was unbearable, and he asked Miss Gold with his hands how she could survive it. The spotlight of eyes burned him. His cue had been repeated, and still he hung in the wings. He was driven out to center stage by the nearing presence of a child with some horror, some mutilation, pending for it, of which its snowfall steps behind the door signaled apprehension.

"Do you know about the baobab tree? Trunks of soft pulp so that when they have been eaten by fungus they can be hollowed out. Diameters of up to one hundred feet. In these hollows the dead are hung, who have not been able to receive consecrated burial. The tree mummifies them perfectly."

"You a baobab tree, Chris, huh?" Jeremiah, hanging on the chimney piece, led the laughter at Victor's sally. A good audience, Jeremiah, and Victor an unquenchably victorious wit, cutting to the bone. Who could best him, among the company? Chris gave him a smile, half proud, forgetful of the terror past, the terror ahead. Both were only glimpses.

"The vertical door, the line of yellow light, slightly bellied, like a cat's eye. If memory lay behind a black rubber wall and the wall had a slit from top to bottom so that when you squeezed it the slit widened . . . this is the simplest way to tell you what it's like. Quick little squeezes, like involuntary reflexes and quick little glimpses of what could be memories. 'Je vois ma femme en esprit. Son regard, Comme le tien, aimable bête'—"

"You repeatin', Chris. Tha' wha' the MAN say, man."

Victor had spoken for them. They waited, no longer patiently. They were a desperate crew, he remembered, all of them defamed and reduced, none but Victor allowed a measure of success, and even he sent back to the stews wearing imprecation like a blinding caul. It was not his body that they wanted. He had offered that to all comers, but only Low had taken it. And Else? Hadn't there been some gossip about the two of them? He turned to seek her collaboration, needing her as evidence that he had *given*, but she was missing. What they wanted was what he had withheld from them throughout the ordeals they supposedly had shared. They wanted his mind.

Else came slowly through a curtained doorway. Her attitude

was penitential at first glance, the bowed head, the lax arms and hands, and then one saw that it was sacrificial.

"Baby —" she said, then, talking over the heads of the others, direct to him, the way a child is prompted to perform, "— fog, rocks, infamy."

A buoy rode beside her, visibly and then audibly.

I AM THE BEAST

Rolling onto the ferry past the attendant he could tell from the sharpening like a perverse greeting in the boy's stare that he was planning further rudeness and determined to have a measure of satisfaction from the encounter that was for once not left entirely to later fantasy.

His was the only automobile to be making the crossing, a primary condition for the unpleasantness which had punctuated the past summer like thrown tomatoes, and he watched in the rearview mirror the boy's movements which bespoke a barely controlled urge to sadism as he manhandled the hawser and clashed the gates together. In his haste and consequent clumsiness he appeared even younger than he probably was. As if he knew this and felt his disadvantage in the older man's eyes, his face, fleetingly seen in the mirror as he turned, was darkened as though by rage. The likeness to a nineteenth-century woodcut of madness, illustrative of a Brontëan theme, was striking and, with the cold black clouds behind, operatic.

Watching the face disappear and the chest move cloudily into view, as though the mirror were a fluoroscope by which he hoped to gauge the virulency of the attendant's turmoil, Driver made a stab, halfhearted because of his own short temper at having to go to the Mainland on a nasty morning at an inconvenient hour, at analyzing the boy's dislike, manifest from the beginning in looks and short words and contemptuous gestures.

Driver had at first considered that the dislike could be his own idea, based on some submerged distrust of ferrymen after an early antipathy to Charon, plus what he had been told of the incivility that was an Island specialty as indigenous as bay scallops. But a high personal quality in the encounters had forced him to settle — as he now did, impatiently, watching the boy's pelvic section in the side mirror — for a snapshot image of his arrival in early spring, convertible piled high with the accouterments of leisure and himself perhaps unnecessarily flamboyant with long scarf whipping in the wind, defiantly top-down in the chilly weather and therefore a summer person. His rather sour, unsatisfactory conclusion had been that, as the first robin catches the early rock of the spring hater, so had he been recipient of the first flush, undoubtedly warming after a hard winter, of zenophobia compounded by the usual envy.

As the boy moved up beside the window, Driver took a deep breath, tasting again the ugly surprise of soured milk, from a bottle newly bought, in his morning coffee, and turned his eyes toward the irritating sound the boy was making by jangling (no sense of rhythm) the coin-changer on his flat hip. The hand abetting the noise was filthy: there was a good half inch of greasy-looking grime under the long nail of the repulsively big thumb.

Disguising with shortness of tone his response, he told the hand, "Round trip," and waited.

Prissily slow, clearly intending to ape Driver's accent, the boy said, "Are you returning to the Island on the same day?"

"The same day as what?"

"What?"

"WHAT same day?"

Slowly the boy said, "Listen, are you coming back on this ferryboat today, mister?"

"Oh, *today* . . . You mean *today*." He heard his vitriol with both relief and disbelief, thinking "I hadn't meant to dip into cattiness" but feeling some amusement at getting at last to the boy's level of insolence. The attendant leaned down and stuck his face in the window; Driver's amusement was replaced by a desire to hit the face hard. Its whiteness, which had done little more than temporarily blush at the sun and wind of summer, had a bluish tinge and a scummy aspect like the milk Driver had poured down the drain.

In distaste and faint disappointment he drew back and shoved without looking his two dollars at the window, half hoping that he would feel his knuckles however softly against the other's nose.

The attendant's murmured words at his ear had the sound of excreta produced under stress. "Are you coming back today, man? If you don't say one way or the other, you won't be getting off this boat on either side."

"No," Driver said, "no, indeed," and flung the door open with such unexpected force that the boy was thrown off balance and tottered backward to the high rail. Without looking at him, Driver went to the ladder that led to the pilot's tower and started up. He heard the boy shouting, faint angry squeaks against the wind like a Lilliputian and saw the pilot's head leaning out, palsied with refusal.

"Can't come up here," the man called. "Whatever it is, can't come up here. Strictly against the rules." The head drew in.

When the ferry was tied up and the ramp lowered and the gates tantalizingly half opened, the boy gave Driver a punched ticket and a quarter change. Driver got into his car and waited patiently, a bit sleepily, while the boy with infinite slowness opened the gates and signaled him through. When he passed from the tossing ferry onto the mainland, Driver held up his hand in farewell and with the corner of his eye saw that it was returned. Both gestures were lethargic; it seemed to Driver that they were like signals of agreement to a later bout made by exhausted adversaries.

Driving to the appointment that had been forced upon him by two needs: his need for financial reinforcements and his former lover's need of whatever magic he might offer her against what she said she felt to be the recurrence of old madness — he thought that the attendant must hate him mainly because of his freedom of choice. The way he had said with such black longing "you won't be getting off the boat on either side" was a clue. He, the driver of a good automobile, could roll off the boat and out into the boundless world of the Mainland, and he could return to the Island at will and keep driving into its heart where his house stood commandingly, but the boy shuttled from shore to shore; when he had shuttled into old age, for him to find his youth it would be necessary to ride whatever vessel then plied the course and stand at the rail and stare down into the water and perhaps glimpse it there where it had been expended without the company of girls or the accompaniment of rock music or even a layer of suntan oil to make the transition smoother. As Driver had been the first arrival on the Island following a winter that must have contained for the boy plans and illusions, so had he remained foremost in the boy's mind as the exemplar of all that was denied him, forbidden desires; and now, according to the local papers, Driver was not to leave at all with the other lemmings but was staying here to eat away at whatever winter illusions the boy might again manage at whatever cost to erect for himself against the coming year. And it was in his remaining that Driver was set apart from others who had occupied the boy's summer thoughts. He alone touched the boy privately by sharing his winter.

The man saw their meeting in early spring as the first-thrown skein of a net. The dark tossing November day with probable madness at the end of the journey could not charm him, as a brighter day might have done, out of such fatalistic imaginings.

She was worse than she had sounded on the telephone. She had built around herself, in her bedroom, barricades of debris, or of respectable objects to which her intent had given the aspect of debris.

She had always, even before they were lovers, repelled him by her nest-building. Her office was a large pleasant room with a fine view, but she had transformed it into a labyrinth through which one threaded one's way expecting at each turn the horns of the Minotaur. When he became her lover he was never quite certain but that his primary motive was to conquer the fear that he, an employee-author in her small publishing house, felt of that labyrinth, for as her clandestine lover the daily threading of secret passageways would become an amusing metaphor, albeit one he could not share with her. But his fear abated only briefly and returned, once he was living openly in her house and had become witness to and victim of the extent and inexorability of her complex, whatever its name might be.

One day toward the end when they had walked home together through the cold twilight and, entering the house, had fallen laughing and shivering onto a sofa, even as they kissed, her hands had been busy behind his back gathering whatever was available and packing it around them. Feeling the objects as clay for the entombment of his ardor, he had torn himself from the claustral place, crying "No, damn it, I will not share your grave," and, freed, had added, for a joke, "Without a martini," and had gone to the bar and mixed drinks for them both. When he brought hers to her he found her obscured to the eyes in cushions, newspapers, bits gathered from everywhere. She lay watching him with such a comical look that he had laughed, forgiving them both, and gone upstairs to bathe. But the parody of an animal in concealment had been the face of insanity, an impudent grimace at Fate paid for with two years of the mind's life.

Standing in her bedroom in the house that she had rented "to be near" him, he observed the elaborate construction at the end of which she waited, and reminded himself that she was quite capable of feigning a recurrence of sickness if that was the only way she could regain dominance. ("A boss lady," he had once said, though not to her, "is evolution's fiercest result, developed entirely on the North American continent and exported, when at all, illegally.")

Looking at her waiting with unusual docility for him to speak, he told her silently, "You madam, are a *result*," and started to her, smiling warmly, saying, "Else, darling," his shortening of Elspeth, which her employees had picked up and used as a malicious threat, "Do this or that or ELSE."

"Dear Else," he said, cautiously moving forward, his feet automatically feeling ahead of him for stumbling blocks.

She lay wanly on the cushions, the gold wash of freckles seeming to float upon her pallor like a school of round goldfish. She was surrounded by pink, a hang-over from the days when it was daring for a red-haired woman to wear that color. He thought that at her age it was once again daring, and ultimately pathetic.

She returned his greeting, holding out her hands like an eager girl and murmuring huskily; he thought that by her voice alone was she recognizable as a boss lady. He dreaded touching her hands lest what was communicated would not be trickery but instead would be the total lack of artifice, the surrender of cultivation, that he believed insanity to be. If the hands lay coolly in his he would relax. But if they burned in their stillness, and the nerves pushed at their thin covering like acid . . . he had held her hands on another occasion when the fingers had seemed to writhe inwardly as though they were gloves filled with insects.

The fingers were warm but reassuringly impersonal and did not loiter in his clasp.

"It's good of you to come. On days like this I need my friends." Was she too suddenly dramatic? "Days like what?" he said, feeling reverberation in his words like the tremors of an echo. He thought that it was because he was still plumbing the depths of the room and imagined himself saying out of nowhere, "Mark twain." His fantasy had overlapped part of her definition *of days like this*, but he tagged onto the end of what was apparently a recital of symptoms. He had an image of the day's terrain piled lumpily about them like an excavation site. Soon he would, another obstacle, have to ask for a drink.

He waited with a look of indulgence because he remembered that an unpleasant or even an impersonal look could set the doors of despair ajar.

Following a longish pause she said, "Of course, you never seemed to care too much for nature." "*Now* where was she," he thought, irritated, but thinking "*You mustn't lie to them*" he said, without emphasis, "Actually, I'm fond of nature. The seasons, to be fanciful, are rather like a big clock —" He paused, considering the policy of continuing, not knowing what simple statement might sound like accusation or worse — surely madness was a state of timelessness — but he knew that her long career as hirer and firer had developed her nose for sniffing out censorship. He went on, "City dwellers never know where they are," and added carefully, "—in a cyclical sense."

She looked interested. "Without legends? Yes, spring is more of a myth in the city."

He could not keep looking at her blankly. He got up from the edge of the bed and walked gingerly to a pile of books, stepping as high as he dared to avoid hidden obstacles. She told him, "Yours is there somewhere, probably about the middle. I keep putting it on the bottom, and it keeps working up to the top, and I have to read it again."

One of the reasons he had only seen her twice, and in company, all summer was his conviction that she would, when they were alone, forfeit all taste and talk about the book. It was a first-person account of a two-year madness in which, in the persona of a man, Chris, he had nonetheless drawn an accurate portrait of her. There was a good deal about her that *was* masculine, and the transformation of a boss lady into a male protagonist was hardly an impenetrable disguise. Still, to be truthful, he had not expected her to recover and read his book.

"Poor baby," she said, and he turned, almost shocked at the genuine maternity in her hard voice. She seemed to him for a moment to be as large and pink and healthy as the archetypal Mama.

"What?"

"*What?*" she mimicked his tone playfully and patted the bed beside her. "Come sit and talk about your days. The clock of the seasons. I like knowing where I am, too. I enjoy it here, la grippe toward one side or the other. The birds tell me the time, the trees suggest the appropriate costume —"

He wished she would not be whimsical or lyrical. Words about seasons and elements and constellations had, in her hermaphrodite's tonality, a touch of the obscene: so might Pasiphaë have spoken on her way to the field, on the night of the Bull.

He wondered why she could not be as direct about his presence as she had been in demanding it. He could not hear himself bluntly reminding her that he was here because she had talked on the telephone in a disturbing way. He could not recall why it had been disturbing; only that the nuances had vibrated darkly, as her voice was doing now, a cicada trilling as she talked, it seemed, of horoscopes. He nodded and nodded and slowly erased her words and placed his own thoughts over them as though mentally forming a palimpsest.

One way to break her bondage to the irrelevant might be to refer, with self-deprecation, to the hour at which she had called last night, for although he had finished work and had eaten supper and gone to bed and to sleep, it was, by her old standards, very early. The telephone had been to his dreamless sleep like a surgeon's knife — in effect, a reverse lobotomy, restoring to him the terror of old thoughts. All at once he had a queer half memory, like an idiot's, of babbling to her, and of tentacle motions, as though swimming in the dark, until his hand found the lamp and switched it on, a gratuity of light, for it seemed as though he had been swimming for another purpose against a current that flowed both back and forward and doubled upon itself.

His mind viewed the strip of black and stormy water that he would have to cross again to reach the Island and the pleasant geometric unclutter of his study, and he shivered. Seeing, in the sudden silence, that she was watching him, he said, "Could I have a brandy, do you think?" and turned back to the books to minimize his need.

There was a long maddening wait in which he tried for a compassionate understanding of her difficulty with sequential thinking. He considered how the word for that condition — sequela — taunted the stolid sequential like a mad mutant offspring. Her season beyond the doors of obsession had muted the snap and twisted the spring of her steel-trap mind. Now it closed on ideas as though made of cotton, without real grasp.

"The bell's broken," she said, and he sighed and asked, "What, dear?" remembering how before the onset of the earlier madness her disjointed sentences had come to affect him as though they were the bloody parts of animals strewn about the room. She said, sounding fretful, "A star for each of us is the best I can manage. Still, there's a star with your name on it, if you insist," and she went on into apology, explanation, reminder, as one by one he erased her words and wrote over them.

Ah yes, you're never too crazy to blame me; now I'm respon-
sible for the malignant heavens. He could not make himself turn
and look at her; to do that he must be armed with brandy.

He heard her get out of bed and tightened his nerves. He listened as she went to the door, her garments whispering like wind
in the labyrinth, and relaxed when she croaked out a request to
the maid for deux cognacs, the French echo from below slightly
altering her pronunciation, and steeled himself again until she
sighed her way back into the bed.

He pored over a book opened at random, the fixity of his attention aimed at discouraging talk, and willed the maid to get a
move on.

He tried to assess the individual weights of their needs, hoping to find an imbalance in Else's favor that would allow him to
give her the comfort she had asked for, in view of her loquacity
an increasingly difficult prospect. He had not realized how much
he had come to hate language and saw his hatred as too complex; surely his goal was to simplify.

At the same time, it exasperated him that he could not remember more of the exact conversation of the night before. They
had talked on and on with, it seemed to him now, suppressed
hysteria answered by soothing, demand met by promise, the direction of the lodestar pointed out time and again to (by) the
disembodied voice. Now and then a cluster of words would
arise from the tonal mass, but still, now as it had been last night,
the main effect was preverbal, or of verbalism. But out of it her
need had come and touched him, scraping at his pity; his urgency, as well, for he had waked at dawn as though to a signal and
found the note he had written to himself and propped against
the telephone: ELSE. EARLY AS POSSIBLE. He had rushed
off, leaving the spoiled coffee, impelled as much by the vague-
ness of the recollection as by the note's insistence.

He was bothered, as he had been on the crossing, by a point
that he could not make fit the case. Experimentally, he said, in-
terrupting her flow, "Sorry I couldn't make it over here last
night," and bent without appearing to, to her reply.

"I am too," she said, "but there was no way to get the money
to you. With me flat on my back, and Josephine can't drive."

Ah yes, the crux; even in her condition she could stress the word *money* in the way — half apology, half reprimand — that was peculiar to her. Of course that was the reason. The night ferry operated on demand only, and cost five dollars, which he had not had. His need had so far been outweighed by hers. Let him consider his own as coldly as possible, especially in the light of her implied contempt for it. *Chat chat chat* he told her silently and closed his mind to her resumed recital *(stars?)*.

He badly needed money to maintain his rented house through the winter; abominable fuel bills, for instance, with the Island winds tearing the heat from the rooms and devouring it as though it were chunks of flesh. He had lived on canned tuna fish, the cheapest brand, for so long that he imagined the grocery clerk was waiting for him to order in cat language. His book, which was to have made him independent, had died with the publisher's debit statement as its epitaph; following on its heels she had arrived and set up this mockingly elaborate house "to be near" him. He saw the debit statement as harbinger of her; as metaphor for her, too, because both were reminders as unemotional as ice of his failure. Her voice came at him on cue, pointing out that she had left the city to make herself accessible to him but that he had not — did she say "confided"? — in her. An odd word, but let it suffice.

"Else, I'm strapped," he said, and she said, quickly, "I know; it's all right." "*Thank you*," he said bitterly, as she rushed in with, "I mean it's no problem, if worse comes to the worst," and he, believing he had not been understood, said, "But it *has*," and swung to her admonishment of "Shhhh" as the maid came in with a full bottle of brandy and glasses on a tray.

Halfturned, he stopped, sickened. Else, with awful brightness, told him, hinting for the maid's benefit at a private meaning, "Just hold on, Buster," as though her eyes were not stark, without the protective clothing of pretense, above the cocoon she had formed about herself while his back was turned.

He glanced at the maid, bearer of particular strength, hoping for another variety from her, a flicker of awareness, a fleck of complicity for the ordeal ahead. He started belatedly to greet her with what affection he could muster as tribute to her silent sympathy in the old days they had shared as unpledged equals in Else's household. She was staring at him like a bird at a snake, entirely primitive in her open terror. His throat relaxed helplessly as he thought *She won't be of any use to me.*

Else snapped at her, "Josephine!" and said wearily, "Over there." The girl put down the tray and fled. Else told him, "Damn it, she's a peasant, really, superstitious, and all the rest of it. They think it will rub off. I'm sorry, dear," and holding out her hand to him, sounding furious, she said, "Oh, my dear." When he could not move she told him flatly, "It was she who answered the telephone last night and talked to you first. I had gone to sleep early."

He gazed into her unclothed eyes that were devoid of that illusion of distance which civilized people are able to set between each other to keep the brute at bay. Surrender of cultivation, indeed. He did not see how he could counter her dissembling, the too-quick onset of delusion that strove even now to reverse their roles.

He poured brandy, keeping his hand from shaking by imagining a statue of himself. He gave her a glass and said, ashamed to reveal weakness so soon (for she would have delved for it later), "Drink this, and Else, please for a minute let's not —" but the bleakness of inadequacy, a return to the subordinate days of employee and lover — and before that, of secret writer to her potentially destructive editor — would not let him finish the request for her silence.

The alcohol, ancient explosive, dislodged from the roof of his memory fragments like painted shale, each containing an image of her in the roles she had either assumed in his life or had been assigned by him. From boss lady to Pasiphaë, in each she was depicted as the stronger (for it was to the queen's design that the bull assumed the two-legged stance of circus performer, the ringed favorites watching and coupling in the deep shade). She had crouched in the heart of his novel, devouring what acclaim there had been. Even his art was not independent of her; thinking to contain her he had found himself contained, with sustenance withheld from him in that place so that his art had died, a starveling. To what was left of him she would administer the killing blow once he was stied by her to her satisfaction.

Sitting down, he waited for her, the Master Builder, to get to work, admitting wryly that without her to indicate the site of his tomb he did not know where to stand so that measurement could be taken for his death. He was here — had come, he supposed, for the purpose of letting her enclose him securely and finally within walls of her own design.

He found himself eager for what she would say, because dread, he knew, could also be an eagerness. He had found when he was writing his book that madness could be like the heaviest magic, a mad person able to draw with a word or an inference responses from the sensitive sane that were close enough kin to be mistaken for madness itself. In the process of writing he had entered into her more completely than he ever had done as her lover; afterward, he had not been able (he had thought it and now saw that it was so) to extricate himself from her, so that his present eager dread of her words and actions was as well dread of his own. Gulping brandy, he thought that if she chose to jam a pillow over her mouth and suffocate herself it would be murder, for she would kill him too.

It was an answer that she might choose over others, other methods, if she was as desperate for the end as he. Yes, what he knew was eagerness more than dread, the waiting having tipped the heavier emotion from the scale.

But the silence was filled only by his gulping, the two stars on the cognac bottle winking at him with increasingly frequency and coyness. He thought it typically perverse of her to choose silence now.

He sought to boost her along with mental reminders, clews, quite certain that she was privy to his thoughts as he had once been to hers. When one of them was locked away — she had somehow managed his willing confusion as to which of them it had been — he used to lie awake, streaming sweat, pondering her brittle bones that had become his own, and wonder what would happen to him if she should maim herself. He looked to her for the answer, feeling like a tired king. He told her, "Now."

As dry as old leaves, Else said, "It's as if I hadn't had a chance to talk, or couldn't, given the chance. Do you know that feeling?" He nodded. She went on, "Last night, after we had hung up, my mind talked on to you. Until dawn, practically. I watched the storm rising and talked to you. It was as if — my mind had found its voice again. I suppose what I've been doing is repeating all that I told you, silently, last night. Maybe you heard me then —" She was not being whimsical, he saw. He nodded uncertainly; she had always made points deviously. She said, "Well, now we don't have to talk at all. It's all been said. I'm tired. I love you." *(What?)* "So — let's just stay accessible to each other. To quote your book, 'Let's keep all the rooms open.' Darling. Yes?"

He looked at her in amazement, finding her expression dreadful; no wonder she had scared the maid. It was the look of the eternal predator, the feeder-upon-but-never-feeding, crouching in her web too intent upon her prey to realize that by a blocking motion she had pointed out the one escape route. He had nearly lost to her; he could not believe his fortune, must claim his winnings and run.

"Water," he said, indicating his glass, seeing at the same time the water plied by the ferry and the empty brandy bottle, more accurate a timepiece than the hourglass. He got up and went toward the door, thinking, tasting the therapy of frivolity, *If thy East Room offend thee, close it off!* With the aid of the brandy stroking him warmly (she knew that wellspring; had tried to keep it from him) he would summon the will to put Else and her needs and wants again from him. This time he would seal the door between. And on the other side, he would set the labyrinth of his own, and not the naïvely simple one of her, construction.

From the top of the stairs he called, for Else's benefit, to the maid, and then went on down. Else called after him words that seemed to be "How nice, coming with seaweed!" and then something more about the stars — "the killer stars" he thought she said, as, uninterested in her meaning, he let himself out the door.

Standing on the doorstep he thought how he had wanted her to recover; had come there, heart-directed, in the hope of somehow being of help to her; last night, or this morning, it had seemed quite simple that her cry from the heart — or his; it had become academic — had to be acted on. But the heart too is chambered, able to close off and conceal its monsters from itself. Treating the line's mystery as gently as though it were his bride's he murmured Pascal's ambiguity: "Le coeur a ses raisons que la raison ne connait pas." His mind embraced the words, felt their trembling withdrawal before he could enter and solve their complexity. Whatever those reasons of the heart were, clearly they belonged to the innermost place beyond which there would lie nonbeing. It was unthinkable, a terrible violation, to "keep all the rooms open," a line written as romantic, commercial hyperbole.

He felt that to admit limitations was a simplifying process, and made more recoverable the clean bright place toward which he yearned, the clean table with the stubby — why stubby? A safety measure, he seemed to recall — pencil and marvelously blank paper and several of that splendid invention, the eraser.

Lately his greatest pleasure and pain, opposite to that of the acquisitive woman upstairs, had been to unclutter, to write as finely as a spider spins and then to erase. Some would call it suicide; some would call it Art before they called it suicide. He supposed it was both infanticide and self-cannibalism, a devouring of his issue while it was still partially enwombed, still attached to him.

He waited, anticipating, until the window above him rose with the screech of old wood. Else called down, "Please come back," the simple words clear to him.

"You need me," he said.

"We need each other," but her confidence seemed to be flagging. He did not want her to give out. He needed her still, to point the direction, to say what she had observed from beyond the small-paned door. He could remember eyes twitching there like insects.

"Storm," she bellowed, "You'll be —" The wind howling up the street like the mouth of a cave-gulped adjective, verb, participle, erased them as effectively as he could have done. His room lay within the wind cave; she had directed him there. Had, by her archaic concern for the physical aspect of safety, also identified herself at last. And him?

He took something from his pocket, it did not matter to him what — something of himself, a sheaf of paper, which was after all what he was — and tossed it onto the stoop. He told her quietly, "There, Ariadne; there's your clew."

He would let her think that he was unwinding the thread behind him, but around the first turn, or the second, when he could do it without her feeling the twitch of severance, he would break the thread. And far ahead he might catch the first glimmer of light emanating from the safe place which they had built for him.

Far up the street he turned and saw her flapping pink in the wind, dutifully bending to his gift, given in emptiness, taken in trust. "Her"; "She"; and yet for all "her" sacrifice in weakly negotiating the stairs, "she" stood faintly flapping like an only barely remembered ghost. Proving his instinct, which he could not let go, even as he stepped as a prodigal into the mouth of the wind tunnel he heard someone calling after him a name that was not his own. To the bartender he said, "No, but honestly — moon, stars, in the most simplistic terminology they're rocks. And a rock that kills has a certain magic, agreed? Even supernatural ability, wouldn't you say? Soooo, the sky is filled with killers. And one of them *has got your name on it*." He leaned over the bar whispering the last line. The bartender moved away smiling. When he did not come back Drinker called to him, "Hey, hey, do you think I ought to call the hospital, or what? Listen, I'm counting on your advice. You fellows are supposed to do everything — advice to the lovelorn, the tired, maimed, poor, weary-laden, beastly sick. Hey, should I call the hospital, do you think? Seriously, now. Hey." The key fit, which was curious but not too curious. He had been drawn to the street, to the car, and the key in his pocket fit the slot. Hands and feet worked, lights sprang on, wheels turned, rhythmic noise filled the spaces around him. Give her her nose, and he did, and out of the roaring dark the boat drew up. Once on it he felt incomplete, a man whose actions have not caught up to him. The dark rushed by parting in wings of sound which he could see, pinions of dark sound, now behind him bearing him up. A killer bird! He saw the pole, pipe, stave-carrying figure, his assailant recalled from a primal place, and when the weapon tore at his metal body causing it to screech, denting it visibly in the dark light, he lunged, backed, lunged, backed, beams of brightness shooting, casting long shadows of his murderer upon the white gate which was suddenly not there, so that the shadow fell over the heaving waves into which he had been supposed to dive. But strategies fail. He saw his old antagonist hurled backward against the night, fall flailing, sink, rise for a moment into light, saw the youth of the illusion strike out, become engulfed.

His own dented grievously wounded body drew up short of the abyss, poised there, rocked, slid on the slickness, drew back. Overhead a mournful keening broke out, crying FOG ROCKS INFAMY. Pilotless the boat shunned the shore, the spilings, headed toward another shore, turned, headed back, turned, headed back. Lights found rocks, tree trunks, tops of trees, night, waves. With the dying of the wind, ruminant thickening fog at the command of the lowing.

Morning

Beatrix, mother of my children, and Jeremiah, gone. Low and Victor vanishing. Others, too, are missing, though I would have to consult someone to find out their names. Life is not entirely without unexpected empathies. Yesterday (?) when I had taken the telephones off the hook, the Ransoms came looking for me. Though they tried to pretend that they were just passing and stopped on impulse, they could not quite hide their concern and admitted, when I asked, that they had tried to call me. Leaving, using the hall mirror as an excuse for the words, Hella said, "There comes that point in life when looking closely at oneself becomes both a burden and a necessity."

I heard it not as a directive, of which I have had enough, but as a hint, a therapeutic tip.

In bed, where I spend the days, the smell of mold is pervasive, having replaced the odor of lilies. I give myself over to it. The sheets, pillows, the bed itself; my chapstick, my water glass, mold. Only my lady's coat in which I bury my nose to sleep is clean of the odor. She woke me barking in the night. I said to her, "Mold?" and the swamp began to retreat. I lay awake thinking about my lack of sympathy for others and had a small moment of self-knowledge: it is because I have none for myself. I was taught to be hard on myself, which I now see is not the same thing; I have misread the directive. But I am so intertwined now with others, some of them Beatrix's inventions, or so I continue to tell myself, that to extract my single thread from the fabric looks an impossible task. To put it as baldly as possible, I do not know now who "I" am.

I dwelled at length on what would seem to be a small thing:

how my lack of sympathy had let me imagine the flesh of others
as having the consistency of cheese. But we are not cheese! I
said foolishly, again and again; our flesh is WON and kept at
great price for all its vulnerability to knives and calumnious
words. The compassion, if that is what it was, for so small a
speck, let me relax and sleep. But today I am able to "see" this:
that the flesh, the bulk, the ironies, are bulwarks against "seeing," others and ourselves, so that if we were cheese, and could
devour each other's flesh, we might expose the hidden cores
which are the inaccessible islands. I feel stripped of flesh, but
cloaked in a garment like a maternity dress, so that the outward
appearance must still be of obesity. To take off the cloak: is it
possible, for me? There are still spectators. It occurs to me that,
in the trial not yet completed, can be found an almost comical
echo of the old Roman custom of lacrimis defendi: the defend-
ant's wife and children, dressed in mourning clothes and dripping tears, dramatically brought in to sway the court.

Night

Victor gone. Low, like ectoplasm, shines in unlit rooms like
the ghost of a murdered boy. Finding him hovering about the
piano I asked him, "Just who are you?" In time he replied, or
tried to: "Hap —" but that was all he could do. Was he trying
to identify himself as *happiness?*

Morning

Alone. To set down reasons. To reason. Ratio. Reckoning. In
dissimili ratione. Pressed by meaning to the earth, crushed beneath the juggernaut of meaning, pushed into the ground: a returning to one's roots, to the roots of meaning, to the reason, the
raison, the raisin, the kernel, the seed: to vanish into language.

FIRST-PERSON BIOGRAPHY

I

What do we call those memories which strike forcefully, usually toward our sleep though sometimes as flashes of lightning, when we, like the storm, are at a peak of activity?

I don't mean the déjà vu, which in its pure form surely is one of the most excruciating experiences one can have ("pure form" here meant to set it apart from those popular, slightly melancholy, and romantic sensings which are decent enough to be sung about). I have known the real thing only once, and when it was over I petitioned that I might never know it again, for during the seizure, which was, I imagined, like epilepsy, I thought my brain would burst.

The memories to which I refer are patently unreal; even in the throes, watching details unfold around the catalyst, we know that they are unreal, yet their reality is strong enough by comparison to overshadow the real objects framing the aperture through which we perceive the memory.

One recent day, seated at my desk trying to write, offended by the cheerless post — catalogs, one bill — I looked around my writing room and saw: on the Apollo, my silver wig, which constricts my thoughts so that I cannot work in it, though it was meant to free me from my own dark brown "reality" with intimations of eighteenth-century courts; under the northwest window, the two-gallon gray pottery crock, blue-painted butterfly, blue painted "2," filled with slowly knotting chrysanthemums; gluttony too was in the room, and danger — the danger of my obesity, for I realized all at once how far one can be pushed by extended panic, and in what direction mine was pushing me. Between the wigged Apollo and the chrysanthemums there is a space of wall with a bookcase spilling its guts, bulging toward the floor in an excrescencelike bellying, with six *Virginia Quarterlies* and four Virginia Woolf's, unplanned companions, fallen onto the floor; and next to the bookcase there is the northeast window. Framed in its lower sash, in the lower middle pane slightly right of the brass handle, is the tub of succulents which sits on the hemisphere of grass between the half circle of graveled drive and the road, under the two maples which I have named Philemon and Baucis. The tub is canker green, the succulents a bit yellower than would be served by "pallid," a word one wants anyhow to use about them.

On either side of the framing pane are the white-fringed curtains that identically mask the jambs of the room's six windows. On five of the windows the curtains on their wooden rings are generally kept folded back into narrow panels, but this one window, the northeast window, is, once the trees have dropped their leaves, kept two thirds blind because of the view of my bare backside its openness would afford to passers-by as I practice those more elongated poses (Suryanamaskar, Sirshasana, Sarvangasana) of my two-hour daily Yoga.

My eyes traveled from hyacinthine wig to chrysanthemums, noting the similarity that was made utterly uncharming because of another factor — age — that caused an equal though hidden dissimilarity: the wig was practically new, hyacinthine by recent design, but it capped the Apollo at least partly because of my age, whereas the chrysanthemums in their age actually resembled me — falling petals, organic shrinkage — and so the surface likeness between the two objects became confusing enough to be maddening. Then my eyes in traveling passed over and returned to the succulents, and memory poured into the room on such a flood, involving all the senses, that I was affronted by the excess.

Later I tried to write about the experience, and it fell into a more or less metered form (I am no poet), and once it was put down I forgot it, or thought I did, and it was today that I found the fragments, which made me recall that I had dreamed the experience solidly into my past, woven it there quite firmly, so that reading the fragments was like discovering an old letter long sought.

One fragment:

> The grass browning toward sleep
> like a child met halfway
> By his dream of fur.

Another:

> But through cracked fringed curtains
> Potted succulents are coffined
> As to a child's horrored gaze carried upon
> Midnight feet to the parlor
> (The last twisting leaves of bright maple
>   the shuddering candleflames)

Followed by:

> Slice memory there like meat;
> Show the tendons but stay
> The feast.

In the "poem," three or four pages of long lines, many of them prose-long, there is a past, the past of someone I do not know and have never known, someone who dwells in a country I have never seen that is filled with carefully detailed artifacts and landscape features unrecognizable to me though now I know them well — and, in fact, knew them well when first I saw them, so that "recognition" must either expand for me and encompass something for which I have no word, or must cease to have any meaning.

For immediacy, I have written as though the experience were virgin: "must either expand...or cease to have meaning...," but I have so many of these nonmemory memories that what was mine and what this other person's, or those other people's, is a thing I cannot answer for. I sometimes believe that I can recall when — those occasions on which — the nonmemories struck me with such force as to seem a form of rape, but I have no way to prove that I am not imagining this about one of my "legitimate" times past, any more than I can prove the converse. Therefore I may be entirely artificial, or entirely "real," as well as many mixtures of each.

What intrigues me most is the possibility that I "exist" only at those times when I am in the throes of a seizure, so that the "reality" (sorry about those endless quotes, but they seem the simplest method) preceding and succeeding the seizure, framing it, as I have said earlier, is part of the seizure too. Then the room that I think I work in, and the house, land, country, have only brief existence in the roles of frames, or supernumeraries. The house that I can describe to you in all its rooms and their details, below stairs and above, may not occupy any space but the space in my head. Perhaps this room only floats here, and the maples and the pot of succulents are pasted there in front in a narrow panel, and what I see, think I see, from the other five windows is either clever trompe l'oeil or a series of nonmemories like fireworks, exploding and unfolding and disappearing quietly as I turn this way and that.

To find yourself unable to prove or disprove anything is a kind of freedom, perhaps not one sought, but then, neither is birth.

I was born, they tell me, in the house of my godmother on the banks of a green river.

Except on occasions when reminders to myself may be necessary, I will dispense with the tiresome quotation marks to frame ironies, as well as with such by now obvious qualifiers as "I think," "they tell me," "if," and so on. I shall henceforth be as deliberate in the writing of this biography as though I were certain of its events, bolstered and supported by rafts of letters, documents, and verbal recountings. But as I do not know myself from the inside I shall continually think of this as biography; let it then be a first-person biography, with "I" as a convenient artifact.

I was born in the house of my godmother on the banks of a green river. I was photographed at nine months in possession of a hairbrush I had stolen. In the photograph I am held by a smiling five-year-old boy, my brother, and am flanked by two sisters, one considerably older than the other children in the photograph, maternally smiling. The other sister is a small solemn creature of three. Another sister is missing, as she is missing from life, being the first of us to have died. One sister is missing because unborn.

I do not have the photograph nor a copy for this reason: it was lost on its way to be copied so that we all might have a piece of the record. Do the others feel as I do, that the loss was as serious as the loss of a memory bank? though I do not think so because of all the others there are many photographic records, whereas that was the only one of me between birth and the age of fourteen. I do not know why this is so. My suspicions are infinite.

Thus I look at the photograph with my mind's eye, which I visualize nastily as being like a stylus that rapidly scans with its single eye the disclike records of my life; a stylus in a groove, or a beam of light, is sanitary and unobjectionable, but the image of eye-on-a-stalk revolts me and goes with me always, and if it looms up when I am in the midst of fellatio I cannot proceed.

I look at the photograph and wonder what features might be discernible in the plump child that could point to pederasty, and late bigotry, and interim beauty, as well as to the precipice where I cling now between twice-daily trips to the post office, having put all other life at a distance requiring that our communications be through the mails.

On Saturday last I murdered a boy, nineteen years old, radiant as a black Apollo, and unless I confess no one will ever know. Where, in the recalled photograph of the plump safe child, is the contour or line, or current between siblings, or between children and missing parents, that, even to a master, even to God, might indicate that murder in the future?

Of course it is necessary to tuck in one of my reminders here (should I write "reminders" and break all vows?) that the memory of the murder could be a nonmemory, but this morning (another nonmemory?) I rang the number he had given me and heard the anxiety and fear in a woman's voice. It was a mature voice, so maybe she was Hap's mother. On the other hand, it is possible that he has sisters as I had who are much older; so it could have been an anxious sister.

What I did was ask for Hap, and hastily, because it was early in the morning, add that I did not under any circumstances desire that he be awakened if he was, and I laughed, unconscious. The laugh was a theatrical touch, neither nervous nor cruel by intent; actually it was an improvisation, and I felt ashamed immediately afterward for throwing others in the cast off their timing. What I had meant to do was try to sense what his environment might be like; voices are eloquent, especially when fearful; and I had meant to sound mature, it was essential that I sound older for I have an adolescent's voice, and I suppose I meant to try to sense what his being missing might mean. In his still life he is like a photograph to me.

My diary was found by a sister who spread it about among the family that I was in love with a male teacher, and thus the designation "abnormal" entered my life before puberty did. It was a curious entrance, not a conventional pain at all as when nails and sharded glass and jealousy entered me. There was no sharpness, but rather a crowding, like fur in the throat. The diary was, of course, found, but the word "abnormal" was truly a found word, for I had been searching for it, had dreamed toward sleep of finding it, knowing that when I did I would know I had.

I had encountered the *word*, for I read a lot, but its application to me had not occurred; Krafft-Ebing on the printed page lay in the future. Encountering words that are descriptive of oneself is a varied experience; it is only then that they become personal, entering us as part of our matter, but the method of entry is various and can be as simple as inwardly riding a caught breath or as complex as emptying Oedipus' eye-socket of its eye.

"Fellatio" is like a banjo tune, lively as a jig; I encountered it years too late, in a spritely mood, and laughed all the way over the top. "Beautiful" was strange and solemn, like the Scriabin *étude* that measured the word into my life, but it is meaningless now, both as applies to me and to its place in the language. Beautiful is not beautiful, it has been superseded by blackness and gayness and extreme situations, many of them pornographic, many of them cruel, many of them as meaningless as the word beautiful.

At a party in the reign of Claudo I was voted out of a fairly formidable assemblage most beautiful, and now hindsight and not a nonmemory informs me that I had been voted most meaningless, because of what has happened to the word.

But the plump child in the photograph was merely uninteresting; the stolen hairbrush was the focal point of the child; his hands attract attention only because they hold the brush. The other three children were infinitely more pleasing to see: the gleeful five-year-old, the maternally smiling heavy-haired fourteen-year-old sister, the serious three-year-old creature with the luminous eyes. But it is a word, eventually, that dominates the photograph, and the word is "stolen." It is the aura, the interest, actually the reason for the visit to the photographer's studio, for those were not the days of the home snapshot.

Thus before I could talk (in the photograph, the tongue lolls suspiciously idiot-large, swollen; has mother's hand only a moment before withdrawn from the camera's range carrying my drool on a handkerchief?) — before I could utter, my life had been entered by a word, *stolen;* by extension, surely, "little thief" as epithet for me was in the photograph, in the air, in my life. But as I have no memory of the deed, the words, the session in the studio, what results is that an actual occurrence of real import and influence becomes my first nonmemory. It presents itself to me framed by artifacts, including, through empathy, Hap's appearance in death, but it is patently unreal.

I go on at such length because it was the first event in my life considered important enough to have been recorded upon film and the last such until, at age fourteen, I won a contest. But it was the school I attended to which (to whom) the award was important enough to record photographically, therefore the only occurrence important enough to assume its place among the sea of family records was my act of theft, and in this I read a directive, printed on the family press. For a nonmemory, I have worried that one quite a lot. And the only proof is missing.

When I was fourteen I won a statewide essay contest. I wrote about the American Indian, his plight, his prospects. I recall an overuse of the word "vivid": sunset over the reservation, Indian skin, eyes, imagery (some examples of this taken from the life), an adjective in fact for everything except his prospects, and I trusted that the words of my plea to change these from dreary to vivid were as vivid as I thought.

I wrote about Indians because I was closely associated with one, an artificial cousin, an unadopted son of an aunt with whom I spent the summers. Everything about him was vivid, from the rectal pain he caused me (until I was ten years old, at which age it mysteriously did not hurt any more, but I had five good years of vivid rectal pain) to the words he used to teach me about nature. He was nineteen, smooth as sweet oil, his rough black hair like a flower, a chrysanthemum, my aunt said. Together we sought the nests of setting hens in haymows, rode animals, even cows, in bareback, sometimes nude, raffishness, swam, caught catfish with our hands, and routed out of muddy ponds creatures not always recognizable, which lumped upon the land like heaving exposed brains, their efforts at locomotion as weighty as thoughts of aloneness. These nameless animals gave to my earliest thinking a respect for the subterranean.

Because of my Indian, I learned that what is ethical need not be moral, may, indeed, be its opposite.

I have spoken of the pain caused me not to gain sympathy, which increases pain and is addictive, but in an effort to make connection between the latest nonmemory, my fragments of poesy, and that first excruciating reality. If I can make connection only once between the real and the nonreal, then I believe the hauntings could subside, and even that I could understand the nonexistence of records of myself when young.

I should interject here the fragments of poetry ("poetry"), the result of nonmemory, for they seem to point the way to an ethical suicide. Everything, it seems by the fragments, can trust itself to wake up tomorrow except the "I":

> The podded mimosa rattling like a sistrum
> Can point to its healed wound and think Spring:
> The buoy in the Creek, through water lightening
> To ice, can feel the tug of the anchor
> And sense that freeze leads to thaw
> And thaw to sails again;
> Elsewhere, and all about, expectancy:

And here occurs the curious line already given:

> The grass browning toward sleep
> Like a child met halfway
> By his dream of fur.

Everything, it seems, except the "I" of the poem has reason to go on, and as the poem's I is the I of this biography, manmade or not, and expresses well enough the doubts of a lifetime for me, there is a certain urgency in the circling and search, though my personal desire for continuity is, as it has been for some time, mainly literary.

Digression can be an acted-upon need for respite, a mask for deep reluctance to unearth the kernels of one's behavioral life. Because of my Indian, I learned that what is ethical need not be moral, may be its opposite, and though I believe it, I glimpsed when I first set the words down a twisting thread setting the pattern for later distortions.

Whether or not at the age of five or six I knew the difference between moral and immoral can't be important. I had learned that it was wrong to hurt someone, particularly someone younger and smaller than you, and I knew from experience that the result was punishment. Thus when I was hurt, was being hurt, and my aunt came into the room having heard a sound, so she said, I, still connected under the covers to my source of pain, had to decide if my pain outweighed his punishment. What he was doing was wrong because it hurt me, but what my confession would do would be still more wrong: I had already been hurt, but he was unscathed; to confess would mean that he would be hurt, and I knew without complicated thought that his punishment would be severe, even horrible. If I knew it because I wished it, which is one path to both learning and invention, I cannot recall. I loved him in the daytime and knew that he loved me at night with a different kind of pleasure, and I could not have him punished for taking his pleasure.

In the scene my aunt is a voice, and while he talked to her, reassuring her, she is the sound of breathing. I do not know why her breaths are so loud. There is no light in the memory, though she may have carried one. If the remembered darkness was pain, or thought, or willful blindness, or because I was buried beneath him, I cannot say. There is no transition. I see us next as viewed through binoculars, two figures far up a road like a riverbed between high banks. It may recently have rained; there is no dust to mark our passage.

Does the foregoing sag in the middle because it is weighted with lies? Are lies then heavy and truth buoyant? Isn't it anthropopathy to invest abstractions with physical properties?

If truth is an abstraction and its natural twin a lie, then a lie is as well an abstraction which would seem to put it out of harm's way. And yet it is much easier to recognize a lie than it is to know a truth on sight. A person possessed of his faculties may, for example, say, "I am dead," and the statement is plainly a lie. But if some people say "I am alive," so many qualifications come into being that we must, even if that person is ourself, give it up as unprovable.

The story does sag in the last section, and I believe this is so because it is crammed with lies. I did not call out to my aunt because I was petrified with embarrassment and was, and knew it by then, a coward. I knew that what was happening was "wrong," but it was my own guilt that concerned me. I was not then, nor ever have been, concerned with morals or ethics. In adulthood I have excused myself on the grounds of membership in that ever-spreading and increasingly undefinable group called artists. In childhood, if I was good, it was because I feared punishment; if I was bad, it was because I believed I could get away with it. The eye of God concerned me sometimes, but far from persistently; it was an unpleasantly stalky thing, not unlike my "mind's eye," poking through clouds and lavatory walls, mainly when I was masturbating. Once it resolved itself into the eye of my real father, but because punishment did not follow, I never again suffered guilt over the practice.

Hap was masturbating when I killed him. As a sensual aid he was employing a bar of soap which he worked into a lather by spitting copiously on it, fresh, young, globous, shining saliva. It was a bar of Bloomingdale's lanolin Carnation, deeply scented, monogrammed with the store's elegant "B." He used so much salivaed soap in his long futile labor over himself that when I noticed it again it was to see that the "B" had been worn away.

Why, one may ask, leave the lie-weighted section in the story if it merely sags? especially the premature nobility (if that mode of behavior is ever anything but). At the "I's" denial of a quest for sympathy through tales of pain one imagines a reader's mouth set in a grin, recalling that a young thing is like Blanche DuBois: he must rely on the kindness of strangers in a world composed of strangers. The child as well as the puppy must waggle and beg for sympathy because the other side of it is something that maims.

I leave the section there because I think that in its willful distortion, in the invention of quite another life and experience, may be discerned the seed, or what comes before the seed, of those hauntings I refer to as nonmemories.

My prize-winning essay, with its overuse of "vivid," replaced the Indian in my life. I had been replaced by a child named Burn, a Fresh Air Kid who came to breathe and stayed to usurp. His name, according to my aunt, meant "stream" in Scots. I thought it meant exactly what it said, and the mark it left was vivid. My essay was filled with good intentions fully realized, through my artistry; with distillations that left only the Indian's nobility; with lies which became official and thus "the truth." My essay, a nonmemory, becomes a memory. Only now, and to whom? do I confess my authorship of lies.

II

My attempt to assay the year with Low (my attempt to "to attempt," in the English that formed me) may have had a root similar to my Indian essay: to analyze pain as though it were a friend, a lover; to find the familiar that lives in all strangeness; finally, to put that pain, that strangeness, in the favored position usually accorded ourselves; to give it precedence over us, physically, morally; or, if that is mentally impossible, as it is for me, then to incorporate it into ourselves so that the Indianness, the birthmark, are, too, our own distinguishing marks.

The distillation of Low that I gave permanent form — the eliding of all his quirks and dishonesties, the romanticizing of his psychopathy — was even more serious an error and misuse of my abilities than the reduction of my complex Indian to a single-strand nobility. At least that maiden voyage was to escape a country in which my life was imperiled. By the time I met Low, I had made so many such voyages to and from so many such countries that my gesture, for him, was mere hedonism: to don his birthmark as though it were a costume for a fancy dress ball. A Mod gesture, in this age of deliberate hideousness, of folk heroes and filmstars who resemble galls.

Could another person have learned differently from Low, have applied the learning differently? I held no brief for or against organized religion, for instance, until I had observed and experienced Low's Christian Scientism. I can see him poring over the weekly lesson, and knowing what I know, my skin crawls at the memory. He used the pap of those writings to sweeten his most ulterior moves. He "studied," hands flying between leaflet, booklet, Bible, only when he was about to cheat, to paw through my things, leaving spoor that my nose easily picked up, or to write one of his shocking letters to some mark in another part of the country.

I recall one long evening of Polaroids, Low coquettish in his poses, his preferred spot, after much trial and error, being beneath the Reynolds over the chimneypiece, the portrait handsome and solemn, perfect "ancestress." A day or so later he asked me to post a number of letters for him, my couriership a necessary part of his game. I felt the snapshots on their heavy backing within the letters, opened one as proof and read the letter.

It seems that he had received a communiqué from the mark in answer to his (Low's) ad in a queer newspaper. Now he was responding with great interest plus the requested photograph taken "under my great-grandmother's portrait in my ancestral home on this remote Island." The cupidity of the letter was appallingly funny. As I read it I saw Low as he had been the day before at his lesson, efficiently looking up Biblical references which undoubtedly told him about the ripeness of time for sowing, or was the ad the seed and this letter, like the first stalks pulled from rhubarb, part of an early harvest?

That is not a digression but an attempt at a theory, upon which the next section will be based. The theory is that in the first person one can own up to anything, one's candor (my dislike for Christian Scientism) being the balm to the wound of shock: I say this about MYSELF, forgive me! — a direct appeal nearly always granted, with the great example of mea culpa the pedestal on which most Western religions (except Christian Scientism) rest. But in the third person, even one's own persona, or alter ego, if monstrous, is held against the author.

Thus I say that which I could not say in the story "The Birthmark": I was constantly repelled by that constellation, that Andromeda of an affliction. It was as though my bride had brought the serpent along, twining breast and back and thigh, the tail resting just above the instep. When Low, and I, Perseus, sat thigh to thigh in the evenings listening to music, and his leg, crossed over the other at the knee, bounced to the beat, I would gaze in a trance of dismay at his trouser cuff above the bare foot, waiting for the music to enliven the snake and cause it to stretch so that its tail could be seen. At such times, when the motion of the bouncing foot hiked the cuff up and displayed the birthmark at the instep, if I was sitting with my arm about his shoulders, as he liked it to be, I would imagine that I could feel the serpent's flattened head lifting on Low's back. An effort of great will kept my arm there, forced it to press harder and harder to kill the snake beneath the shirt, which Low would take as urgent sexual need. Revulsion can be an aphrodisiac, too, as I learned that year with Low.

Hap's chest was a mass of scars, healed in ropes of exposed and twisted muscles. One thigh, from groin to knee on the inside, was made up of a piece of flesh different in color and texture, hairless; it was like a piece of black lamb fell, or a black snake's shed skin. His tongue was cleft! These wounds were the result of a fall of one hundred fifty feet in a canyon. In the fall a memory bank had been wiped out. Hap spoke haltingly when formulating sentences, but when he referred to the loss of a memory bank the technical terms he had learned came pouring forth as though from the groove in a record. At times his tongue lolled, fat and forked, from the corner of his curly mouth. The sensation of placing the tip of my tongue in the groove of his was like (rather than causing) déjà vu; it was like a waking dream of bestiality. Once he crouched on the floor tongue-touching with my dachshund. I spoke to him sharply. It seemed to me that her excitement in the game was unnatural. (It was later that he spoke of mounting her, tried to penetrate her with his finger: the fatal move.)

By equating, however ineptly, Hap with Low, I am trying to do one of two things, or so it occurred to me in the break represented above by space which represents another telephone call, this time to a phone said not to be a working number (all evidence of Hap now faded or fading):

1. To give Hap the spurious substance I have given Low, which is to make him more literary than not, a metaphor;

2. To place Low in Hap's position, which may be: murdered by me, the snake successfully slain and belly-up at last.

In that phrase "belly up at last" rests another possibility, a purely sexual wish, one, if a wish, unrealized with Low, and I might add with Hap. Both had severely afflicted thighs, the blisters of Low's matched by the parchment deadness, paper brittleness, of Hap's, so that to have placed the face in that

274

vicinity would have been unaesthetic. Hap tried to force my head there; Low, when naked, covered himself there with cupped hands like a parody of a virgin. The two impulses are aligned, at this moment overlapping. Just so are Low's passivity to buggery and Hap's fighting rejection of it and effort to become the buggerer curiously superimposed, a perfect fit with no edges to be trimmed with a scissors. Between these two transparent layers I can see myself pressed, the three of us lined up for a photograph which when developed depicts only one — but one what? Urge? (Photographable nowadays in the offices of neurologists and in courtrooms.) Thumbprint? — the thief and liar, the hustler, the criminal lobotomized by nature (Hap was running from justice, seventeen-year-old fugitive, among Colorado labyrinths) revealed as one? If so, I state in some excitement (literary) that the nonmemories are essentials, fillers for the missing memory bank, and for Low's dread that his birthmark, too, was missing.

In unconsciously choosing "photograph" as a condition by which the three of us are revealed to be one, I have finally made a connection with myself, with my own perhaps only important loss, the photograph of me as a child.

In its place, I am astounded to consider, I have so far without regret, remorse, or actual recall, been pleased enough to put a squeamish murderer. Is anything, then, better than nothing? Or just how important to the sake of identity are tangible records? Vagrants, without geographical or provable familial associations, regularly confess to crimes that they did not commit; some die for crimes which are surely nonmemories. Sometimes, as recently in the case of Whitmore, or Whitimore, justice, however by default, prevails and they are set free, but it was the black's nonmemory that won him several years behind bars. *Won* — le mot juste; it was a prize avidly sought. If I succeed in convicting myself here, my own words will be my jail, which will be no change at all in the status quo.

As each corridor and chinkhole must be assayed, are these nonmemories, then, my effort to break out of my word-jail? Listing in the order of their importance to me, if I could amass, invent: enough colors, primary or dilute; strains of melody; artifacts singular either because unflawed or monstrously flawed; some people — food producers and sex providers, mainly; and finally a series of psychological moments like bursts of fireworks — all these to furnish and make habitable a small, tapestry-like world, I would step into it with no backward glance at a world which for too long has been 8½ x 11 inches. This world I have peopled with the spectrum of human aberration, but its grisaille renders it jejune. The effect is prevailing weariness pierced only by need which, when satisfied, produces more weariness.

My mother: it was as if tiredness were pressed into bricks, like the gold at Fort Knox, and carried with her everywhere, looped in strings and bundles about her body, dangerously weighing her down but too precious to be left behind.

Those words are from another essay, written when I was in military school. Ostensibly they are an effort to understand my mother's peculiar lack of other than musical vitality, but I see them now as autobiography, a veiled attempt to set down my own misery for the discerning eye to discover, and in it I discern both my mother's and my masochism. Of all she may have taught me, the primary idea that remains is her rejection of all human bonds except the bond of mortality, shrinkingly acknowledged. The certainty of her own death was, perhaps, her sole comfort, and her famous suicide complex, under whose shadow we somehow grew, I now see as a velleity. She was a voluble woman, and always her words were substitutes for actions. Do I write as she spoke: to avoid gesture? She talked sometimes of loving us, but I can recall no caress.

My fantasy that her hand had just withdrawn with my drool before the photograph was taken was an attempt at a loving nonmemory. But again, this is an easy way out, causalities too readily found: the rejected child equals the (adult) murderer, ultimate act of rejection. But rejected children also equal the most driving successes we can point to: tycoons, movie stars, scientists, sexual athletes. In my sort of game, as you may see it if I ask you, just as in the game of hide-and-go-seek, only the most diabolically hidden, the child in the burrow, musters our best efforts. Sympathy, like coitus interruptus, spoils the climax. Or, continuing and altering the figure, I don't want to win through delicacy; only rape will satisfy.

My mother's "bond of mortality": growing up, when I could think about it, without the dictation of a mind that had learned to view any variety of permanent closeness with profound distaste, it could be moving, peculiarly undegrading, even when the fellow creature was a reptile. Words from a forgotten book, "Your little dark day of life," could be seen to apply to reptile and man, idiot and genius. Once I addressed a snake which had severely frightened me (and been frightened by me; released from our mutual thralldom, it had shivered away like a filament of detached nerve): "Under mortality we are blood kin." My mother taught me this, so that I might teach her, so that the rope might, almost, paraphrase it for me.

Pride too often litters the path of understanding like a rock-fall, but weariness, temporary defeat, especially, can be heavy enough machinery to push the rocks aside, and in relief at having been spared mortal concussion I can acknowledge the bond. I know fully now, and accept, that Hap's loss of a memory bank is linked to the loss of my photograph. For a moment I am able to believe that Hap and I are, were, the same person. But if his murder is only a kind of literary suicide, another try at the rope, I am still caught, as my mother was, in velleity.

I was brought up on the following quote from F. Scott Fitzgerald: "The best people are always hard on themselves." At some moment in my education I came upon those words in *Tender Is the Night* and was astounded by their context: Nicole's sister had danced until two A.M. with an icebag strapped to her side under her evening dress, was operated on at seven the next morning for appendicitis. The reason for her masochism was that she had *three royal princes on her dance card.* Therefore the lesson I was meant to learn was: *the best people are snobs.*

Among the creative acts of my time — how hard I worked to avoid the quotes around creative; such mental endeavor, the

mind pushing against itself, must fall in the category of iso-
metric — we have witnessed one painter erasing the work of
another, possibly greater painter. As snobbism is an ultimate
reduction to its lees of ego, then this act is one of basest snob-
bishness. Destructiveness in art, self-destructive machines, self-
defeating artists, are now a fixture of what I will again refer to
as my time, though to claim this time as my own is another
destructive gesture, in the sense of my contribution to it and its
influence upon me. Surely a person, even a thalidomide baby,
is the result of creative endeavor, therefore an Art object. In my
extreme snobbism I have, may have, joined the Movement by
destroying Hap. We are said to be made in the image of our
creator(s). Hap's beauty could have led one to believe in a
radiant God, his flaws only the reversal of coloration and texture that one finds on a photographic negative. I should like to
have seen the negative of my baby photograph. More than that,
I should have liked to have sensed its oppositeness, the reversal
of values: little thief become little philanthropist, for example.
The projection into the future of those negative values would,
of course, have turned little pervert into Little Square. At this
juncture, to become my own opposite is the only way I can
visualize for myself a measure of salvation. My dimensions,
when cubed, enclose me in a prison of self. The clear plastic
walls stop me from further outward movement, though I may
stand at the barriers and see beyond them the paths that I may
have taken stretching to, for me, impossible horizons. I see my
projections trudging, leaping, advancing with dignity, flying,
burrowing, while I, fossil in amber, maintain — maintained —
illusions of freedom: of movement, of choice, of thoughts, the
three fates from whose loins issue the whole of life.

One longs for acceleration, longs to have done with the
Jamesian equivocations, the parenthetical clauses, the ifs, ands,
perhapses, buts. The desire to *make connection* is as acute as
sexual need, if sexual connection permanently altered one's
state; as it is, my body tautens to receive that first alien touch,
my mind dilates to receive the images that sustained will finally

push me into the climax and beyond, into a kind of peace. For as in the aftermath of sex there is no escape from knowing that aberration was achieved and so one is forced to make one's peace, so I long for the No Exit of the past tense: I DID, I WAS (and therefore I am.)

I dream serenely. In my dreams all is contained within the past. When I walk in a dream it is down a road traveled long ago. Figures of the past crowd my dreams, even though I know that I have never seen them before. Nonmemories such as those never-seen figures cast no cloudy projections on the road before me. My world is contained, so that a densely treed country road affords glimpses of deep chairs, sofas, marble pools with heated towels nearby. Even the rain falls from the roof of my contained world, my house. A dusty mill beside a bleak river is part of the furniture; a pasture gate leads into a carnival area, one of whose rides is eternity, so that my house contains achieved death. All the people I have known in life stand below looking upward where, in the cockpit, my dachshund and I ride forever. In my dreams I have made connection with everything, and the peace of the No Exit of the past tense settles constantly over me like clouds of yeast spores borne to an arbor of grapes. Like ripeness, the past is immanent.

III

I think I have not confused these nonmemories with the inventions I call stories, which are nearly innocent of events. I can imagine that a writer with a "tapestry" of characters and scenery, foreground and background carefully woven, might in some late remembrance recall his inventions as having had flesh and blood. I am a dealer in words only: I am confined, not always willingly in the past, to the belief that the sole movement in my stories may be only the motion a word may have. When I write "he ran," I see neither him nor running; I see two words. In the stories of a handful of other writers, sunlight "lights," flowers "bloom," sometimes a "house" has rooms, verandas, history. Thus some of these others have "gifts" for writing while I construct sentences which have "grace," for instance, only if they contain the word. In some lexicon with private application to me, a "graceful" writer is one who uses the word "grace" to excess.

This limitation, imposed upon me (I see it this way: $\frac{\text{limitation,}}{\text{me}}$ allowing the line, in a reckless mood, to represent "upon") could be either from skepticism or fear. I acknowledge that spoken or written sentences can hurt even when they do not contain the word "hurt"; therefore they must be able to kill, or so this theory could, if allowed, run.

But nowhere does this digression bring me closer to an answer (compulsively, I set down here that the only way, in my terms, that "me" can be brought closer to "an answer" is to move it there, as in "give me an answer," the imperative move resulting, not surprisingly, in an imperative), unless by denial I have managed to remove a fragment of some barrier (which in my increasing compulsion is accomplished by removing "fragment" from the sentence, which, anyhow, was not a part of "some barrier"). Removing fragments, in the sense of letters, from "some barrier" would be to admit the existence of an actual barrier within the words, with the letters seen as stonelike fragments, and though I can discuss it, I cannot see it, and so the action would be foolish.

In this sort of indulgence the only activity comes to lie entombed within parentheses; words and I are divorced from each other, and the game is between the typewriter, instrument of removal, and the self-erected barriers of parentheses, which, unlike the words "some barrier," do resemble fences; so that finally the page is filled with (   ) (   ) (   ); then the pages, the book. A new art form, like Rauschenberg erasing De Kooning? Or madness? No, it is only page, pages, book, filled with parentheses, lines, marks, ('s. Finally one learns to leave the paper as it was found, unmarked; and then one does not bother to find it.

Among my compulsions is counting, which someone said was calculated to take the place of thought, and though I said that thought was required to count — mainly any parallel lines, or sets of symmetrical figures: stair risers, squares in wallpaper, windowpanes — really I lied because it had become so automatic that it was not counting but a sort of assessment by intuition: a sweeping glance across a newly encountered window and one is somehow emotionally informed of something which the nerves, probably, register. Balance, it seems, becomes the object: one is either reassured or disquieted by the sense of proportion, or angered, or, as has happened, sexually aroused. There were rooms in the world that I could walk into and relax with, the relaxation the result of old neural assessment, though these rooms were very rare. Usually my nerves armed themselves at thresholds against the emotional horrors of architectural imbalance. There were no new books, for example, no matter the publicity, that I could open without that forearming, and very few old ones. The dictionary, which "contains" "emotion," but also has "none," was safest for me in certain moods, though the Random House one left here was so full of errors that it contained emotion in quite another sense.

This is how I see the personal part of that sentence: "was" "safest" "for" "me" etc. In other words, there is "safety" but there is no safety.

"I" "must" "stop" "this." How do "I" "stop" "this"? Obviously, "I" cannot, but the typewriter can erase it, thus:

"I" "must" "stop" "   ."

       and

"I" "must" "   ."

       and

"I" "   ."

       and

"I"

       and

"   ."

Murder by subtraction.

But then one comes to rely solely upon punctuation, otherwise the murder would be unnoticed . . . For a moment, such is the nature of hope that has led one to write in the first place (to write "in the first place"!) there is a little upspringing of belief that such a story might be "written," composed entirely of punctuation. One thinks of it as the ultimate (up to now, though someone is undoubtedly working on it) collaboration between author and reader, for though supplying punctuation, the author does not dictate whether, for instance, ! is to indicate surprise, joy, anger, emphaticness, command, or plea, among other possibilities. ? may seek knowledge, or confirmation of what one already knows, or may merely take the place of such a sentence as "He waited politely, eyebrows raised, for her to continue." In music there is a kind of composition which gives options, of melody, rhythm, key, to the performer. In such a book as mine, "serial" would acquire an entirely new meaning: title, *The Serial Songbook*.

As the typewriter easily eliminates "I," so does my new method eliminate the ideas ("I"deus) of author/creator. He now could fuse with typesetter, who drunkenly has been his collaborator since the invention of type. Thus, vanishing, the author gives sanction to the murder of words.

Or, choice still persisting like some vestigial organ, one arrives back at the blank page which one may now fill with words, this time punctuationless. And so it does   the seesaw   le mot juste   for the choice is finally confined   as it was in the beginning   to stasis and illusion   static on the ground   illusion of flight on the brief surge   and so it reduces to emotion   mood up   mood down. (Finality must retain its mark willy-nilly.) To obtain evenness on the seesaw   the device functionless then   is to stand   you and opponent   without moving   the plank between the legs.

Finally, you will notice how hopefully I have used "finally," as though the cluster of letters held within them the mysterious ability to draw to a conclusion the events defined by the words that follow "finally." Finally, one has reduced oneself to words that contain no movement or possibility of movement, so that one also is without the capability of movement. "Murder," then, surely, defines only itself, which is to say, its parts: m,u,r,d,e,r.

The only possible movement, action, surrounding the word is of accumulation, a letter at a time, and this accomplished, it lies upon the page, harmless, erasable.

Erasable, yes; harmless, no. As words have histories of associations, they have futures that may contain influences exerted. There is a great terror, in putting down words, that the influence, in some future time, may be a bad one. That the words may maim, depress, lead to acts the reverse of what one thought one meant. Hate, on a page intended for the printer, must be carefully, so carefully! put in perspective so that for the reader there is no possible confusion that might let him see hate as a directive. Thus moral conclusions must be drawn, or clearly implied; the artist is never freed from this obligation. Never. Every word written swims before my eyes in this curious drowning death stripped of camouflage. I see, knowing that the reader has seen, the deadly directive posing as satire; the racial epithet no longer hiding behind compassionate or "cleansing" usage, the prurience kerneled within the "liberated" scene: nothing is more painfully pornographic than sex described by a Christian in whom natural lasciviousness is endlessly being punished by a puritan upbringing, a kind of ageless schoolmarm whose birches are one's very own roots. Simile, metaphor, corrode from the acid of sudden vision and flake away, and the supportive rod, brutish weapon, stands alone.

Before I abandon, or am abandoned by, this newest futility, here is a scenario upon which a lifetime may have been based. It contains the sunlight of perpetual summer, wears the aura of privilege, and in spite of these, may, through reversals and adjustments, substitutions and cutting, be seen as simplistic enough to bear the code stamp Universal. It places blame, but where? I do not know. I know only where it led both my farmer-sailor and me.

Cousin Margaret was adopted, which made her not a cousin at all. But his mother, when explaining how he came at the age of eight to have acquired a new twelve-year-old relative, told him that because of Margaret's being less fortunate in her origins than he, he must treat her with especial care and kindness. "Why?" he asked, finding in the vague directive the seed of an idea that was counter to what he had been taught and what he had further deduced about the nature of privilege. His mother, smiling, said, "It's a tradition, based on condescension," and turned back to the piano and Bach, which she used as others used soap and water. He had decided to be very kind and careful with his new Cousin Margaret.

The first time they were left alone to play, Margaret said, "I know a game I bet you've never played." "Why haven't I?" "Because I made it up." "Oh, all right." "It's called Naughty Child. Would you like to be 'it' first?" He, thinking to smother Cousin Margaret with kindness, agreed. He waited for an explanation of the rules, but all the adopted girl did was stare at him, eyes unblinking, body unmoving, until his fingers and mouth sought to comfort each other in an all but forgotten gesture.

"Naughty Child!" shrieked the girl and swooped down upon him like a bird, digging one set of claws into his scalp as though to uproot his hair, and with the other palm curved to produce resonance, she slapped him about the cheeks and ears until he burned and rang like a fiery church steeple. He had never been touched in anger or violence, therefore the violation of his person was, at least in the truth of his imagery, like the sacking of a holy place. His emotions reached far beyond outrage, into the center of shock where they kerneled and grew a tough husk, all accomplished so quickly that a moment later he scarcely remembered feeling more than the normal desire to retaliate.

"Now you be 'it,'" he told Margaret, perfectly calm, thinking he would strike her on her large and brittle-appearing nose. She sat down on a stone bench (they were within the garden maze, his favorite place) and crossed her ankles and hands and said, "Very well. But you have to catch me doing something naughty," and did not move a muscle until his Aunt Emily, Margaret's mother, came to fetch the orphan home.

The next time they were together the game was not men-

284

tioned, and they strolled around the gardens and fields in a stupor of politeness, burdening each other with considerate acts, outdoing each other in pleasantries and compliments. Finally he stopped and said, "Look here, Cousin Margaret, I'd like very much to hit you on the nose," and she, murmuring "Naughty Child," came at him with furled talons and pommeled his face until his nose ran, but so scientifically that an hour later there was no sign of the beating and none the following day. Once again she turned to stone, or to some inner contemplation so satisfactory that breathing was hardly necessary to sustain her until her foster mother came for her.

"Is Margaret still underprivileged?" he asked his mother.

"Cousin Margaret," she corrected automatically, continuing to play the bass of the passacaglia he had interrupted.

"Cousin," he said. "Is she?"

"Financially, not at all. Far from it, at least in her prospects."

"Well, is she still inferior?"

"I can't answer such questions for you." She sighed, bidding Bach one of the infinitude of little good-bys that seemed to be their common daily fate. "But we can discuss it." She turned about on the piano stool, coolly accessible. He took a seat opposite her.

"Less fortunate in origin means inferior, doesn't it?"

"I mean it that way." His mother was nearly always oblique, which pleased him because it allowed him to draw inferences.

"Then I'll mean it that way, too."

"You may want to be more precise," said his mother, and despite her disinterested tone he thought he could see a distant pleasure in her eyes.

"Well," he said, " 'less' means not so much, which could mean 'below,' and that's what 'inferior' means. From the Latin inferus."

"Below what? Be precise."

"A fixed—" he groped about — "standard? A norm of some kind?"

"Fixed by whom?" she asked. "Disinterested persons, do you think?"

"Does that matter?" He surprised them both with the hardness of his tone. "Does disinterested matter?"

"Not to me," she said, smiling, "for I am a beneficiary, and that's important to me, more important than the idea of bias against someone else. But that doesn't make me particularly admirable. Perhaps you'd rather be admirable and care about such things."

"Would you admire me, Mother?" She made a stopping gesture.

"We can say 'I am' and 'I was.' We cannot say 'I will be' except —" her eyes grew darkly brilliant, "to say 'I will be dead.' Still, I imagine that what you want to know is if an Act of the Courts, such as adoption, for example, can make a socially inferior person superior suo jure. No, of course not. But since Uncle Bruce and Aunt Emily have given her their name, we must give her our good will, which could mean the benefit of the doubt, which could be stretched to mean that we would come to imagine that her natural parents were the equals, in all ways, to yours. Mind you, I have spoken conditionally. As for myself and my private thoughts, I shall go on believing that Margaret springs from a union of loups-garous in a time of extreme famine." She turned back to the piano and rubbed her fingers over the keys as though to work up a lather.

The next time he and Margaret were together: "Please, Cousin Margaret," he began, not knowing what the plea was for. "Whining?" she said. "Naughty Child," and slapped him with cupped palm until it seemed, when she struck his ears, as though it were a gesture of priming that would draw from him the last drop of his hearing. It was the third beating she had given him but the first during which he cried for real pain, which overshadowed his submerged rage.

"I cannot hit her," he thought. "I cannot hurt her, I cannot hate her. Poor unfortunate." Aloud he cried, "I love you, Cousin Margaret!"

As though only tales of cruelty, seeds of murder, could draw him, he returned, my farmer-sailor, my seed, myself-when-old-before-born, the evolutionary stage from which I veered. I saw him; he stood beside me; I wrote to his dictation:

ALL THERE IS, IS FRAGMENTS, because a man, even the loneliest of the species, is divided among several persons, animals, worlds. To know a man more than slightly it would be necessary to gather him together from all those quarters, each last scrap of him, and this done after he is safely dead. To know him slightly, for to know him well is not vouchsafed even God, who has receded aeon by aeon, propelled by the shocks of astoundment and *mea culpa* at what he has wrought.

If you could gather the man together and somehow piece him out there might be revealed a design, a pattern, for all your troubles, and there might not.

Because the church said — churches always say, which is one reason to stay clean of them — "Brother So and So was fine, upstanding, God-fearing," and his inlaws might say he was a wife-beater, and his wife . . . though that's an opinion that would count for least, favorable or no, because to survive, those bound in daily forbearance must soon enough cease hearing, looking, or to a large extent, feeling. Then his best friend says, and his prime enemy says, and his old sweetheart and teachers and shipmates and his Spanish woman. Yes yes yes, voices in the wind all aiming at his carcass like arrows, each one in self-importance believing his is the bull's-eye. But what about the eyes that took some of him in passing on a windy corner one dark night and enshrined that fragment of him like a holy relic and yearned over it and prayed to it for days and years, his eyes being the only ones to have mentioned the beauty in *her* scarred face, or made *him* feel that men together were not freaks, Euphemism being the name of a special province inhabited by sailors and the races of the Dark Corner.

Those fragments of himself that he gave to music — an entity, possessed of mobility and nerve and eery intelligence—those pieces would be scattered beyond reclaiming; and concerning what he left of himself in books, perhaps a particular page marked with a smear of him like jam, the possibly one time when the meaning of words was received like a welcome knife; concerning those pieces of the man, what? Fragments. Fragments: even to himself, that's what a man is.

2 a.m.

In failure, some crisis is immanent, for though I go about among my fellows, acknowledging kinship — explosive, murderous, with a raging, joyless sexuality — no ray escapes to burn them or give them warning. In the post office I "accidentally" brush another's flesh with mine, expecting revulsion, but am smiled upon. Only my lady, tonight, shifted away from me, putting space between us. When I awoke a while ago I found her on the opposite side of the bed barely within arm's reach. When I touched her her muzzle trembled, infinitesimally hitched upward like an Austrian blind, revealing her fangs. She has not done this since the fierce long-abandoned games of puppyhood. I feel as though she is telling me that she now requires notice so that she may prepare herself for my caress. Yesterday as we walked near the woods thunderous with the sounds of autumn slaughter, I felt the formation within me of a persona, that of a mass murderer. I stood as it were pressing my ear against the woods, listening through to death moving in the dry leaves, and for a spell I became Death, all the murderous impulses of the legion of hunters concentrated in me. When I returned to reality it was to find that my lady was fleeing down the wagon road, tail tucked between her legs.

p.m.

I walked with my feet in the cold Atlantic and wept; wept because I had not swum there this past summer; wept for my

lady's beauty as she stretched her neck, sniffing the salt, a dachshund dreaming of swans; wept for our masquerade, ineffective
and soon over, for it seemed to me a time of summing up and
casting aside. The quiet water encroached in the guise of other,
new continents, self-stenciled on this old one, that I felt I would
be leaving, destination unknown. But not as a stranger; no
longer as a stranger. I and my companion will no longer hide
within the skins of others. Like island hoppers, we have leaped
from life to life, discovering in the spaces between that cruci-
fixion has many forms, that self-crucifixion is the most un-
pardonable sin; that I stand guilty before my self at last, which
may be, before God.

Today had the sound of holocaust. The ubiquitous hunters
have swelled to a regiment; the police slam away at targets on
their range beyond the bamboo grove; the Mmes, the Ms'es and
the Misses commandeered the skeetshoot in butt-sprung khakis,
leather jackets, and boots; spraddling in the tussocky field waiting their turns, they would ease their crotches as though the
weight there had grown to a dreamlike heaviness. (Peace, Beatrix! my first-born, boy-girl, mistress, spouse, dear nemesis.)
Timing my shots to theirs I blew holes in the tires of all the
parked automobiles and walked home, an innocent hunter
among hunters, tipping my cap to all I met along the way. How
approvingly they greeted me, seeing me similarly burdened.
Rapacious-eyed, they could not look through my identical
mask to the thunderhead of catharsis building on the horizon.
Flensing the beasts in the field without respect or thanksgiving
or need, they were a perfect reflection of myself lately found,
a metaphor for all acts, including writing, which are performed
without charity. Compared to what they do, and I have done,
I am able to admit to charitable murder, murder as an act of
love. Seeing their blunt surgery under the wintry trees, I imagine another kind of surgeon. Would Beatrix, would my lost
Miriam — both with hearts as stout as the Magdeburg hemi-
spheres — approve? Both were, at core, sentimental, which may
be that they suffered an excess of humanity. So then will Sajic,
through whom I could recover.

"If I could make pronouncements, unequivocal and commanding like those products of secure societies, the English, the Bostonians, I would say that Sajic is a good man. His morals, like mine, have been called into question. Like me, he has been condemned without trial (though his has not been self-condemnation; keep this in mind.) But, parallels done with, his actions, public and private as far as I can guess, are based on and in regard for others. Even his notorious affair with Heather, from which seed his condemnation grew to tower above him and put him perpetually in shadow, was surely an act, mutual and absorbing, of supreme regard. Having observed him working around the grounds here while the affair flourished, I saw the sunniness of its effect upon him. His craggy face wore an astoundment of light, like those mystics whose beatitude comes from gazing at the sun long after blindness has smitten them, the inner sun so bright that they do not know they are blind. His squared-off hands can touch a seemingly dead tree and feel the secret sap still coursing; their touch on a human body must be galvanizing."

Is such a man strong enough to take me into his own persona and be used by me, and survive? My face already knows the weight of his cragginess, my desires, his wholesomeness; my

Moselle

hands, mouth, eyes, genitals, know his despair at losing ~~Heather.~~ My blood knows his tides.

"All the summer and late into the fall, Sajic worked on the grounds of the old house. Like a surgeon he broke and reset the limbs of the osage orange to make an archway. He trained flowering crab to grow in fan shapes against brick walls, thinned out the Belgian hedge of espaliered pears and apples, formed a summerhouse from the old grapevines, lopped and caulked the two great maples which his employer called Philemon and Baucis. He worked in blaze and light rain, hating to miss one day in the regeneration of the place that had looked essentially the same to his great-grandfather. He had worked for nearly two years at his job and could not help wondering at the extremity of the aloneness of the man who employed him: the man and his dachshund, not another soul in two years, and a house full of telephones that never rang. Sometimes music raged from the windows, but mainly, as though the house were a refuge for woodpeckers, there was only the sound of the typewriter, which sometimes the man would bring into the garden still connected to the house by a long umbilical extension cord."

Keep self out, maybe a peripheral glimpse. This is Sajic's story His tides, which you claim to know, would be like the ocean's: anarhithmon gelasma; Polyphloisboio thalasses. When he falls in love it is like the ocean and the shore: nothing can keep him away.

"He had thought, right up until the end, that he was going to be allowed life."

THE SURGEON

He had thought, right up until the end, that he was going to be allowed life.

That last evening he listened to his wife and thought about Moselle. His mind branched into twigs and buds and leaves, though a striving for singleness of idea and intent had pierced him with continual pain for a long time.

Once he had thought it the essence of the miraculous the way a mind could keep separate and distinct so many pieces of itself, those twigs and leaves and branches, no two alike; the likeness of a man to a tree was his clearest article of faith. He practiced it when he was tending wounds, lopping branches, painting, cementing, caulking winter's ravages and the galls of time.

A MAN IS LIKE A TREE could have been the wording on his shingle, if he had had a shingle. Now, even as sap was swelling fibers, nourishing new growth, so did his own sap still mindlessly push up and out when he thought of Moselle.

For the first time in two years his wife was giving him a signal, one long sought, even prayed for, and to fight the sudden terror of the signal, he thought about Moselle.

He thought about Moselle and listened to his wife, and then it was as though he were listening to Moselle (with his sap, his blood) and thinking of his wife, as she had been: never a nag, over a respectable span of years; never one to administer advertent hurts, for even after the trouble she pained him through inadvertence, sometimes ignorance, a forgivable failing. He had thought she had tried her damndest to be a mother and a lover,

293

and yet he had tried time and again to leave her, first mentally, in sporadic dry runs, and then spiritually and bodily. He began to see, as she spoke and signaled, that she would have to leave him first, she, and the kids.

The signal was outwardly simple, inwardly cancerous: she was willing. Behind the signal and the meaning he saw the reason for all the unwilling lives around him, that puzzled and finally broke him: lives begun from such willingness rendered by time devoid of meaning. Such offspring would be, were, true inadvertencies, without roots.

His thoughts focused, gathered like moss on a tree around the central idea: she would have to leave him first, she, and the kids.

"She, and the kids" had always been divided by a septum. Leaving his wife was one thing, renouncing his kids meant another, a denial of the fruit of his manhood, a reversal, a renunciation of his great natural function, his dehiscence. A man in middle age, setting out to produce a second family from the womb of a young wife — as part of an enforced new order, that was all right. But for a man voluntarily to do it . . . and arriving at that point he always would force himself to see that what he mainly felt for Moselle was a kind of unconquerable lust, needles in the hide, fire in the bowels, a seizure like epilepsy. What he felt for his children was a thing too big to be tagged, a something as horizonless as night.

He saw the world: an immense hollow globe, reverberating with the roar of winds and restless directionless energies. And then he saw his children as tiny as seeds set down smack in the middle of the hollow ball, which he recognized as a fancy figure for his mind, and those tiny objects calmed the acoustical anarchy, softened and deadened the huge sounds so that a whisper could be heard — "Pa"— and he was at peace. Over the tumult of Moselle he would think to himself about his children: *They are the furniture of my mind.*

Self Argument:
A man can live without furniture. The further into the Eastern hemisphere you go the sparser the furnishings of a man's house, and black tribes get along with a pot in one corner to

cook their messes in. Furniture is a part of acquisitiveness, stand-in for desire too abstract to be formulated, maybe a shadow of a shadow of lust for the souls of one's fellows. A house is a copy of a brain, divided into chambers. The living room is the conscious mind and from there one moves downward: the lethal bathroom with shelves of death and tools of murder and suicide is probably the subconscious, and the bedrooms have equivalences peculiar to the occupants. The kitchen will mean one thing here, another in that household: Julia Child's kitchen and the Borgias' being example enough. Such as reading rooms, pantries, storage areas, music places, stand for various protuberances and depressions of the brain, individual to each man. At times in a man's house one can feel, on the threshold of a room, what that room means to the host, and it is usually a piece of furniture gone graphic as country speech that gives the meaning away.

Thus, without furniture — is this a syllogism? — a man would be safe from detection.

A Trial Predicament:
Caught and tried. He saw the courtroom, his judge-wife, the jury of three, two towheads and one as swart as Heathcliff: he'd be the troublemaker. First son: try those words on the tip of your mind, leaving the heart, that satchel of confusions, out of it, and if you are straightforward the words are like salt on meat, drawing juices to the surface, heightening discernment. Divorce emotion, pack it off without alimony, leave Pride penniless, give Traditional Expectations five minutes to get out of town, then feed to the computer-cold mind the equation FIRST SON. Whirr whirr as each bin is dipped into, each band pillaged, every bank robbed of infinite associations. FIRST alone is an agitator of large dimensions; SON alone rouses the sleeping rabble of atavism; FIRST SON is a major revolutionary figure with an aura of Christ and death. And of eternal life.

To be tried by your own children, to be granted or denied freedom by them, unbiased weighers of evidence; if this were standard procedure, would a man so freely seek release? To be tried by a jury of his peers . . . but how difficult to imagine yourself the equal of your children when you are attempting desertion, how the scale tips, then! No, not difficult; impossible. And so a trial becomes unthinkable because undemocratic and thus its own antimatter.

What you are really dodging is evidence — having to present it or witnessing its presentation to your first-born: that the co-respondent, Moselle, is closer to his age than yours; a high-school sophomore who waves to you, as you greedily wait each day at noon, surreptitiously flapping her hand behind her back at the cafeteria window, the cafeteria of the same building that holds his eighth-grade agonies, his gallant losing bouts with parsing and Pythagoras.

"*Moselle?*" You hear his incredulous voice that shards like a brittle urn which held his childhood. Moselle, who shared his classrooms and study halls in the small Island school, who marched with him in the band. His comic's voice that betrays his pains as nothing but jokes, that soars and plummets and plops with the hollow smack of a bladder, saying, trying out the words of imaginary introduction with Moselle as their object: "This is my *mother?*"

History:
Moselle was seventeen that January when the words of a song he liked, about needing more than wanting, and wanting for all time, became reality.

She had been his lover for a year. They celebrated her birth-day with love in a field, a night when the populous sky was like a city. His shadow across her was mystical to his eyes, the shad-ow of a century raping an infant year, the abstraction of an eclipse, the sere breath of low-ebb January.

That night he operated less from lust than at any time with her. His new tender, terrible awareness of *who* she was to him made her seem fragile, recalled to him her two-year absence from school with the weight and aftermath of a curious fever upon her, her emergence as pale as the wine of her name, but as mysteriously matured, so plainly so that a fellow worker, watch-ing her pass, said to him, "How'd you like to try that vintage?"

He saw that day that she was not beautiful, not voluptuous, but what he saw was a knowledge to match his own, that only the knowing can detect in others: of the relationship between death and life-as-sexual; the cavern between death and sanity. And he saw her desire to contain and be contained by the knowledge. She was not flirtatious when he stepped forth, formally, and they spoke for a while. She was direct in speech and her gaze was like a Fourth of July sparkler on his spine, for it seemed to tell him of her need. Not for some man; for him.

In a fantasy which may have had to do with middle age, dangerous in a man, it was said, he had watched her watching for his truck from the store porch, the tall girl two years behind in her classes, conscious of being with younger people. Their first alliance, they discovered, had been formed thus, with eyes that pretended to others not to see, and through a fantasy that each imagined was his or hers alone. But one day, as she walked home from school and he down-shifted to stop and offer her a lift, her back told him that she knew who he was, and that she was ready for him.

She told him in her pale voice how she had come to know the sound of his passing as she lay bald and listless before the fever had gone, and how she imagined that the fever had only moved down her body and settled where it remained, for him, because when it seemed to go and she overheard that she was to live, she had been thinking of him and not of dying, and the new fire of life was in her sex because of him; and she came to believe that thinking about him, and wanting him, had saved her from death. She told him this when they were one body and her breath and words were as hot as desert air on his face. The skin of his face had seemed to tauten with her whispers; all of his body had tightened and hardened until his bones were all he was aware of. It was as though her words had stripped him down to his essential self like a tree in winter. There was nothing superfluous, he was all bone and need to survive, and survival meant that she should flesh him out like leaves and cover his bones.

The first and consequent times with her, he had worn her thin pliant body like a foliage whose heat he had not imagined.

He had been an early lover, had never been celibate even as a pubertal boy. From early boyhood, which he placed sexually-retrospectively at about nine years, a spoken word or a written one, a glance between people, a thought, all were flint to his tinder. But the heat of Moselle's responses and the actual heat of her inner body exceeded his most hopeless imaginings. Thin, white, blue-veined, fragile; and an equator in her loins and upon her tongue.

When he had finished his first labors with her, she had collected moisture from him and with her fingers had rubbed it on her lips, and with no restorative pause he had plunged again.

Enclosed with her in the safety of their passion like a high impenetrable wall beyond the reach of laws, he told Moselle that in another time she would have been called lewd and lascivious and condemned to burn for a fraction of what she said and did with him. She was solemn at his jest, engrossed, he somehow knew, in plans to further prove him right.

One of her solemn pleasures was in his mystification: he had taken her as a virgin with ample proof of virginity, not only blood but a hymen as thick as a monastery wall, and her scream, turning inward, became part of the deep implosion that seared and claimed him. But eventually she told him that she had never touched herself, except with her mind; with him in her mind. Yet, with him in her mind, through the long illness and the liberating delirium, feeling her hair grow and the paling of the shell-like marks on her face, her sole moments of rationality brought about by the penetrating sound of his truck, there was nothing she had not done, and in doing, perfected.

His sensuous life had been copious as to partners, but circumspect, limited by the willingness of others, which had proved limitation enough. Therefore in a way he and Moselle came together as equals, truly experienced only in their imaginations. He, preoccupied with nature, had thought it a vain dream to find another person so free that deep roots were necessary to keep that person from diving headlong into heaven. He felt his own roots, deep and dark, as such essentials. Moselle, floating in the delirium, growing filaments of hair, obsessed him.

The Surgeon Attempts a Philosophy:
The natural, or pagan impulse, then, was toward a rivening ecstasy with heaven its goal, or perhaps, the ecstasy itself was the

heaven, and the essential order was in the fostering and placement of roots. He could envisage a world new in creation where
trees floated in the still-heavy air, their fibrils silklike, and as he
gazed, these thickened and grew and touched earth, drawing
the trees downward and placing them firmly. It was God's plan,
that taste of freedom before order, and it was out of such a
memory that the dream of airy heaven was formed. Counter to
it was the underlying order, a conspiracy between God and the
human race.

It was in the subsurface that enduring relationships took place,
down where the roots met, and increasingly in his life he had
come to suspect that others lacked such fundamentals, and until
Moselle he had groped for that chthonic mystical touching with
growing bewilderment. It was as though others sought to be
blown away by the first storm to bid for them.

He said that it was wars that did it, so many wars in his lifetime, dispersing people over the face of the earth with their
roots left behind in other countries, other times. He did not
mean family, for frequently they migrated en masse, nor did he
mean race, for the same conditions applied. What he meant was
that mental tag in Latin or Greek that told you what you were.

A tree spore carried to a distant place by the wind took hold
and produced itself a network of stability, but people no longer
seemed to do the same. They appeared, in fact, to long for any
chance to disassociate themselves from their pasts and from each
other. As he observed them, on television and in newspapers and
in person on the Island as summer brought them in hordes, they
invented chances and reasons. It invaded their educations, this
need to live on air, their books were composed of it, and their
sentiments and clichés, songs and slogans.

The massier the movement, the less connection there seemed
to be just under the surface between its proponents. No unity
prevailed, and at last, whatever the cause, there were factions
broken off from factions without a fiber to show where the
splintering had occurred, proof to him of the lack of connection
to begin with.

But Moselle and he were Philemon and Baucis, and in the
darkness of the earth they touched, and when he thought that

way, his children — their need for him and his need for them — became finally the airiest spirits of an upper region, in no way bound or binding, and they and he were free of each other, and there was only himself and Moselle.

Trained to detect unsoundness, he found the sophistry, and despaired. He saw his despair as the denial of God, as essential disbelief in maintained order. Caution without purpose became pointless.

Moselle and the tree surgeon were discovered one warm May night, entwined beside the fresh-water pond, by a mob of her contemporaries. There were giggles and some vituperation and a hail of small stones from the boys. One stone each marked the man and the girl, he on his face, she on her breast. As a townsman remarked, after the courtroom exposure of Moselle's breast, "It's a good thing it wasn't the other way around. Who'd have wanted to see *his* tit in court."

The Surgeon Sums Up:
Love is condemned. It has been taken from us and condemned publicly. It was immoral, amoral, criminal, punishable. It was a third creature on trial, it was love that received the sentence. He and Moselle were only its parents, perpetrators, owners or trainers of the beast gone wild, rampaging, trampling civilization.
A high part of the trial, to which he had been brought by Moselle's parents, was when the tree surgeon spoke haltingly, seeming to address his words to his first-born, about roots, one of which he said was love between man and a fellow creature. A voice called out: "It's your root that got you in this mess," and court had to be dismissed for the day.
The sentence was commuted, as sentences frequently are in small islanded communities, out of consideration of the scarcity of good men to do the necessary work. But the man and the girl were marked, butts of jokes and crude epithets, and the girl, pregnant, was given in marriage to an off-Islander and moved away.
The man Moselle married was no bad bargain, a little older

than her lover, the owner of good property and a sound house, and he had little or no lust in him. As he told her father, what he mainly wanted was a good housekeeper and an heir, and in Moselle, miraculously, he had found both. He was secure enough in his relationship with church and community not to care about gossip, and he promised Moselle's mother that he would keep his wife busy enough, once the baby came, not to have time to think about her past, and her good example, in church and out, would influence others to reform.

The tree surgeon saw the death of her youth as his own murderous act.

He moved his family out of the house that had witnessed his birth and his father's birth, and his wife's bewilderment that was a kind of birth, too, for she had emerged from the trial and the revelations a bent and bitter tuber, forced to the surface by elements and deformed by prolonged exposure. The familiar rooms held darkness for her. He would find her standing by a window, and seeing or hearing him in the room she would begin to speak in a low voice, recalling how she had stood thus waiting for him past midnight, past many midnights: the night in May when he and Moselle were discovered; the January night when he said his truck had broken down on the Shore Road; the night was in the house with them. In the familiar house the sun no longer stood above the horizon of its windows. Within it was always mörketiden, which, as her forebears knew, infected the brain.

When, in need or dreaming, he turned her to him, she cried out in her sleep. She could not be penetrated. Lying in the darkness, talking softly, she would recall for him how she had labored at his body's need, forcing pliancy when each bone ached after the long day's work. She told him how after the wedding night she had suffered the prospect of a life spent in that particular service. As she razed the structure of their mutual illusions, the darkness seeped deeper into him like a blight. At last, afraid the house would not withstand the inner pressures, he sold the old place and moved his family into the manor house of a sea captain turned farmer, dead a hundred years.

The house was nearly two hundred years old, but in elegant

repair, thanks to the money of the last occupant — owner, still — a known queer. The house stood on a traveled road, and its tall windows sucked in the first and the last sun of the day. The surgeon had barbered its old trees, saved its new mimosas wind-riven at the crotch in their third year, broken and bent and arched into an allée the toxic spiney limbs of its great wall of osage orange, which the man told him was called bodark in the South, a corruption of bois d'arche. The owner had called the finished walkway, bricked and bordered beneath the arches with sun-shy mountain flowers, his Via della Spina. As the tree surgeon worked about the place, the owner and his birthmarked lover walked hidden within the vaulted greenery, shirtless. Once, as though teaching a baby to venture further into the world, the man had drawn his lover into the sunlight, and the tree surgeon had seen the curious formation on the lover's back: the map of an unfamiliar world that could still stir the memory.

He came to love the house, and when the owner had gone, re-fusing, by staying on an extra winter, the scandal the Islanders tried to force upon him, the tree surgeon continued to minister to the gardens and orchard, and after his own ordeal he saw the house as a refuge. He believed that no aura of perversity, or of the one-hundred-fifty-year-old murder whose stains were still in its attic, could so badly discolor its light and air as his own house was discolored by events of the past years. He could pic-ture his wife in the sewing room, lit by the southern sun, and he thought he could hear her humming. He could see his children carefree in the orchard and himself pruning the espaliers, apt examples of deformity transformed into beauty.

Making the move, he concluded that he was joining the hu-man race, for he was cutting off his own past to become a liver-on-air, to save his life and the lives of his family.

The Surgeon Concludes:
In so doing, an act of enormous unnaturalness for him, he lost his final connection with them. Only Moselle and he were still joined, the runners of their union having pushed beneath the waters of the separating Sound, and he saw that it was not so,

not possible; that it was only his memory posing as the solution when it was the problem. It was Moselle he would find in the sewing room, pale full-bodied wine sparkling in the sunlight, a decanter he could never again touch. In the orchard it was Moselle and his child romping in silhouette, refracted in the blossoms, while his wife rocked by a window in a north room, guarding the possibilities of her womb until no guardian would be necessary.

Like a pointing finger, one fact was protrusive: in two years no Island child had been born. The only child formed of an Island union lay secure by Moselle's side in a house whose acres touched the edge of the sea.

No young of any age were enticed by the full moon to make love by the fresh-water pond, and he knew if they stumbled on love they would denounce it. In his brooding conclusions he saw that this was worse than loveless venery, fornication, all the excesses of old destroyed cities.

In solitude, the Islanders spent their evenings in front of individual television sets (the only rooted things left, their cables an intricate tracery under the soil), took their solitary meals there, living with Lucy, an old ghost no longer comprehensible to them. As he prowled around their houses, watching them through windows indifferently uncurtained — who had anything to conceal? — no laughter at the clown, except the laughter on the soundtrack, was heard. Lucy's predicaments, innocent and predictable, were founded on man's delight at his saving vulnerability. The tree surgeon's neighbors were invulnerable on their islands, invulnerable to gunshots and screams, moans and confessions and pleas for mercy. He watched them stolidly eating off trays, expressionless, lone but unlonely, and saw in windowpane and mirror the reflected violence from the T.V. screens, sometimes in color, mostly in the pale gray of nothing, of fog, limbo, and his ashen deductions.

And yet some old rationality persisted in him and made him suspect his conclusions, which seemed, after two years of nocturnal research, too final. As a man of the earth, he did not, had not believed in finality. Checking on himself, he climbed ladders, broke into outhouses, rowed out to boats promisingly bobbing in the harbor. A flashlight became an extension of his hand. He was already a criminal; nothing was beneath him.

That night, two years after Moselle had gone, when their child would be a year and five months old, that May night of anniversary lit by a full moon, the tree surgeon, pointedly rejecting his wife's signal, gone old and weak as a radio wave from another solar system, sent his family to bed and took his shotgun, his pick-up truck, and a small arsenal. One by one, slowly and with grace of motion and intent, for it was an offering, he killed everyone on the Island, five hundred and seventy-two people. He was a perfect shot, taking his roebuck, his ring-necked pheasant, his mallard in season with one clean shot, but he had never before taken so large a bag, and when he was finished his shoulder was torn and bleeding freely.

Before he killed his own family and himself (it was then past dawn, the horizon that pearly hue of a great dangling raceme of honey locust) he treated his barked shoulder with tenderness, and bound it. A momentary thought of precedence occurred: who first? but it was only an echo of order across the chasm of chaos.

Before he shot them, he grouped his family together so that in case he was wrong and there were still roots, they might intermingle long after flesh and the last signs of their blood had vanished.

The promise of the warm barrel in his own mouth was as sweet to him as the memory of Moselle's nipple.

Spring!

My lady is hiding from me, probably stretched out on her back in some deep pool. Of sunlight, joining gold to gold. In jubilation: spring and the completion of what seemed an endless voyage, I called her to come and ride with me to the post office, but the usually irresistible lure of CAR could not fetch her from her heaven. As it turned out, the post office was tight closed, the postmistress possibly off somewhere with the rest of the Islanders practicing some arcane vernal greeting. If so, they worship silently. I would have joined them, if asked! I feel, quite curiously, a sense of oneness with them and want, if practicable now, to know them. I hope my long silence has not made this a vain dream.

As a love offering, my "Surgeon" may not be acceptable – to them, if they could read it, or to my agent, to whom I tried to mail it today. I wrote that there was a chance that Sajic might not be able to take me into him and survive me, but as it turned out, eternally apt, it was I who took him into me, and my empathy has painful proof: I write with *left* arm so sore that I am tempted to examine my shoulder for his ruinously barked flesh (for I am left-handed.) I love him, and thus myself, and by what would once have been an unthinkable extension, I love the tired hunter who abandoned his battle-scarred rifle at the railing of my porch where it leans as though in penitence. One feels his shocking fatigue at dawn, as though he had hunted all night... I hope I am not going to overdo the empathy bit (Clytie, hello!) in the manner of all reformed Scrooges. At least his season is over and his shots will not madden my days and perturb my nights.

It is too late for morals, but like Margaret Fuller and the universe, I accept myself, knowing that it is the same thing; or: that all I will know of the universe I must and shall find within myself: life and death, love and hate, sin and redemption; and the reconcilement of Jew and Christian, man and woman, old age and youth, if I am to prevail. Emily Dickinson's lines on the house within the house within et cetera, with which this odyssey began (it was written then that it might turn out to be a novel, and one still does not know the measure, or total lack, of success), will do much better than anything I can write on that inner chaos:

> One need not be a Chamber
> to be Haunted
> One need not be a House
> The Brain has Corridors surpassing
> Material Place
> . . . .
> Ourself behind Ourself, concealed
> Should startle most
> Assassin hid in our Apartment
> Be Horror's least.
> etc.

I recommend the poem to all who have ideas about the simplicity of man (persons).

Settling into one's environment as unprotestingly as possible is an old virtue, approaching, in its antiquity, a lost technique of Art. Memories of other lives, or of possibilities of lives not ventured, hold tenuously to one's imagination. The experience is like a sleepy attempt to plan one's dreams. Desirously but gracefully yielding, settling in, one gives soft rein to fleeting old images long abandoned, allowing them duskily to play out some *rejected* scenario. Here is a fragment, and my last apology to you, Beatrix, for "rejected" is the operative word, and the best I can do.

In a commanding house in the middle of an island a man

wakes up and hears a horn crying softly, fog, rocks, infamy.
The doleful sound, growing louder, makes the man wonder,
sleepy and inclined to self-indulgence, what lost soul can be so
inconsiderate as to wake the Island, though from his bed he can
see no lights at other windows. "Nothing can reach our Island,"
he thinks snugly, and goes back to sleep.

In other words, I will heed the call. Love, Chris.

Before I seek out my lady to venture forth to (into) the profound revelations of spring, I must lay the deeper past to rest
and with it the unquiet ghost of my farmer/sailor/murderer,
who, I see now, has been the real guide to my passage through
the chambers of mind. His life has — reader, beware! — coin-
cided with mine in ways not always accessible to the rational
seeker, and the major coincidence I cannot acknowledge save
through innuendo (it was his stepmother) and pluralizing a
terrifying and bleak noun. Some corners of some chambers
must remain forever in shadow, enigmatical even to ourselves.
Examine euthanasia. Consider complicity: what guilt attaches
to turning your head?

Noon has passed, and for once the event has not been marked
by sirens from the firehouse. It is as though, if they did not
notice it, this first day of the year's paradise would not tell out
its hours on the inevitable string, and they could keep it forever. One sees the Islanders static, like the hunter's gun leaning
against my porch, aware that if they do not move, act, breathe,
it will always be afternoon on a spring day. One sees them face
up, rapt under the sun.

I have always looked forward to the revelations of afternoon,
and so will place my nineteenth-century man there, an hour
before sunset; this is selfish, typically, for it allows me to have
the pleasures twice, the imaginary and then the real. I wish my
lady could share this double enjoyment, for it would mean two
five o'clock dinners for her. Thinking of her, all at once I know
where she is, for I view the stairs in my mind as they were when
I returned from the post office, and see, as then I did, but subliminally, the drops of blood on the carpeting. She has gone

307

into heat. Thus do we sexual creatures leave trails by which we may be found.

Some compulsive neatness or need, some awareness of the circularity of events, perhaps, insists that I end this composition, before the coda, as it began. *I live in nightmare. My primary activity is concealing that fact. I am less and less successful.*

For my loving murderers, surcease, now, and a return to, if not innocence, pre-experience when the mind holds all the world but the world is good.

HE STOPPED *on the little rise that in his childhood his mother's gardening hands had blanketed with a patchwork quilt of low-growing, bright flowers, and watched his wife as she took the washing from the line, making of the wind an accomplice in the task of folding sheets. She grasped a sheet by two corners and allowed the wind to think it could snatch it from her, and just at the moment when she seemed about to let go, when the sheet lay out flat upon the wind and tugged most forcibly at her hands, she rushed forward, folding the sheet in half; then a quarter turn, repeating the process. The final fold was made against herself, using her body as a board upon which to smooth out the wrinkles. Her head bent and nodded in satisfaction as though thanking the wind for allowing her to use it so. He wondered if there was bitterness also in her knowing that her flat body was, by circumstances of their ages, reduced to the category of laundry appliance on which she changed muslin covers for the same reason that she changed those on the ironing board, of which attractiveness was not a requirement. He wondered if, when she bathed, it was as though she were scrubbing down a counter.*

There was no movement of any kind in what he viewed except that of his wife's collaboration with the wind. Noth-

ing invited his eyes to stray from that center of vigor and ingenuity where, it seemed, his wife had captured all turmoil in a basin, for the trees did not invite him by bending to the corners of his eyes. The tall wind-burnt lilac bushes were still, in the lower limits of his vision. And yet he looked as though called toward the attic window, toward the Wind's Eye. It lay shadowed under the eave, without reflection, a cool dark eye without sight. And then it gained a pupil, as he watched, and an iris: a woman's face surrounded by a bonnet.

The sun lay, an hour from setting, behind the house, so that the house extended long arms of shade into which he walked and was caught up like a child and pressed to the house's bosom. Finding the door was, because of the age he felt himself to be then, devoid of sexual metaphor; entering it was like being lulled to sleep, shown the door to dreams.

He walked down the tenebrous hall, glancing into the parlor where the child's lamp of tinware waited for darkness, pausing only at the bottom of the stair, thinking, I did not tell her good night. Then, with little regret at the omission, he mounted the stair into shadows that were both deeper and beginning to be light.

The door into the attic was closed — the final door just this side of dreaming always is — but a gentle push set it ajar, and beyond it, turning slowly as though with reluctance to abandon the beauty of a darkling landscape, he could see her. She tilted her head, peering, and from her smile he could tell that she recognized him, and was glad that he had come.

Wondering how they would address each other, after so long a time to think about it, he went into the attic and closed the door behind him, firmly.